**Black Sporting
Resistance**

Critical Issues in Sport and Society

*Michael A. Messner, Douglas Hartmann, and
Jeffrey Montez de Oca, Series Editors*

Critical Issues in Sport and Society features scholarly books that help expand our understanding of the new and myriad ways in which sport is intertwined with social life in the contemporary world. Using the tools of various scholarly disciplines, including sociology, anthropology, history, media studies and others, books in this series investigate the growing impact of sport and sports-related activities on various aspects of social life as well as key developments and changes in the sporting world and emerging sporting practices. Series authors produce groundbreaking research that brings empirical and applied work together with cultural critique and historical perspectives written in an engaging, accessible format.

For a complete list of titles in the series, please see the last page of the book.

Black Sporting Resistance

Diaspora, Transnationalism, and Internationalism

JOSEPH N. COOPER
Foreword by Gerald Horne

Rutgers University Press
New Brunswick, Camden, and Newark, New Jersey
London and Oxford

Rutgers University Press is a department of Rutgers, The State University of New Jersey, one of the leading public research universities in the nation. By publishing worldwide, it furthers the University's mission of dedication to excellence in teaching, scholarship, research, and clinical care.

Library of Congress Cataloging-in-Publication Data

Names: Cooper, Joseph N., author.
Title: Black sporting resistance : diaspora, transnationalism, and internationalism / Joseph N. Cooper ; foreword by Gerald Horne.
Description: New Brunswick, New Jersey : Rutgers University Press, 2025. | Includes bibliographical references and index.
Identifiers: LCCN 2024027122 | ISBN 9781978839854 (paperback) | ISBN 9781978839861 (hardcover) | ISBN 9781978839878 (epub) | ISBN 9781978839885 (pdf)
Subjects: LCSH: Athletes, Black—Political activity. | Black people—Ethnic identity. | Sports and globalization—Social aspects. | Racial justice. | African diaspora. | Black nationalism. | Pan-Africanism.
Classification: LCC GV706.32 .C666 2025 | DDC 303.6088/796—dc23/eng/20240815
LC record available at https://lccn.loc.gov/2024027122

A British Cataloging-in-Publication record for this book is available from the British Library.

Copyright © 2025 by Joseph N. Cooper
All rights reserved

No part of this book may be reproduced or utilized in any form or by any means, electronic or mechanical, or by any information storage and retrieval system, without written permission from the publisher. Please contact Rutgers University Press, 106 Somerset Street, New Brunswick, NJ 08901. The only exception to this prohibition is "fair use" as defined by U.S. copyright law.

References to internet websites (URLs) were accurate at the time of writing. Neither the author nor Rutgers University Press is responsible for URLs that may have expired or changed since the manuscript was prepared.

∞ The paper used in this publication meets the requirements of the American National Standard for Information Sciences—Permanence of Paper for Printed Library Materials, ANSI Z39.48-1992.

rutgersuniversitypress.org

Contents

	Foreword by Gerald Horne	vii
	Introduction: Beyond Boundaries—Sport as a Site for Black Resistance	1
1	Black Sporting Resistance	20
2	A Collective Consciousness: African (Black) Diaspora Sporting Resistance	44
3	They Lived on Their Own Terms: Black Transnationalism Sporting Resistance	75
4	Revolutionary Consciousness: Black Internationalism Sporting Resistance	125
5	A Radical Imagination of Future Black Sporting Resistance	160
	Acknowledgments	175
	Notes	177
	References	199
	Index	215

Foreword

It is long past due to acknowledge the obvious: *sports are more than a game*. This is particularly the case in the United States, where breakthroughs in sports often have prefigured steps forward in society as a whole. This was the case when Jackie Robinson desegregated baseball in the aftermath of World War II, bringing the national pastime back to where it began in the late nineteenth century. Robinson's advance was a harbinger of what occurred in 1954 when the U.S. Supreme Court ruled that Jim Crow—domestic apartheid—was unconstitutional. And both the Robinson case and the high court opinion were driven in no small measure by a changing global climate: Washington found it difficult to win "hearts and minds" in a decolonizing world when people of color, and African Americans most notably, were subjected to atrocious third-class maltreatment.

We espy a similar trend in 1970 when the ebony running back of the University of Southern California Trojans—Sam "Bam" Cunningham—trampled the proud Crimson Tide of the University of Alabama on the football gridiron, compelling Alabama's Jim Crow squad to move more aggressively to recruit Black athletes in order to compete more effectively. However, the idea that the Trojans did more to desegregate the calcified Tuscaloosa campus than Dr. Martin Luther King on his best day is largely apocryphal—but does reflect the state of mind of those who have spoken in those inflated tones as they leveraged sports mania on behalf of wider goals. But even before the age of decolonization and desegregation Black athletes were blazing a progressive—often radical—trail.

Such was the illustrative example of pugilist Jack Johnson, born in Galveston, Texas, in 1878. He would become a target of obloquy after he became heavyweight boxing champion a few decades later. This led to a search for a "Great White Hope," a man to knock this "Negro" off his throne in order to restore—it was thought—the racist status quo. Trumped-up charges were generated against Johnson, compelling him to flee the country. He wound up in Mexico during that country's revolutionary decade—1910–1920—where he sought to establish a citadel against Jim Crow, rescuing African Americans from the torment of lynching and racist oppression. Alas, regime change compelled him to return to his homeland and a stint behind bars—but afterward, his wanderlust and progressivism continued.

His successor as boxing champ cum hero, Joe Louis, was not known for his political stances. By the late 1940s, though, Louis was aligning with forces on the left before the advent of the Red Scare. He joined with Black businessmen as he sought to make inroads into the business side of the sport but was stymied, not least because of the intervention of organized crime and capital affiliated with it. This illustrates yet another roadblock faced by minoritized groupings that seek to countervail the status quo. And, of course, there is the better-known Muhammad Ali, who in the 1960s and 1970s quite famously shunned conscription during the U.S. war against Vietnam and barely escaped imprisonment as a result.

A direct result of the uproar ignited by the fierce battle against Jim Crow was a more searching scrutiny of various forms of bigotry, including male supremacy. This led directly to Title IX of the Education Amendments of 1972, a federal legislative measure meant to increase athletic opportunities for women in sport. This contributed to the growth of professional opportunities for women in basketball, tennis, golf, and other sports. This laudable trend also illustrated the by-products of sport of which women had been systematically deprived, Black women not least: the ability to sacrifice for the collective and the greater good, the importance of discipline and teamwork, and the essentiality of sound physical condition as a lifelong ambition.

This well-researched and thoughtful work by Professor Cooper forces us to think more deeply about the profundity of sports and, particularly, its impact on racism and sexism. Make no mistake: it is a major contribution.

Gerald Horne

GERALD HORNE is the John and Rebecca Moores Professor of History and African American Studies at the University of Houston. He is the author of over thirty books, including *Revolting Capital: Racism & Radicalism in Washington D.C., 1900–2000* and *The Counter Revolution of 1836: Texas Slavery & Jim Crow and the Roots of American Fascism*.

**Black Sporting
Resistance**

Introduction

Beyond Boundaries—Sport as a Site for Black Resistance

> Cricket had plunged me into politics long before I was aware of it. When I did turn to politics I did not have too much to learn. (James, 1963, p. 71)

> Sports has the power to change the world. It has the power to inspire. It has the power to unite people in a way that little else does.... Sports can create hope, where once there was despair. (Laureus, 2000, p. 1, citing former South African president Nelson Mandela)

The first quote above from internationally renowned Trinidadian intellectual, activist, and cricket enthusiast Cyril Lionel Robert (C.L.R.) James suggests there is an inextricable link between political affairs and sporting practices whereby power relations and sociocultural implications are ever present. This critical view of sport posits these activities are more than mere leisure engagements designed to promote social harmony; rather, these spaces constitute sites of contestation where values, cultures, and ideas are simultaneously reproduced and resisted. James's analysis and articulation of sport emerged during the pre–West Indian independence era in the early to mid-twentieth century, and his political views were informed by revolutionary thinkers such as William Edward Burghardt (W.E.B.) Du Bois, Marcus Garvey, Karl Marx, and Leon Trotsky (James, 1963).[1] Although James sought racial justice through the desegregation of cricket (as opposed to promoting separatism), he was a staunch anti-colonialist who challenged European racist beliefs and systems. By comparison, the second quote above is from another human rights champion, former South African revolutionary and president Nelson Mandela. These iconic words were delivered during a legendary speech at the inaugural Laureus World Sports Awards in Monte Carlo, Monaco in 2000. Mandela's view of the role of sport in societal affairs was based on the fact that he had secured Black leadership in the South African government by the mid-1990s. In 1995, Mandela famously donned the jersey for the then all-White South African Springboks national team at the Rugby World Cup to signify his commitment to racial reconciliation through sport.

Both James and Mandela are widely revered as revolutionaries for their dedication to human rights in general and Black liberation more specifically. James is lauded for his anti-colonialism efforts on behalf of the West Indies (currently known as the Caribbean region or nation-states) and Mandela is lionized for his anti-apartheid leadership in South Africa during the mid- to late twentieth century. Notwithstanding the fact of their respected legacies, it is important to contextualize these revolutionaries' unique perspectives and approaches to sport. As an African diasporic person, James's view of cricket was shaped by his experiences growing up in an environment that had not yet experienced decolonization despite the fact that Black West Indians constituted a majority of the people who lived on the islands.[2] Thus, consistent with other colonizing forces across the West Indies, the politics embedded in cricket mirrored the colonial ideologies in the broader society and served as a contested terrain for national sovereignty, racial pride, and human dignity.[3] Since cricket had been desegregated by the mid-twentieth century (albeit inequitably), James's sport activism focused on providing fair access to captaincy positions and improved social conditions for West Indians on and beyond the pitch. On the other hand, Mandela, as a continental African, expressed his view of sport after being unjustly imprisoned for nearly three decades and following a successful social movement that dismantled apartheid in a multiracial South Africa. As such, Mandela's approach to racial reconciliation promoted an integrationist philosophy whereby Black and White South Africans could come together to participate on the same teams, which he felt would lead to the eradication of racism in South Africa and subsequently across the globe. Both approaches were shaped by their respective and evolving contexts, personalities, and political philosophies. In addition, both approaches contributed to tangible gains in the fight for Black liberation and self-determination while also containing their own limitations. The presentation of these two Black revolutionaries' perspectives and approaches underscores one of the aims of the current text, which is to analyze the heterogeneity of resistance efforts in and through sport enacted by Black people across time, space, and context.

Moreover, popular clichés such as *Keep politics out of sport*, *Sports bring people together*, *Sports are the great equalizer*, and *There is no race on the playing field* have been commonplace in sporting spaces dating back to the Ancient Greek Olympic Games and continuing through the twenty-first century (Maguire, 1999). The notion that sport must be apolitical and color-blind is the sacred oath of engagement for participants and spectators, particularly in neoliberal capitalist societies. Sport purists or traditionalists endorse a functionalist interpretation of organized physical activities whereby these spaces benefit everyone and maintain social stability (Coakley, 2017; Sage, 1998). Mandela's belief that sport could reduce racial prejudice and discrimination reflects his internalization of the functionalist approach. In addition to social benefits, the concept of "muscular Christianity" was grounded in the idea that a healthy mind, body, and spirit could be developed through sport participation (Sage, 1998). Character development, mental and physical fortitude, moral integrity, manhood, and nationhood were and remain synonymous with sport.[4] Advocates of this perspective highlight athletes' "rags to riches" stories, heroic performances of strength and perseverance, multicultural fan bases, internationally celebrated athletic events, and sport philanthropy as evidence of the social benefits of these activities.

In contrast to sport purists, critical sport scholars have argued these activities are inherently political and primarily serve as tools of ideological hegemony (Brown, forthcoming; Carrington, 2010; Coakley, 2017; Davis, 2016; Douglas, 2018a, 2019; Edwards, 1973; Eitzen & Sage, 2012; Joseph, 2017; Sage, 1998). Antonio Gramsci is widely credited as one of the prominent theorists who conceptualized how capitalist societies, led by a conglomerate of leaders, establish and maintain dominance over the masses through passive consent with economic systems, political influence, religion, education, media, and other forms of social control beyond coercion via military violence (Gramsci, 1971; Sage, 1998). Related to hegemonic ideologies, Sage (1998) explained how the effective transmission of these beliefs involves social institutions and cultural practices reflecting and legitimizing them. Stated differently, sport scholars who study hegemony argue that sporting spaces primarily serve as sites for reproducing dominant ideologies (Carrington, 2010; Edwards, 1973; Maguire, 1999; Sage, 1998). For example, sport scholars have documented how the globally dominant modern-day sports were largely spread internationally through European imperialism, colonialism, and militarism (Danylchuk, 2012; Mwaniki, 2017).[5]

Given the diasporic, transnational, and internationalist foci of the current text, I echo Mwaniki's (2017) assertion that the critical examination of sport enables us to make visible and subsequently deconstruct the taken-for-granted inequities embedded within a global society that has suffered from the ravages of European imperialism and colonialism.[6] Moreover, although European colonization extended to all parts of the globe, given the pronounced influence of the transatlantic atrocity involving the mass enslavement and exploitation of African people, the current analysis focuses on Black sportspersons' resistance against anti-Black and Eurocentric ways and systems of thinking, being, and doing. Consistent with the Black radical tradition (Robinson, 1983/2000) and research on Black athlete activism (Cooper, 2021; Edwards, 2016), my project centralizes Black resistance against the most prominent oppressive force Black people have faced over the past four hundred years, which is White racist settler colonialism and capitalism (Horne, 2016, 2018a, 2020b).

More specific to race and racism, Carrington (2010) surmised that the racial signification of sport was created to reinforce biological myths attributed to racial groups, specifically White superiority and Black inferiority. As a result, in neocolonial contexts organized sports were and remain grounded in socially constructed hierarchies (Brown, forthcoming; Carrington, 2010; Coakley, 2017; Davis, 2016; Douglas, 2018b, 2019; Edwards, 1973; Eitzen & Sage, 2012; Hylton, 2008; Maguire, 1999; Sage, 1998). Unlike sport purists, Edwards (1973) posited that sport sociologists are principally concerned with examining "the functions of sports . . . to understand the intricacies of social organization" (p. 9). Dating back to the early nineteenth century, sport participation in colonial societies was limited to White male economic elites because they possessed the leisure time and resources necessary to engage in these activities (Sage, 1998), whereas those in the proletariat or working class as well as those who were enslaved spent most of their time laboring against their will.[7] As an extension of labor exploitation, in the limited instances when working-class and/or enslaved males were allowed to participate in sport, it was intended to serve the exploitative interests of White elites (Carrington, 2010; Cooper, 2021; Edwards, 1973; James, 1963; Maguire, 1999; Wiggins & Miller, 2003). Hence, from their inception, modern sporting practices have been rooted in racial, gender, and class domination.[8] This fact serves as the context by which Black sporting resistance is explored in this book.

Black sporting resistance is defined as the embodiment of epistemological, ontological, and/or axiological empowerment against anti-Black racist and intersecting oppressive ideologies, systems, and practices in and through sport.[9] Consistent with my philosophical and political orientations, Black sporting resistance is an extension of the Black radical tradition (Robinson, 1983/2000) whereby Black lives and experiences are centralized and contextualized within an intergenerational global context. In previous work I delineated the concept of *resistance* from that of *activism*, whereby the former term is defined as "intentional and/or unintentional actions by individuals, groups, organizations, and/or institutions that challenge oppressive systems and ideological hegemony" (Cooper, 2021, p. 7). Different types of resistance include agency, pioneering, advocacy, hybrid, activism, social movement, revolution, and sustained cultural empowerment. Building on my previous work, which was largely focused on African American athletes and sport activism *within* the United States (Cooper, 2019, 2021), the current text engages a more global analysis of Black sportspersons across the world who have utilized sport as a tool for resistance and empowerment.

Moreover, sporting resistance has been reflected epistemologically via Black sportspersons' knowledge of self, their capabilities, their cultural foundations, and their native environments across time and distinct ecological conditions.[10] Throughout history, the achievements of Black sportspersons have been minimized by racist assertions that suggest they were naturally predisposed to accomplish certain feats (Cooper, 2019; Edwards, 1973; Hawkins, 1998; Sailes, 2010).[11] Referencing Gardner's (1983) seminal work on multiple intelligences theory, I have asserted that Black athletes have resisted White epistemological oppression through their application of logical-mathematical, visual-spatial, and bodily kinesthetic intelligence (Cooper, 2019). In addition to athletic performance, Black athletes have also demonstrated their epistemological prowess outside of sport by articulating their counter-hegemonic political stances and astute analyses of systemic injustices. Hence, despite racist conjectures, Black sportspersons have embodied sporting resistance by perpetually debunking the notion that they are mindless athletes or dumb jocks with no cultural foundations or political proclivities (Carrington, 2010; Cooper, 2021; Edwards, 1969/2017, 1973; Hylton, 2008; James, 1963; Wiggins, 2018; Wiggins & Miller, 2003). Another mode of epistemological resistance highlighted throughout the book is grounded in African spirituality whereby Black sportspersons understand and embody their actions in and through sport as being deeply connected to spiritual sources, beliefs, and values, as opposed to these actions being devoid of or separate from spiritual significance.

Ontologically, since the onset of European colonialism and imperialism, Black people in general and Black sportspersons more specifically have been resisting dehumanization. These pressures of dehumanization were imposed in myriad ways including through enslavement, land theft, economic deprivation, familial destruction, cultural erasure, medical malpractice and neglect, sexual abuse, and environmental violence (Fanon, 1952/2008, 1961/2004; Hartman, 1997; Rodney, 1972; Williams, 1974/1987). More specific to sport, Black athletes have been subjected to exclusion, objectification, commodification, and exploitation at different times for the benefit of the White gaze (Carrington, 2010; Cooper, 2019; Edwards, 1973; Henderson, 1939; Hawkins, 2010; Smith, 2009). In response to these pressures of dehumanization, Black sporting resistance has been exemplified through participation, achievement, resource mobilization, innovation, and dignified disposition in the face of intense overt racism.[12]

Axiologically, the meaning of sport participation for African people has historically and contemporarily reflected their cultural values, which have been distinct from European cultural orientations (Yehudah, 2020). African cultural values have centered on spirituality, communalism, harmony, and balance whereas European cultural values have prioritized competition, individualism, domination, and materialism (Nichols, 1974/1987/2004; Robinson, 1983/2000; Rodney, 1972; Williams, 1974/1987). Within sporting spaces, Black sportspersons have resisted European cultural values through their refusal to separate their athletic identities, successes, and experiences from the broader Black liberation struggle in society. One example of this type of Black sporting resistance occurred in 1993 in Australia when Nicky Winmar lifted his jersey, pointed to the color of his skin on his stomach, and verbally expressed his pride in his First Nations Aboriginal identity *and* his embracement of his Blackness (Osmond & Klugman, 2022).[13]

Another example occurred during an interview following the 1968 Olympics protest when U.S. athlete John Carlos, the bronze medalist in the 200 meters, said his children, Black communities, and working-class people cannot eat medals (Edwards, 1969/2017). Although they grew up in different parts of the world and possessed different ethnic backgrounds, Winmar's and Carlos's shared diasporic experience with anti-Black racism compelled them to engage in Black sporting resistance against White racist neoliberal capitalism that values material goods such as medals and money over Afrocentric and Indigenous values that prioritize human relationships and harmony.[14] Hence, their articulation of the meaning of their sport achievements illuminates how Black sporting resistance is significant only insofar as these actions advance the plight of Black communities and Black freedom struggles more broadly. Relatedly, I contend that Black sporting resistance, as an intergenerational and global phenomenon, is a part of the Black radical tradition. In his seminal text *Black Marxism: The Making of the Black Radical Tradition*, Robinson (1983/2000) conceptualized the Black radical tradition as " the continuing development of a collective consciousness informed by the historical struggles for liberation and motivated by the shared sense of obligation to preserve the collective being, the ontological totality" (p. 171).

The un/sub/consciousness of Black sportspersons and their subsequent resistance actions has been and remains connected to historical and concomitant broader Black social movements. The perennial challenging of anti-Black racism and interconnected forms of oppression in and through sport highlights how these spaces serve as important sites for the embodiment of Black ontological totality.

Significance of This Book

The purpose of this book is to explore and connect how Black sportspersons across geopolitical contexts have embodied diaspora, transnationalism, and internationalism to resist anti-Black racism and interconnected oppressive forces. These efforts were and remain driven by the desire to exemplify their humanity, cultural heritages, political ideologies, and spiritual beliefs.[15] In disciplines such as Africana studies, history, philosophy, military sciences, political science, sociology, anthropology, and cultural studies, there has been extensive research on Black resistance in international contexts (Fanon, 1952/2008, 1963; Gordon, 1996; Carmichael & Hamilton, 1967; Horne, 2015, 2016, 2018a, 2020a; Rodney, 1972; Swan, 2020, 2022; Williams, 1974/1987). However, there is a dearth of scholarly literature in sport studies that has centralized Black resistance in and through sport across national borders (Carrington, 2010; James, 1963; Joseph, 2012a, 2014, 2017; Mwaniki, 2017). Building on the contributions of critical sport scholars of the African (Black) diaspora (Carrington, 2010; Hylton, 2008; James, 1963; Joseph, 2017; Mwaniki, 2017), a unique intervention of this book involves the application of the sport resistance and activism typologies (Cooper, 2021; Cooper et al., 2019; Cooper et al., 2020). The sport resistance typology includes the categories of agency, pioneering, advocacy, activism, hybrid, social movements, revolutions, and sustained cultural empowerment (Cooper, 2021). Examining different types of resistance enables a nuanced understanding of the direct, indirect, convergent, and divergent factors that contribute to anti-colonial outcomes such as African nation-state independence from colonial rule and Black human and civil rights gains across international contexts.

The sport activism typology includes the categories of symbolic, scholarly, grassroots, mass mobilization, economic, political, legal, media, music and art, and military activism (Cooper, 2021; Cooper et al., 2019; Cooper et al., 2020).[16] Religious activism is also introduced as a counter-hegemonic action within this expanding typology. Activism is often synonymous with public protests, but I surmise this type of resistance is exhibited in numerous ways and yields different outcomes based on the context, actors, and execution. The international analysis of activism in and through sport provides a more comprehensive understanding of the complex interplay between ecological systems, counter-hegemonic efforts, and observable social outcomes. More specifically, the expansive examination of diverse forms of resistance across international contexts accentuates the connection between broader Black liberation and empowerment efforts and those that occur within sporting spaces.

Another novel aspect of the current text is the inclusion and contrasting of diaspora, transnationalism, and internationalism. In Carrington's (2010) groundbreaking text, he introduced the term *sporting Black diaspora* to refer to the global impact of the Black athlete in the twentieth century on conceptions of racial difference and the (counter-)hegemonic tensions therein. His text primarily focused on Black male athletes across Europe and North America in boxing, track and field, and fútbol/soccer. In another African diasporic athlete analysis, Mwaniki (2017) examined how Western media outlets depict migrant black African athletes such as Mario Balotelli (Ghanian-Italian fútbol player), Tirunesh Dibaba (Ethiopian distance runner), Didier Drogba (Ivorian fútbol player), Tamba Hali (Liberian-American football player), Telga Loroupe (Kenyan distance runner), Mwadi Mabika (Congolese-American basketball player), Dikembe Mutombo (Congolese-American basketball player), Catherine Ndereba (Kenyan distance runner), Christian Okoye (Nigerian-American football player), and Hakeem Olajuwon (Nigerian-American basketball player).[17] Specifically, Mwaniki (2017) highlighted how, as a part of a global neocolonial project, "foreign black Otherness" is disseminated in mainstream Western media via misrepresentations of African athletes' transnational identities, experiences, and embodiments (p. xi). In another examination of Black migrant athletes, Joseph's (2017) application of Gilroy's (1993) Black Atlantic concept explored the role of migration routes and cultural exchanges between Afro-Caribbean cricketers in Canada and their diasporic connections throughout North America, Europe, and the Caribbean regions. A significant influence on these works is the contributions of C.L.R. James, who understood the political power and significance of sport beyond the boundary lines of the pitch. In his internationally acclaimed book *Beyond a Boundary*, James (1963) examined the relationship between cricket and West Indian anti-colonial efforts. He emphasized how cricket matches in Trinidad, England, and Australia were more than symbolic racial and cultural events, but rather inextricably linked to political resistance for liberation from colonialism in the West Indies. Similarly, the current text explores the influence of Black sporting resistance within and beyond the boundaries of the athletic milieu across global contexts.

Carrington, Mwaniki, Joseph, and James are a part of a legacy of Black international and critical sport scholars who understood and exercised the political seriousness of sport for Black liberation within and beyond nation-states.[18] Collectively, these works have expanded the discussion of how sport, politics, and race intersect locally and globally. Notwithstanding the benefits of these works, one overlapping limitation is the lack of delineation between and analysis of the concepts of diaspora, transnationalism, and internationalism. In several instances, diaspora and transnationalism were used interchangeably. Within the current text, I define each of these terms, highlight their uniqueness, and demonstrate how each inform one another in meaningful ways particularly as they relate to Black sporting resistance. For example, Black internationalism as a concept has been infused in various disciplines (Burden-Stelly & Horne,

2020; Bush, 2005, 2009; Featherstone, 2013; Swan, 2020; Thomas, 2013; Wilkins, 2007), but one field where the concept is conspicuously absent is in sport studies. Given the significant role of sport during the interwar period (1919–1938), Cold War era (1947–1991), South African apartheid regime (1948–1994), and African continental and diasporic independence movements (1847–1965), it is important to connect the activism enacted by Black sportspersons during these eras to the actions of emancipatory political efforts beyond sport. Hence, this book fills this gap.

Another unique contribution of this book is the expansive sporting analysis. Instead of focusing on a single or a handful of sports, the current text explores Black sporting resistance across boxing, fútbol, cricket, capoeira, track and field, baseball, basketball, rodeo, tennis, hockey, racing, and rugby/Australian football. This broad analysis facilitates a nuanced exploration of when, where, why, and how different forms of resistance contribute to specific outcomes across diverse sporting spaces. The cross-sport analysis also assists with understanding how the nature of the sport influences—or does not influence—perceptions of resistance and contributions to broader political movements. In addition, this text builds upon the application of the Black Atlantic (Abdel-Shehid, 2005; Carrington, 2010; Gilroy, 1993; Joseph, 2017), but also extends the analysis beyond the United States, Canada, Caribbean nation-states, and England to also include influences in contexts such as South Africa, Angola, Nigeria, Democratic Republic of Congo (formerly known as Zaire), Australia, First Nations, Brazil, Japan, and Mexico.[19] As such, Black sporting resistance is examined as a global phenomenon rather than a hemispheric occurrence.

Moreover, unlike texts that position Black sportspersons as assimilationists or passive reproducers of the racialized social order, this book incorporates historical, comparative, and critical sensitivity (Sage, 1998). Specifically, this approach is employed to better understand how, when, where, and why Black sportspersons have strategically leveraged their platforms, resources, and influence to challenge hegemonic status quos. Regarding historical sensitivity, Sage (1998) characterized this approach as an understanding of the relationship between events, cultures, and political forces across time and context. More specific to the current text, Carrington (2010) explained the historical role of sport in Black liberation efforts: "Thus, sports have historically provided an opportunity for blacks throughout the African diaspora to gain recognition through physical struggle not just for their sporting achievement in the narrow and obvious sense but more significantly and fundamentally for their humanity in a context where the structures of the colonial state continue to shape the 'post/colonial' present" (p. 5).

In concert with Carrington's (2010) analysis, I demonstrate historical sensitivity through the contextualization of Black sporting resistance within broader historical events. In particular, I explore the connections between Black sporting resistance and concurrent broader social movements such as the Black Liberation Struggle, Pan-Africanism, Black Nationalism, and Black Radicalism. Emphasizing these connections fosters a more in-depth understanding of the antecedents and catalysts for different types of resistance and subsequent outcomes.

In a related vein, Sage (1998) notes that the application of comparative sensitivity "help(s) us understand that the popularity and meanings of different sports vary across cultures" (p. 7). The examination of Black sport participation and resistance in and through multiple sports across the African diaspora reflects comparative sensitivity. Although I aim to avoid ethnonational essentialism (Gilroy, 1993), I do acknowledge the role of ethnic, cultural, and geographical differences as they relate to contextual resistance efforts.[20] Critical sensitivity involves the challenging of taken-for-granted myths. This approach requires interrogations of the social construction of human inequalities and explores the complexities and contradictions therein. Given the vast influence of White racist neoliberal capitalism in global societies, I problematize the ways in which sport has been viewed primarily as a reproductive space and emphasize how for select Black sportspersons these spaces serve as sites of resistance, reimagination, and replacement of hegemonic norms and conditions with more equitable structures and arrangements.

Foundations for Black Sporting Resistance: Black International Resistance beyond Sport

In order to understand Black sporting resistance, it is necessary to contextualize these actions within a broader historical and socio-ecological apparatus. Throughout history when faced with imperial and colonial antagonists, Africans have consistently engaged in resistance efforts to protect their humanity, communities, culture, and land (Asante, 1990, 2003; Asante & Mazama, 2005; Carruthers, 1999; Diop, 1974; Fanon, 1952/2008; Hilliard, 1998; James, 2012; Rodney, 1972; Williams, 1974/1987). Resistance manifested in multiple ways including militaristically, politically, economically, culturally, intellectually, psychologically, and spiritually. Within this section, select Black ideologies and social movements are highlighted to contextualize how collective diasporic actions contributed to liberatory and empowering outcomes for African people both locally and internationally. Social movements are defined as "sustained collective efforts against oppressive forces and systems by an oppressed group for a concentrated time period typically (albeit not exclusively) lasting for one year or more" (Cooper, 2021, p. 90). These social movements reflect what Faist (2010) described as transnational spaces, fields, and formations given their symbolic, ideological, and material impacts across borders. It is important to note that African resistance is not limited to social movements, but these pronounced and protracted efforts provide a useful framework to examine how hegemonic disruption occurs across time, space, and context.

Moreover, Gerald Horne, renowned historian and internationalist, has argued and substantiated through his expansive research that the advancement for African people in the face of anti-Black (neo)colonial forces has been made possible by diasporic relationships and political alliances with countries and groups that shared a common adversary (Horne, 1985, 1994/2020, 2013a, 2014a, 2015, 2016, 2018b, 2020b). For example, Horne (2020a) explained how the Haitian, Algerian, Cuban, South African, and other African-led revolutions were possible due to support from anti-colonial forces, including diasporic Africans across the Americas and Caribbeans, continental Africans, and non-diasporic allies such as Indigenous groups, the former Soviets, the People's Republic of China, and select sects of socialists and communists across Europe, Asia, Latin America, South America, and Australia. In each instance, there was a broader social movement led by Black people that was driven by their desire for liberation from colonialism. Green (1982) captures the overarching aim of these resistance movements that were grounded in combating anti-Black oppression as well as other forms of inequality: "At the heart of the struggle in all these strands—Négritude, Afrocriollo, Pan-Africanism and Black Power—the objective is to reduce social and economic inequalities, to ensure freedoms and justice, as well as to erode the amorality of systems of exploitation that reinforce racism" (p. 58).

In contrast to viewing African resistance as disconnected nation-state projects, I concur with previous Black internationalists who surmised that African humanity is best understood through an international lens (Du Bois, 1903/2003; Horne, 1985, 2016; Robeson, 1958/1998). Given the fact that European imperialism and colonialism were and remain international crimes against humanity, African resistance is inherently a global endeavor. Hence, all social movements outlined in this section illustrate international connections that enabled African people to mitigate the literal and proverbial chains of White racial oppression. Concurrently, these social movements exemplified African self-determination, resilience, excellence, and collectivism, which are foundational to intergenerational Black resistance in all spaces including in and through sport.

Across various disciplines scholars have explored Black social movements such as the Black Liberation Struggle, Back to Africa, Black Nationalism, Pan-Africanism, Négritude, Black Power, Civil Rights, Black Freedom, Rastafari, anti-apartheid, African independence, and Black Lives Matter (Burden-Stelly & Horne, 2020; Gordon, 1996; Green, 1982; Hine et al., 2006; James, 2012; Joseph, 2006, 2007; Ogbar, 2020; Singh, 2004). Although all Black social movements are important and meaningful, not all of them directly influenced

Black sporting resistance efforts in tangible ways. For example, the Black Power movement had a major influence on the revolt of the Black athlete in the United States during the late 1960s (Edwards, 1969/2017), compared to the lack of pronounced influence of the Rastafari movement on sporting practices across the Caribbean region in the 1930s (Davis, 2009; Joseph, 2017; Marqusee, 1994/2016; Riley, 2011; Wilde, 1994). In concert with other Black radical thinkers (Gordon, 1996; Horne, 2020b; Kelley, 2002; Rabaka, 2020), I assert all forms of Black resistance across international contexts, including those that are more visible and those actions that are less visible, are all part of an intergenerational legacy of political and cultural struggle. Given the focus on Black sporting resistance within the current text, the following social movements are highlighted: a) *Black Liberation Struggle*, b) *Black Nationalism*, c) *Pan-Africanism*, and d) *Black Radicalism* (Anderson, 2012; Hine et al., 2006; Horne, 2020; Moore et al., 1982; Ogbar, 2020; Rodney, 1972).

The global *Black Liberation Struggle* (BLS) was birthed out of the spirit of African people who sought to resist oppressive forces, particularly those from Europeans.[21] Dating back to the fifteenth century, European colonization and imperialists' aims were directed at exploiting non-Europeans such as Africans as well as the land resources of Indigenous and Asian people where these groups were living (Horne, 2020a, 2020b; Moore et al., 1982; Rodney, 1972).[22] From his analysis of the ontological impact of colonialism, Carrington (2010) offered the following summary: "The conditions of colonialism produced a space of denial for black self-hood; a denial of subjectivity, a denial of freedom and a denial of humanity. The black self that struggles to be recognized is therefore engaged in a struggle to be known, to be seen, to be free, to be human" (p. 104).

The cumulative effect of intergenerational colonization was collective underdevelopment. Preeminent African diasporic scholar activist Walter Rodney (1972) described the European enslavement of Africans and corresponding environmental resource theft as the foundation for underdevelopment in Africa. *Underdevelopment* refers to the exploitation of people, land, economies, cultures, political systems, educational processes, and other resources for the benefit of a colonizing or imperialist entity or entities (Rodney, 1972).

In 1884, a group of European countries met at the Berlin Conference to divide the continent of Africa into nations designated for colonization—consequently, the existing African tribes and territories were devastated, and the modern African nation-states are a by-product of this European invasion (Byrd, 2020; Sherwood, 2012). Liberation from all forms of slavery was pursued from every shore of Africa to the waters of the Atlantic and Pacific Oceans to various lands in the Americas and in the Caribbean and Pacific regions (Horne, 2020a; James, 1963/1989, 2012; Swan, 2020, 2022). Revolts such as the Stono rebellion in South Carolina in the mid-1700s and the Seminole Wars in the early to mid-1800s in the United States were commonplace throughout the enslavement period. These courageous acts signified African and Indigenous resistance to European colonialism (Franklin, 1947/1974; Horne, 2013a, 2014, 2015, 2018a, 2020a). In the Stono rebellion, a group of Africans enslaved in South Carolina coalesced to plan an attack on their enslavers in a broader effort to escape to freedom (Horne, 2014a). The Seminole Wars lasted nearly half a century, during which organized Africans and Indigenous people fought off multiple groups of Europeans including the Spanish and British (Horne, 2013a). The success of the latter revolts resulted in U.S. government peace treaties that allocated lands for Seminole territories (Horne, 2013a). In concert with the significance of these revolts, scholars have described the Haitian revolution of 1791–1804 as one of the most internationally impactful resistance efforts among enslaved Africans (Horne, 2015; James, 1963/1989, 2012; Robinson, 1983/2000). During the Haitian revolution those who were formerly enslaved violently upended their European oppressors including the French, Spanish, and British. This revolt illuminated the collective power of organized Africans, in partnership with allies, to disrupt the system of European settler colonialism and tyranny. The ripple effect of this revolt contributed to future African liberation efforts across the Caribbeans, Americas, Africa, and Oceania in symbolic, epistemic, and material ways (Horne, 2015; Swan, 2022).

Another important dimension of this revolt as it relates to subsequent Black sporting resistance efforts was its disruption of the economic structure of slavery. In his analysis of the political economies in the late eighteenth century in the United States and the Caribbean region, Horne (2015) emphasized how although Africans were viewed and treated as property and less than human, essentially their labor/corporeal production fueled the lucrative international cotton, sugar, and tobacco industries.[23] Thus, Africans who resisted these oppressive conditions were exhibiting a form of class struggle, which carried significant domestic and international implications (Horne, 2015). These industries would spawn numerous economies around the globe that would form the backbone of modern White racial capitalism (Kelley, 2002; Robinson, 1983/2000). Related to this structural arrangement, modern neoliberal commercialized sports (Hawkins, 2010; Smith, 2009) rely on Black athletes to serve as the primary wealth-producing laborers while White economic elites (e.g., league and team owners, corporate sponsors, etc.) constitute the most enriched benefactors.[24] I posit the effective disruption of White settler colonialism via revolts by Africans who were enslaved in the seventeenth through late nineteenth centuries is integrally connected to the various boycotts enacted by Black athletes during the twentieth and twenty-first centuries that sought to disrupt White racial capitalism (Cooper, 2021; Hawkins, 2010; Robinson, 1983/2000).

I recognize the vast differences between the material conditions facing Africans who were enslaved during the eighteenth and nineteenth centuries and their descendants who would become athletes in the twentieth and twenty-first centuries, but in accordance with Hawkins (2010) I emphasize the persistent presence of anti-Black racism via exploitative structural arrangements and corresponding power dynamics. Thus, the comparison here is more about the ideological and structural domination that has been intergenerational and the ways in which Black people have resisted this oppression through the use of their bodies. This sporting resistance includes both the removal or withholding of their bodies from sport participation (i.e., boycotts) as well as instances when they chose to engage in sport participation under specific contested conditions (i.e., separate Black sport leagues and teams). In each instance, the economic power of Black collective resistance was exercised to disrupt an exploitative status quo (Edwards, 1969/2017; Cooper, 2021) and thus the Black ontological totality was reified (Robinson, 1983/2000). Stated differently, the intergenerational reenactment of the Black struggle against oppressive forces in diverse contexts reflects the reclamation and embodiment of this group's ontological, epistemological, and axiological prowess. The connections between the foundations and strategies of the BLS and subsequent Black sporting resistance across geopolitical contexts throughout the nineteenth, twentieth, and twenty-first centuries are highlighted throughout chapters 2–4.

As an extension of the BLS, the roots of Black Nationalism emerged with the efforts of the Outlayers, Maroons, Cimarrons, and Geechies during the sixteenth century throughout the Americas and the Caribbean region (Ogbar, 2020).[25] During the transatlantic atrocity, there were multiple African tribes who were forced into chattel enslavement (Williams, 1974/1987). In an analysis of this hybridization process, Ogbar (2020) noted that "The transportation and forced amalgamation of hundreds of different African nationalities resulted in creolized communities of Africans in the Americas" (p. 91). These processes and outcomes have been conceptualized with various terms ranging from *creolization* to *hybridity* to *liminality*. For example, Gilroy (1993) referred to this process and outcome as *hybridity*, which refers to the mixture of cultural ideas and groups across the Black Atlantic. Relatedly, Haour (2013) defined liminality as a subjective state of being an outsider as a result of psychological, cultural, and/or physical displacement from one's homeland and native culture. Thus, Africans who were displaced through the transatlantic atrocity experienced liminality in their new locations in the Americas and the Caribbean region.

These amalgamation processes resulted in new identities being formed. Specifically, these African diasporic groups created their own societies and territories after revolting against European colonizers (Ogbar, 2020). These successful revolts were a by-product of strategic alliances between other oppressed groups such as the Seminoles as well as common allies at different periods of the seventeenth, eighteenth, nineteenth, and twentieth centuries (Horne, 2018a, 2020a).[26] The militant philosophy of these groups centered on "armed self-defense, self-determination, and territorial separatism" (Ogbar,

2020, p. 91). The use of physical resistance has been emblematic of Black freedom struggles for centuries. Although a comprehensive exploration of how these militant strategies emerged across diasporic groups is beyond the scope of the current text, the primary point here is to underscore how Black people have perpetually fought against their oppression via physical force at the local, regional, national, and international levels since the onslaught of European colonization in the fifteenth century.[27]

In concert with military resistance, an integral goal of Black freedom efforts was self-determination and sovereignty with territorial separatism. The Cimarrons, Maroons, Outlayers, and Geechies were renowned for ferociously fighting off European colonizers and establishing their own communities throughout the Americas and West Indies (now known as the Caribbeans) (Horne, 2014a, 2015; Ogbar, 2022; Robinson, 1983/2000). The continuation of this tradition of pursuing territorial separatism was illustrated by the famous request from the Black Panther Party for Self-Defense to the United Nations (U.N.) in the late 1960s, in which the group sought to supervise a plebiscite whereby Black people in the United States could create their own community and pursue self-governance away from a tyrannical government (Nelson, 2011). Hence, these core values of self-defense and self-determination are emblematic of the spirit of Black Nationalism from the fifteenth century through the present day. More germane to the current text, the ethos of Black Nationalism and the creation of separate societies influenced Black sporting resistance via the establishment of separate sport organizations to demonstrate Black people's self-determination and desire to exist in affirming and safe cultural spaces (see chapter 3).

In addition to the creation of separate communities and institutions, another aspect of Black Nationalism focused on emigrationism (Ogbar, 2020). Popularized by Paul Cuff in the early nineteenth century, numerous Africans expressed the idea of Black emigration back to Africa as being the best path forward for race relations for those living in colonial societies.[28] Despite these efforts, a mass emigration that parallels the extent of the forced migration during the transatlantic atrocity has yet to fully manifest. Nonetheless, the spirit of emigrationism in terms of being spiritually, culturally, and physically connected to Africa as a homeland remains salient across the African diaspora in the twenty-first century. The notion of shared identity and connections (real and imagined) to African homelands is foundational to the concept of African (Black) diaspora sporting resistance (chapter 2). Relatedly, the concept of transnationalism among Black people, including sportspersons, has roots in the emigrationism movement whereby racial and cultural connections were (re)established and strengthened via migration flows and exchanges (chapter 3). In addition, the symbolic connections to Africa also informed Black internationalist sporting resistance efforts from the mid-twentieth century through the twenty-first century (chapter 4).

Black Nationalism is also closely associated with Pan-Africanism. The roots of Pan-Africanism date back to African revolts in the fifteenth century (Horne, 2014a; James, 2012). From Toussaint Louverture of Haiti to Martin Delany of the United States to Marcus Garvey of Jamaica, African revolutionaries understood that the strength in resistance and transformation lies in coalition building along racial and cultural lines (James, 2012). Settler colonialism and global racial capitalism were and remain by-products of Pan-Europeanism and inter-class collaboration (Horne, 2020a). In response to this formation, Pan-Africanists seek to combat Pan-Europeanism locally and globally by prioritizing racial solidarity over religious, political, and other social identities (James, 2012). Carmichael (1971) captures the intersectional underpinnings of this African-centered political philosophy: "Pan-Africanism is grounded in socialism which has its roots in communalism" (p. 221). In concert with Kwame Ture and former Ghanaian President Kwame Nkrumah,[29] my philosophical and political orientation is grounded in scientific socialism and Pan-African communalism. Although I acknowledge the important contributions of Marxism and Leninism, particularly their critiques of capitalism, prescriptions for revolutionary change, and influence on and by African revolutionaries,[30] my political orientation and philosophical approach align with Robinson's (1983/2000) assertion that these political theories do not *fully* account for the role of racialism in the social, economic, and political realities of Black people across the world. Along with Robinson (1983/2000), I argue any resolution for Black people must centralize, as opposed to peripheral analyses, their historical, cultural, social, political, and economic conditions and experiences across and within specific milieus. Thus, my Pan-African scientific socialist orientation and my alignment with the Black radical tradition are rooted in historical and contemporary embodiments of African communalism (Carmichael, 1971; Nkrumah, 1973; Robinson, 1983/2000; Rodney, 1972).

Arguably the most successful example of Pan-Africanism was the establishment of the Universal Negro Improvement Association (UNIA) in 1914 in Jamaica under the leadership of Marcus Garvey (Adi & Sherwood, 2003).[31] At its height in the pre–World War II era, the UNIA claimed worldwide membership of over eleven million Africans across forty countries, with two-thousand-plus divisions in locations such as New York City, Limon, Costa Rica, and Cape Town, South Africa (Byrd, 2020; Tolbert, 1975). Among the UNIA's most successful endeavors was the 1918 creation of the politically mobilizing publication outlet *The Negro World*, which boasted two hundred thousand subscribers in its first year of existence (Byrd, 2020). Another achievement of the UNIA was the short-lived Black Star Line steamship company, which was created to optimize resource trade and repatriation efforts between diasporic areas and Africa (Byrd, 2020). In 1920, the UNIA adopted the red, black, and green flag (Byrd, 2020; Ogbar, 2020), in which red represents the blood of African ancestors who fought for liberation and empowerment and the common bond among African people, black signifies the power of African collectivism, and green reflects the power of the environmental resources on the continent of Africa. Symbolic representations of Black Power and African unity serve as counter-hegemonic tools that communicate the message of self-determination. The hybrid resistance typified by Pan-African organizations such as the UNIA illuminate the power of strategic deployment of different types of counter-hegemonic actions such as media, music, art, and sport. Stated differently, Pan-African organizations of the early twentieth century provided a blueprint for the effective Black sporting resistance efforts that are highlighted throughout this book (chapters 2–4).

In 1900, a group of African diasporic leaders from Haiti, Ethiopia, Liberia, Trinidad, the United States, and other nations met at the first Pan-African Conference in London (Burden-Stelly & Horne, 2021; Munro, 2008; Ogbar, 2020). One of the lead organizers, Henry Sylvester Williams, stated that the purpose of the conference was to promote and strengthen global liberation efforts for African people. The following goals were outlined:

- to secure civil and political rights for Africans and their descendants through the world;
- to encourage friendly relations between the Caucasian and African races;
- to encourage African people everywhere in educational, industrial and commercial enterprise;
- to approach Governments and influence legislation in the interests of the black races; and
- to ameliorate the condition of the oppressed negro in all parts of the world. (Sherwood, 2012, p. 107)

Subsequent meetings were titled Pan-African Congresses (instead of Conference) and hosted in Paris (1919), London, England, Brussels, Belgium, and Paris, France (1921), London (1923), New York City, (1927), Manchester, England (1945), Dar es Salaam, Tanzania (1974), Kampala, Uganda (1994), and Johannesburg, South Africa (2014) (Munro, 2008; Sherwood, 2012). Common themes across these meetings involved the removal of detrimental European forces and influences in African countries, self-government by African people, and the stabilization of African economies and political organizations. These same themes are prominent among Black transnational sport organizations (chapter 3) and Black internationalist sporting resistance (chapter 4) throughout the twentieth and twenty-first centuries, and so the current text outlines the genealogy of Black resistance within and beyond sport and the recursive relationship between the local and the global.

Another strength of these Pan-African meetings was the intentional merging of racial and class interests, with particular emphasis on unions and workers' rights (Burden-Stelly & Horne, 2020; Byrd, 2020; Horne, 1985, 1994/2020, 2013a; Robinson, 1983/2000). The demands outlined at these meetings were also relevant to various groups who suffered from the pillaging of European imperialism. These Pan-African meetings coincided with African nation independence efforts. Between 1847 and 1965, over forty African countries declared their independence from European colonizers such as Britain, France, Spain, Belgium, the Netherlands, and Portugal (James, 2012; Wallerstein, 1961/1967/2005). On July 10–13, 1969,[32] Pauluu Kamarakafego, a Black internationalist and environmental justice activist, organized the first international Black Power Conference in Bermuda (Swan, 2020, 2022).[33] This conference highlighted issues impacting the Black World globally. The 1,500 conference attendees came from Africa, Asia, Europe, and the Americas (Swan, 2009). C.L.R. James was the keynote speaker of the conference, and he served as a mentor to Pauluu Kamarakafego (Swan, 2009). Hence, the twentieth century was the period where Black Nationalism and Pan-Africanism loosened the chains of European colonialism through international coalition building and coordinated counter-hegemonic efforts. Likewise, concurrent movements were taking place in sporting spaces across the Americas, Caribbeans, Africa, and Australia, and these efforts are explored throughout this book.

Another primary ideology that informed Black international social movements is Black Radicalism (Ogbar, 2020). Black Radicalism is distinct from Black Nationalism and Pan-Africanism due to its proximity to communist and socialist philosophies. One example of this orientation was the African Blood Brotherhood, which was established in Harlem, New York, in 1919 by Cyril Briggs, Richard B. Moore, and Otto Huiswood (Byrd, 2020; Ogbar, 2020). This Black leftist organization included numerous World War I veterans, and it established alliances with the Socialist Workers Party and Communist Party (Ogbar, 2020). One of the strengths of Black Radicalism is its ability to galvanize anti-racists with anti-capitalists and anti-fascists (Anderson, 2012; Horne, 1985, 2013b). Black Radicalism would continue through the mid-twentieth century in the United States with the formation of organizations such as the Black Panther Party for Self-Defense, which adopted a Marxist-Leninist philosophy in 1968 (Newton, 1973; Ogbar, 2020; Slate, 2012). Beyond the United States, the Black Power movement influenced the creation of scores of radical organizations in Trinidad and Tobago, Guyana, Israel, New Zealand, Polynesia, and India (Slate, 2012).[34] Similarly, Black Power leaders in the United States were also influenced by revolutionaries in Cuba, China, North Vietnam, and African countries such as Algeria and Ethiopia (Carmichael & Hamilton, 1967; Slate, 2012). Prominent Black radical leaders such as Kwame Nkrumah of Ghana, Kwame Ture of Trinidad and the United States, Walter Rodney of Guyana, and Steve Biko of South Africa all adopted and embodied leftist politics. Black Radicalism is foundational to the emergence of Black internationalism in the mid-twentieth century (Byrd, 2020; Burden-Stelly & Horne, 2020; Patterson & Kelley, 2000), and its philosophical and strategic impact on numerous Black sportspersons is explored in chapter 4.

Summary

In this introduction, I situate the role of Black sportspersons within a broader sociopolitical and sociohistorical ecosystem. In contrast to notions of sport being an apolitical space, I argue alongside other critical sport scholars that sport is inherently political and particularly for Black sportspersons it is often a site of resistance against oppression. This analysis builds upon the legacy of scholarship from critical sport scholars of the African (Black) diaspora such as C.L.R. James, Ben Carrington, Janelle Joseph, and Munene Franjo Mwaniki to name a few. The introduction of the Black sporting resistance concept is informed by these works while also adding nuanced insights. Unique contributions of this book include the application of the sport resistance and activism typologies to international sporting spaces; the infusion of diaspora, transnationalism, and Black internationalism within the Black sporting resistance framework; the exploration of a broader range of sports where resistance efforts were enacted; and the expansive inclusion of Black sporting resistance beyond the Black Atlantic, including in regions such as Australia, Latin America, South America, Africa, and Asia. The historical, comparative, and critical sensitivity within the book also facilitates the recognition of connections between Black sporting resistance and international Black social movements such as the *Black Liberation Struggle*, *Black Nationalism*, *Pan-Africanism*, and *Black Radicalism*.

1
Black Sporting Resistance

That is, to consider sport as a particular racial project (that would include the rules of the game, the actions of the players, fans and coaches, the sports media, institutional governing bodies, as well as sports discourse itself) that has the effects in changing racial discourse more generally and that therefore reshapes wider social structures. Sports become productive, and not merely receptive, of racial discourse and this discourse has material effects both within sport and beyond. *Sport helps to make race make sense and sport then works to reshape race.* (Carrington, 2010, p. 66)

Since the mid-twentieth century scholars have explored the intersection of race, sport, politics, resistance, and activism across various disciplines including sport sociology (Bass, 2002; Brown, forthcoming; Cooper, 2021; Edwards, 1969/2017; Hartmann, 1996; Magrath, 2022; Sage, 1998), cultural studies (Abdel-Shehid, 2003; James, 1963), sport history (Wiggins, 2018; Wiggins &

Miller, 2003), sport communications (Anderson, 2023; Brown, 2020; Hatcher, 2021), and sport journalism (Bryant, 2018; Zirin, 2008, 2021). These various contributions have expanded collective understandings of how hegemonic practices have been challenged in subtle and more pronounced ways both within nation-states and transnationally. Nonetheless, there remains a need to explore Black sporting resistance efforts across geographical, political, temporal, and sociocultural spaces using a multilayered framework that accounts for the complexity of shared and hybrid identities (real and imagined), political alliances, migration experiences, and overlapping goals.

In accordance with Bauböck and Faist (2010), I seek to incorporate the concepts of diaspora, transnationalism, and internationalism in this text in complementary yet distinct ways to produce conceptually rich analyses with evidenced-based propositions. I posit all examples of diaspora and internationalism are inherently transnational, but all examples of transnationalism are not inherently diasporic and/or internationalist (see figure 1). The primary difference in the concepts is the extent of connectedness across distinct geopolitical spaces (physical and psychological) and the level of intentional radicality in challenging prevailing hegemonic ideologies, systems, and practices. For example, Black internationalism involves a more radical orientation to challenge intersecting oppressive realities compared to diaspora and transnationalism. Relatedly, diaspora and Black internationalism have a more pronounced political aim whereas transnationalism can also have a political agenda, but not inherently.[1]

In an effort to connect conversations across multiple disciplines, the Black sporting resistance framework (BSRF) was created. The BSRF is an approach that centers African (Black) epistemology, ontology, and axiology in and through sport as oppositional forces against global anti-Black racism and related forms of oppression. In concert with Gilroy's (1993) critique of ethnonationalist absolutism, I argue Black resistance transcends nation-state boundaries and corresponding citizenship. Relatedly, as Horne (2004, 2014a, 2018a, 2020a, 2020b) posited, the advancement of Black people within any nation-state, particularly in neocolonial contexts, has been a product of international forces and alliances. These alliances include alignment along racial and cultural lines, as with the Pan-Africanism movement, as well as other intersecting identities including political, religious, and social class, as in the case of the Black internationalism movement. In other words, the shared enemy of European imperialists, colonizers, fascists, and capitalists has contributed to the international alignment of multiple marginalized groups.[2]

Despite being minimized in non-sport-centric disciplines, I argue along with my critical sport scholar colleagues that sport has played and will continue to play an integral role in resistance efforts against European settler colonialism, imperialism, and White racial capitalism (Carrington, 2010; Chen & Mason,

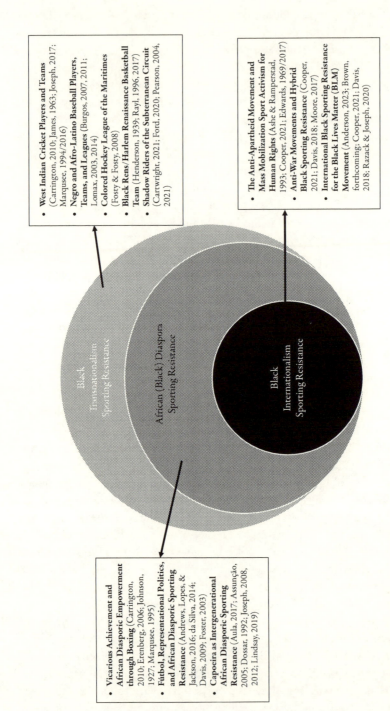

FIGURE 1 Black sporting resistance framework

2019; Hylton, 2008; James, 1963; Joseph, 2017). Given the global impact of these oppressive ideologies and systems as well as the far-reaching ideological power of sport (Coakley, 2017; Edwards, 1969/2017, 1973; Sage, 1998), the BSRF includes analytical concepts that enable an in-depth analysis of African (Black) diasporic, transnational, and internationalist resistance in and through sport. Hence, the BSRF incorporates the following key conceptual dimensions: a) African (Black) diaspora, b) (Black) transnationalism, c) Black internationalism, d) sporting resistance typology, and e) sport activism typology (see table 1).

African (Black) Diaspora

The concept of diaspora has been explored in disciplines such as philosophy, history, anthropology, sociology, international relations, communication, comparative politics, geography, biotechnology, and ethnic and cultural studies (Bauböck & Faist, 2010; Cohen, 1997; Fazal & Tsagarousianou, 2002; Gilroy, 1993; Safran, 1991). The term derived from the Greek words *speiro* and *dia*, which translate in English to mean *to sow over* (Cohen, 1997; Faist, 2010; Patterson & Kelley, 2000; Safran, 1991). A key component of diaspora refers to the dispersal, in many cases through forced migration, of a kindred group of people across different geographical spaces. In academic scholarship, the term *diaspora* was originally used to refer to Jewish people who were dispersed due to violent coercion by antisemitic regimes. Over time the definition of diaspora has evolved. For the purposes of my current analysis, I utilized Hamilton's (1995) definition: a "global aggregate of actors and subpopulations differentiated in social and geographical space, yet exhibiting a commonality based on shared historical experiences conditioned by and within the world ordering system" (p. 394).

One benefit of Hamilton's definition is its malleability in terms of being applied to multiple diasporic groups. For example, although the term *diaspora* was originally attributed to Jewish people, it subsequently has been used to refer to the experiences of multiple religious, ethnic, and cultural groups such as Armenians, Africans, Palestinians, Indians, Chinese, Lebanese, Sikhs, Zionists, and Caribbeans.[3]

Moreover, Faist (2010) described how all diasporas include migration or dispersal, cross-border experiences between homeland and new land of settlement, and levels of integration with land of settlement. Diaspora scholars such as Safran (1991) and Cohen (1997) highlighted how collective memory and myth of homeland, ethnic distinctiveness, desire to return to homeland, and contested experiences in land of settlement are common features of diasporic groups. In all instances, the connections to a real or imagined homeland and an adaptive reenactment of traditional cultural values, beliefs, and

Table 1
Black Sporting Resistance Framework (BSRF)

Conceptual Frame and Definition	Black Sporting Resistance Examples	Key Conceptual Framework Characteristics
Diaspora[a] "global aggregate of actors and subpopulations differentiated in social and geographical space, yet exhibiting a commonality based on shared historical experiences conditioned by and within the world ordering system" (Hamilton, 1995, p. 394)	• Muhammad Ali's conversion to Islam, support of the Nation of Islam (NOI), and solidarity with African diasporic and continental people as well as anti-Islamophobia groups worldwide (Ali & Durham, 1975; Cooper, 2021) • Joe Louis's high-profile fights against Max Schmeling during the interwar period (agency/stealth racial empowerment)[b] (Erenberg, 2006) • Brazil winning the World Cup in 1958 with Afro-Brazilian players (pioneering) (Davis, 2009) • Jack Johnson's support for the Australian Aboriginal Progressive Association (AAPA) and the Mexican Carrancistas (advocacy) (Horne, 2005; Maynard, 2005) • Social justice–oriented capoeira classes in urban environments (grassroots activism) (Lindsay, 2019) • All African Games (sustained cultural empowerment) (FEI, 2022)	• Cultural distinctiveness/collective identity (Bauböck & Faist, 2010; Gilroy, 1993) • Race and ethnicity (Bruneau, 2004, 2010; Faist, 2010) • Entrepreneurship (Bruneau, 2004, 2010; Faist, 2010) • Geosocial displacement (Davies, 2008; Hamilton, 1995) • Social oppression (Davies, 2008; Hamilton, 1995) • Endurance, resistance, and struggle (Davies, 2008; Hamilton, 1995)
Transnationalism "everyday practices of migrants engaged in various activities . . . reciprocity and solidarity with kinship networks, political participation not only in the country of emigration but also of immigration,	• West Indian cricket players, leagues, and spectators (agentic participatory sporting resistance, stealth migrant sporting resistance, symbolic activism, grassroots activism, collective cultural resistance) (James, 1963; Joseph, 2017; Marqusee, 1994/2016)	• Cross-border mobility and migration (Faist, 2010) • Social formations (Faist, 2010) • Building communities and networks, including for business and social

Table 1

Black Sporting Resistance Framework (BSRF) (continued)

Conceptual Frame and Definition	Black Sporting Resistance Examples	Key Conceptual Framework Characteristics
small-scale entrepreneurship of migrants across borders, and the transfer and re-transfer of cultural customs and practices" (Faist, 2010, p. 11)	• *Colored World Series of the Negro Leagues* between the 1920s and 1940s (mass mobilization activism and economic activism) (Lomax, 2014) • *Colored Hockey League of the Maritimes* (grassroots activism and economic activism) (Fosty & Fosty, 2008) • *Harlem Rens* sue to have Black players participate as members of the Original Celtics in the 1920s (legal activism) (Rayl, 2017) • *Shadow Riders of the Subterranean Circuit* (grassroots activism, economic activism, pioneering, media activism, and advocacy) (Cartwright, 2021; Ford, 2020; Pearson, 2004, 2021)	movements; social and symbolic ties with native and migrant destination countries; reciprocity and solidarity with kinship networks (Faist, 2010) • Nongovernmental organizations (Faist, 2010)
Black Internationalism[c] "a response to slavery, colonialism, and white imperialism. It is a political culture that prioritizes the liberation of and collaboration among people of color the world over. It is about embracing struggle and making common cause" (Byrd, 2020, p. 548)	• *Sir Isaac Vivian Richards of Antigua* declining invitations to cricket events in South Africa during the apartheid era (symbolic activism) (Davis, 2009) • *Black press coverage of the anti-fascist and anti-Vietnam War efforts*—Chicago Defender—in the 1960s–1970s (media activism) (Cooper, 2021) • *Eroseanna "Rose" Robinson's boycott of representing the U.S. in track competitions in Russia during the Cold War and her refusal to pay taxes for militarism* (political and symbolic activism) (Davis, 2018; Moore, 2017)	• Anti–white supremacy/continental unity • Anti-colonialism/self-determination • Anti-imperialism/revolutionary transformation • Anti-capitalism/socialism • Anti-sexism/radical black humanism • Anti-war/durable peace (Burden-Stelly & Horne, 2020 Horne, 2014a; Swan, 2020)

(continued)

Table 1
Black Sporting Resistance Framework (BSRF) *(continued)*

Conceptual Frame and Definition	Black Sporting Resistance Examples	Key Conceptual Framework Characteristics
	• *Paul Robeson's anti-war, anti-racist, and anti-imperialist musical performances* (music and art activism) (Robeson, 1958/1988)	
	• *Naomi Osaka, Guen Berry, Raven Saunders, Lungi Ngidi, Lewis Hamilton, and Nicky Winmar expressing their support for the BLM movement* (symbolic and political activism) (Fischels, 2021; Katwala, 2021; Moonda, 2020a; Morse, 2021; Osmond & Klugman, 2022; Razack & Joseph, 2021)	

[a] The definition of *diaspora* presented here is broad and applies to multiple diasporic groups. I define and apply the concept of African (Black) diaspora as people who possess and embody an explicit connection to Africa as a homeland; collective identification with the racial and political categorization of Black and/or related terms (e.g., Afro-African American, West Indian, Caribbean, Geechee, Maroon, Moor, Negro, Black Pacific, Dalit, Scottish ethnic minorities, Aboriginal Australians, and other Indigenous peoples); connectivity to African worldviews, spiritual systems, and customs; and a resistant disposition to anti-African oppression. Thus, as a specific type of diasporic group, I explore how African diasporic sportspersons enact resistance in myriad ways to connect the local to the international.

[b] A type of agentic resistance I call *stealth racial empowerment*; this concept is described in chapter 2.

[c] I acknowledge there are multiple definitions of *Black internationalism*, including Burden-Stelly and Horne's (2020) definition: "a conceptual framework that illuminates ecumenical anti-capitalist modes of analysis, struggles for liberation, and efforts at worldmaking emerging from the local, national, and global conditions for African people. It centers political economy analysis; theorizes the international character of Blackness as a special condition of surplus value extraction; interrogates intra-racial class conflict and antagonism; insists upon the importance of culture in the history, progress, and self-emancipation of African descendants; and strives for the eradication of white supremacist capitalist imperialism" (p. 70). Although I agree with Burden-Stelly and Horne's (2020) definition, Byrd's (2020) broader definition of Black internationalism is most relevant to the examples highlighted in this text. For example, Burden-Stelly and Horne's (2020) emphasis on anti-capitalism is not as clear with all examples outlined in this text (yet when it is clear I highlight its presence). Because the complexity of Black participation in modern-day sport is grounded in capitalism and neoliberalism, these activities are rife with contradictions and challenges (see Andrews, 2020; Hawkins, 2010; Rhoden, 2006; Smith, 2009; and Yehudah, 2020, for more expansive discussions on this topic). Hence, Byrd's (2020) broader definition of Black internationalism is used while select characteristics from Burden-Stelly and Horne's (2020) text are applied when applicable. Furthermore, in chapter 4 I highlight the saliency (and concurrent lack thereof) of the different components of Black internationalism in sporting resistance while maintaining alignment with the spirit of the paradigm.

practices are essential for the intergenerational sustainability of diasporas (Bauböck & Faist, 2010; Bruneau, 2004, 2010; Cohen, 1997; Faist, 2010; Joseph, 2017). Using a sociological perspective, Cohen (1997) offered the following description of the significance of diasporas across geopolitical contexts: "They bridge the gap between the individual and society, between the local and the global.... Diasporas themselves articulate their demands in terms of human rights or 'group rights'" (p. 196).

In concert with Gilroy's (1993) concept of the Black Atlantic, I centralize the connection of African people from the precolonial period through colonial dispersal and more recently to post-/neocolonial diasporic existence. The term *African (Black) diaspora* has been conceptualized in a multitude of ways over the past several years. Here, I will provide a brief overview of these definitions, highlight their similarities, and offer my own definition of the concept for the purposes of the current analysis. The African Union refers to people of the African diaspora as those who possess genetic and cultural lineages to the continent irrespective of their current nationality or citizenship and demonstrate a commitment to the uplift of Africa (African Union, 2022). Related to the de-emphasis of current nationality or citizenship, Cohen (1997) described the conditions that informed the manifestation of the African diaspora concept in the twentieth century: "the forcible transhipment of ten million people across the Atlantic for mass slavery and coerced plantation labour in the Americas provided the defining and constituent elements of the African diaspora" (p. 27).

In more concrete terms, Patterson and Kelley (2000) conceptualized the African diaspora as both a *process* of racial imperialism, capitalism, and colonialism and a *condition* of wretchedness, displacement, and resilience in the face of oppressive conditions. The process is continually re-created through movement, context, expression, and political resistance, and the condition is recursively connected to these processes (Patterson & Kelley, 2000). The African diaspora as a collective group that has been dispersed across the globe perpetually seeks to embody what Gilroy (1993) described as an "imaginative humanity" under dehumanizing conditions (p. 201).[4] The extent and nature of this infamous period in human history created a distinct shared experience among African people as a result of their encounter with the violent and immoral actions of Europeans across multiple generations.[5] Correspondent with this colonial project came the invention of Whiteness and Blackness as dichotomous ontologies whereby the former constituted everything good, pure, and correct and the latter represented everything evil, undesirable, and incorrect (Battalora, 2021). The creation of Whiteness along with the colonial project instituted a global system of White supremacy that continues to exist in the twenty-first century;[6] hence, the intergenerational presence of African (Black) resistance.

Moreover, Joseph (2017) emphasized the aspect of imaginary or socially constructed communities in her definition of African diaspora. According to Joseph (2017), African diaspora refers to "real or imagined communities scattered from a homeland over multiple sites ... the racial, ethnic, local and national (imagined) communities and cultures that span borders as a result of historic and contemporary migrations" (p. 10). Beyond the focus on dispersal, Davies (2008) explained how the African diaspora is integrally connected to upending colonialism. Specifically, the author posited that the African diaspora is "linked to decolonization activity and therefore has political intent, and that is to account for the 'status and prospects' of various peoples of African descent scattered around the world, who are often denied their humanity" (p. xxxvi). Each of these definitions informed my understanding of African (Black) diaspora as an analytical concept.

My use of the term *African diaspora* does not adhere to the strict criteria as outlined by Safran (1991) or Vertovec (1999), although these guidelines are useful. Due to the unique plight of Africans who were affected by the transatlantic atrocity and continental pillaging of Africa by Europeans, the concept of African diaspora transcends nation-state boundaries and specific ethnic applications and traverses into the racial (Black), cultural (Pan/Trans-African), and political (anti-colonial) spheres. This collective identification, both imagined and real, is a by-product of precolonial ties, shared colonization experiences, and overlapping cultural practices. European colonizers sought to destroy Africans' cultures and identities through enslavement, pseudoscientific claims, intellectual theft and distortion, land theft, murder, abuse, and other forms of violence (Asante, 1990, 2003; Asante & Mazama, 2005; Carruthers, 1999; Rodney, 1972). Despite these efforts, the traditions, beliefs, values, and systems of traditional African culture have sustained over time (Asante, 1990, 2003; Asante & Mazama, 2005). As such, I define the term *African diaspora* to refer to people who possess and embody an explicit connection to Africa as a homeland; collective identification with the racial and political categorization of being Black and/or related terms;[7] African worldviews, spiritual systems, and customs; and a resistant disposition to anti-African forces. This definition is not geographically bound, but rather bounded by historically situated events and sociological conditions.[8]

The widespread nature of the transatlantic atrocity resulted in difficulties for African diasporic descendants to determine their exact homelands and familial lineages across the continent. It is widely understood that a majority of Africans who were enslaved in the Americas and Caribbeans were of West African descent (Franklin, 1947/1974; Williams, 1974/1987).[9] However, throughout the nineteenth and twentieth centuries, symbolic homelands referenced for African people included Ethiopia, Guinea, Liberia, and Ghana (Cohen, 1997; Patterson & Kelley, 2000). Specifically, during the emergence of the Pan-African movement in the early twentieth century, the biblical scripture of Psalm 68:31, which states that "Ethiopia shall soon stretch out her hands unto God," was a rallying cry for Africans globally to embrace their historical roots and combat European colonialism and fascism (Patterson, & Kelley, 2000, p. 14). When discussing the symbolic significance of Ethiopia for African people globally during the early twentieth century, Patterson and Kelley (2000) explained that "Ethiopia as the metaphor for a black worldwide movement against injustice, racism, and colonialism lay at the heart of the early historical scholarship on the role of African peoples in the making of the modern (and ancient) worlds" (p. 14).

As noted earlier, Davies (2008) surmised how the concept of African diaspora is inextricably connected to decolonization movements for African people and thus inherently a political descriptor rather than merely a cultural reference. As such, I contextualize the manifestation of the African diaspora through Black sporting practices as a form of resistance against anti-Black racist ideological hegemony.

Related to African diaspora, Gilroy's (1993) conception of the Black Atlantic is another instrumental concept for the BSRF. In an effort to challenge and demystify notions of national absolutisms, Gilroy posited that the Black Atlantic is a "theorization of creolisation, métissage, mestizaje, and hybridity" (p. 2). Specifically, Gilroy focused on intercultural exchanges and relations (also referred to as flows and circulation of people and ideas) and how these occurrences inform(ed) identity and cultural (re)formulations in different geographical contexts yet interconnected with one another. He explained the importance of this focus: "The history of the black Atlantic ... continually crisscrossed by movements of people ... engaged in various struggles towards emancipation, autonomy, and citizenship—provides a means to reexamine the problems of nationality, location, identity, and historical memory" (p. 16).

This point is particularly relevant to the examination of prominent Black athletes from the United States such as Jack Johnson and Muhammad Ali. They fought several of their high-profile matches outside of the United States, which amplified the resonance of their identities, personalities, demeanor, and performances with African people globally. They signified Black humanity, liberation, and empowerment whether it was their intention or not.

Furthermore, Gilroy's (1993) emphasis on cultural kinship over nationality aligns with my approach to exploring how the accomplishments of Black athletes and teams galvanize African people across different nationalities and citizenships, including those within the Black Atlantic world. Building on Gilroy's (1993) analysis of the impact of the Black Atlantic through music and Joseph's (2017) application of the Black Atlantic with Afro-Caribbean cricket players in Canada, I explore Black sporting resistance across the Black world including across and within the Atlantic and Pacific regions.[10] The examination of Black sporting resistance beyond the Black Atlantic reflects an extension of Gilroy's (1993) and Joseph's (2017) work rather than a departure from it, because all of our approaches focus on flows, exchanges, and connections beyond nationality, ethnic identity, and citizenship.

Key components of diaspora in chapter 2 are cultural distinctiveness/collective identity, race and ethnicity, entrepreneurship, geosocial displacement, social oppression and endurement, resistance, and struggle (see table 1) (Bauböck & Faist, 2010; Bruneau, 2004, 2010; Davies, 2008; Faist, 2010; Gilroy, 1993; Hamilton, 1995). Given efforts to dehumanize African people through enslavement and genocide, symbolic representations, cultural iconography, and collective identity have served as powerful sources of resistance. Patterson and Kelley (2000) described this collective identity as a "political imperative... formation of political and cultural movements premised on international solidarity" (p. 19). For example, interracial sporting contests during and post-enslavement period constituted political, ideological, and spiritual battleground sites whereby African humanity, dignity, self-determination, and resilience were undeniably on the line and proven (Carrington, 2010; Cooper, 2021; Edwards, 1969/2017; Henderson, 1939; James, 1963). Regardless of an African person's nationality or citizenship, the shared identity of being marked as subhuman as a result of one's distinctive phenotypical features, homeland, and/or cultural heritage creates both a real and imagined community among the oppressed. In contrast to transnationalism, in which mobility is the primary unit of analysis, my diaspora analyses in chapter 2 centralize collective identity across time, space, and context.

Relatedly, Bruneau (2010) posited that iconography is integral for the intergenerational transmission of diasporic identities, particularly regarding the sustainment of social networks across geographical spaces post-dispersal.[11] Cultural practices such as music, language, literature, cinema, media, community, and family life are important configurations of diasporic identities (Bruneau, 2010). Another important aspect of diasporic identities, albeit to varying extents across different groups, is sport. Within his *sporting Black diaspora* theory, Carrington (2010) purported that sport was essential to the creation and contestation of racial differences and identities during the twentieth century. Aside from social ties, diasporas can exist through memory of or an imagined desire for a homeland or a common destiny of liberation from oppression (Faist, 2000). More specific to sport, the symbolic victories and participation of Black athletes and teams have been associated with Black people's vicarious achievement and shared imagination of Black liberation from oppressive realities. In other words, Black sportspersons' success, particularly their pioneering interracial feats, signify a deeper affirmation that Black people are indeed human and capable of accomplishing greatness when a proverbial leveled playing field is established (Cooper, 2021; Wiggins & Miller, 2003). In concert with Carrington

(2010), I surmise sport figures and achievements elicit memories, affirmations, and connections to real or imagined homelands and a time when African people were not colonized or oppressed. In chapter 2, I highlight select instances where Black sporting accomplishments, identities, and actions resonated across the African (Black) diaspora within the context of broader geopolitical occurrences.

(Black) Transnationalism

The terms *diaspora* and *transnationalism* have often been used interchangeably, but over the past few decades scholars have begun to explicate how these terms are related yet distinct (Bauböck & Faist, 2010; Bruneau, 2004, 2010; Faist, 2010). Two primary differences between the terms include the impetus of the concepts and the focal units of analysis. Diaspora was developed as a concept to describe the impact of group *dispersal* as a result of exile and/or trauma and the corresponding *collective identity* created in connection with respective homelands (Cohen, 1997; Faist, 2010; Safran, 1991). Transnationalism, on the other hand, refers to a broader range of migration experiences that focus on *continuous cross-border mobility, establishment of networks in settled lands*, and *reciprocal connections with homelands* (Bruneau, 2010; Dahinden, 2010; Faist, 2010).[12] Moreover, Faist (2010) defined transnationalism as "everyday practices of migrants engaged in various activities. These include ... reciprocity and solidarity within kinship networks, political participation not only in the country of emigration but also of immigration, small-scale entrepreneurship of migrants across borders and the transfer and re-transfer of cultural customs and practices" (p. 11). According to Bruneau (2010), transnationalism includes networks, kinship groups, and migrant organizations as well as diasporas. Hence, diasporas are a subset of transnational experiences, but not all-inclusive of the transnationalism phenomenon (see figure 1).

The concept of transnationalism as a phenomenon of widespread scholarly interest emerged in the early 1990s (Glick et al., 1995). Transnational spaces are stabilized environments where dense ties of social groups are sustained within and beyond nation-states; in fact, the homeland, settled land, and migrant groups create a triangular structure of exchanges and flows via cross-border processes (Faist, 2010). Migrant formations emerge to formalize transnational connections and develop what Faist (2000) labeled as a border-crossing expansion social space. Therefore, no transnational migrant fully assimilates into a new culture, but rather integrates selective aspects of each space they traverse. Related to this point, transnational citizenship refers to the political realm whereas transnational syncretism is associated with the cultural realm (Faist, 2010). Scholars have outlined four domains of transnationalism: the economy, politics, culture, and religion (Dahinden, 2010; Vertovec, 1999). Transnationalism is integrally connected to the process of globalization whereby ideas, peoples, goods, services, and other resources result in the integration of economies and societies (Aninat, 2002; Faist, 2000). Although colonialism was a part of globalization, Pan-African resistance was and remains a part of globalization as well. For example, Gilroy (1993) explained how Black experiences inside and outside of modernity involve cultural mutations, hybridity, and intermixtures despite neocolonial oppression. The enactment of these transnational practices by Black sportspersons is highlighted in chapter 3.

Furthermore, mobility and locality enable information and resources to be exchanged on a routine basis (Dahinden, 2010). Transnational migrants establish businesses and organizations in settled lands that either rely on or provide support to similar entities in their respective homelands. Given their cross-border identities, transnational migrants and communities are inherently politically driven (Dahinden, 2010). The motivation for mobility extends beyond individual desires and reflects a commitment to collective empowerment. The locality of transnational migrants allows them to establish stable relationships with networks in the settled land as opposed to being nomads or transient migrants. Concomitantly, their mobility enables ties to the homeland to remain intact in tangible ways as opposed to imagined connections (Dahinden, 2010). Transnationalism also ranges from being highly institutionalized within entities such as churches or political organizations to being enacted through informal relationships such as family and non-biological connections (Faist, 2000).

Key components of transnationalism in this text include cross-border mobility, social formations, reciprocal kinship networks for social and business purposes, and nongovernmental organizations (see table 1) (Faist, 2000, 2010). More specifically, I incorporate the concept of transnationalization, which refers to small group reciprocation, circuit exchanges, and solidarity within and across communities (Faist, 2000). Kinship bonds include family, friends, religious members, associates, and business partners. Within sport research, migrant laborers have been the most studied group of transnational communities (Bale & Maguire, 1994; Magee & Sugden, 2002; Maguire, 1999). However, less attention has been paid to the formation of sport leagues or organizations as transnational communities (Burgos, 2007, 2011; Joseph, 2012a, 2017; Lomax, 2003, 2014). The institutionalization of Black sporting spaces by migrants reflects the phenomenon of transnational social spaces. Faist (2000) outlined key factors that contribute to the creation of transnational communities: "Factors conducive to the formation of transnational social spaces not only include favourable technological variables, troubled nation-state formation and contentious minority policies in the developing world, and restrictions such as socio-economic discrimination. Instead, political opportunities such as multicultural rights may also advance border-crossing webs of ties" (p. 191).

Moreover, Bruneau (2010) posited that transnational communities (also referred to as diasporic transnationalism, Dahinden, 2010) are composed of individuals who possess migration expertise, and this essential aspect of their identity facilitates the creation and sustainment of networks across borders. A keen focus on transnational practices within these communities reflects my social constructivist orientation whereby historically situated and contextually grounded knowledge and relationships are examined as complex phenomena as opposed to monolithic generalities. The transnational popularity of sport as a cultural practice with political implications underscores the power of Black transnationalism in sporting resistance whereby racist beliefs can be challenged and upended in (neo)colonial milieu; hence, the location and modalities of resistance are emphasized with this type of sporting resistance. In chapter 3, I explore the experiences of Black sportspersons, teams, and leagues that embodied key components of transnationalism.

Black Internationalism

The concept of Black internationalism emerged in the mid-twentieth century in response to Cold War politics (Burden-Stelly & Horne, 2020). Although Black internationalism has roots in the Black radical tradition, it diverges from traditional Pan-African philosophies with its explicit leftist, anti-capitalist, anti-nationalist, communist-friendly, and socialist-friendly political stance (Byrd, 2020; Burden-Stelly & Horne, 2020; Patterson & Kelley, 2002). Black internationalism as a movement and paradigm manifested during the interwar period when the Russian Revolution and New Negro movement in the United States embodied a radical leftist posture toward European imperial powers (Burden-Stelly & Horne, 2020). Historical Black internationalists include Paul Robeson, Eslanda Robeson, William L. Patterson, Ben Davis, W.E.B. DuBois, Shirley Graham DuBois, Marcus Mosiah Garvey, Amy Ashwood Garvey, Claude McKay, Ferdinand Smith, Walter Rodney, C.L.R. James, George Padmore, Sylvia Wynter, Cyril Briggs, Lovett Fort-Whiteman, Richard B. Moore, Otto Eduard Gerardus Majella Huiswoud, Claudia Jones, Zora Neale Hurston, Kwame Ture, Huey P. Newton, Bobby Seale, Angela Davis, Aimé Césaire, Pauluu Kamarakafego, Kwame Nkrumah, Patrice Lumumba, Nelson Mandela, Malcolm X, and Muhammad Ali (Burden-Stelly, 2022; Burden-Stelly & Horne, 2020; Byrd, 2022; Horne, 1985, 1994/2020, 2013a, 2016; Ransby, 2022; Swan, 2020). More recent Black internationalists include Cedric Robinson, Gerald Horne, Robin D. G. Kelley, Barbara J. Ransby, Quito Swan, Keisha Blaine, Charisse Burden-Stelly, Sundiata Cha-Jua, Clarence Lang, Roderick Bush,

Minkah Makalami, and Cheryl Higashida (Burden-Stelly & Horne, 2020; Kelley, 2002; Quan, 2019; Robinson, 1983/2000; Swan, 2022).

These Black internationalists of the past and present understood the power within and across racial group alliances. For example, Byrd (2020) articulated the origins of Black internationalism and its grounding in cross-cultural coalition building: "At its core, black internationalism is a response to slavery, colonialism, and white imperialism. It is a political culture that prioritizes the liberation of and collaboration among people of color the world over. It is about embracing struggle and making common cause" (p. 548).

Black internationalists express solidarity with anti-colonial, anti-imperialist, and anti-fascist countries, groups, and individuals (Burden-Stelly & Horne, 2020; Byrd, 2022). Organizations such as the African Blood Brotherhood for African Liberation and Redemption led by Richard B. Moore, Cyril Briggs, and Otto Huiswood and the American Negro Labor Congress led by Lovett Fort-Whiteman embodied the ethos of Black internationalism during the 1920s through their support of anti-colonial and anti-racist movements in the Caribbeans, Africa, Asia, and the United States (Byrd, 2020; Horne, 1985, 1994/2020). A distinct strength of Black internationalism in comparison to previous Black social movements was the pronounced alignment with non-African labor, communist, socialist, and anti-colonial organizations. Black internationalists view European imperialism, colonialism, fascism, and capitalism as the primary antagonists and thus seek to build alliances with any groups who share this disposition (Burden-Stelly & Horne, 2020; Byrd, 2020; Horne, 1985, 1994/2020). This political view enables different alliances to be established across time, space, and context based on mutual aims or interest convergence, in contrast to building alliances on predetermined factors such as race or proximity.

Beyond the United States, Black internationalism emerged as a formidable philosophy and movement during the mid-twentieth century. Kwame Nkrumah's Organization of African Unity (OAU) and the Négritude movement in France and the francophone world signified the far-reaching sentiments of anti-colonialism across the African diaspora following the infamous Berlin Conference in 1884 (Byrd, 2020). As noted earlier, the 1945 Pan-African Congress emphasized labor rights, leftist politics, and militancy (Burden-Stelly & Horne, 2020). Ten years later, another historic event occurred within the Black internationalist movement on April 18–24, 1955, with the Bandung Conference (Burden-Stelly & Horne, 2020; Horne, 1985; Byrd, 2020). This six-day conference included twenty-nine representatives from African and Asian countries and signaled the growing alliances between these major continental entities (Byrd, 2020). In 1961, the Non-Aligned Movement (NAM) was established to organize developing countries who sought independence from the United States and Soviet Union (Byrd, 2020). As a result of these partnerships,

Burden-Stelly and Horne (2020) conclude that Black internationalism is a global left *and* Pan-African movement committed to Afro-Asian solidarity, Third Worldism, and Tricontentialism.

More germane to the current text, Burden-Stelly and Horne (2020) outlined six core elements of Black internationalism: a) anti–White supremacy/continental unity, b) anti-colonialism/self-determination, c) anti-imperialism/revolutionary transformation, d) anti-capitalism/socialism, e) anti-sexism/radical Black humanism, and f) anti-war/durable peace. Anti–White supremacy refers to the explicit and perpetual resistance against beliefs, systems, and actions that promote White superiority. In concert with Pan-Africanism, Black internationalists view continental unity as the solution to ending White supremacy. It is important to remember that a major reason why the underdevelopment of Africa was able to occur was through the lack of collectivism among and within different African tribes who subsequently were subjected to European deception and exploitation (Rodney, 1972; Williams, 1974/1987). In other words, although Europeans viewed Africans collectively as inferior savages, African people during ancient times spoke many different languages and upheld customs that varied across tribes and regions. This lack of continental unity was exploited by Europeans, which led to the current state of Africa as a resource-rich continent, but also one that is economically and politically vulnerable.

Relatedly, anti-colonialism refers to the recognition, challenging, dismantling, and replacement of colonial systems and practices with humane and equitable structures (Burden-Stelly & Horne, 2020). All aspects of a society including land and other resource allocations, economic systems, language and meanings, intellectual property/contributions, laws, educational institutions, political arrangements, and cultural norms must be changed if the vestiges of colonialism are to be eradicated. Black internationalists surmise African self-determination is the goal. Examples of African self-determination include the creation of Black labor organizations such as the Brotherhood of Sleeping Car Porters and American Negro Labor Congress, the pre-1940 tenor of the National Association for the Advancement of Color People (NAACP),[13] the establishment of the UNIA in 1914, the pre-1994 African National Congress (ANC) in South Africa,[14] and the organization of the Pan-African Congresses between 1900 and 1953 (Byrd, 2020; Hine et al., 2006; Horne, 1985, 1994/2020, 2013a, 2016, 2019; Munro, 2008; Sherwood, 2012). Beyond destructing colonial ways of doing, being, and thinking, self-determination also involves replacing these norms with more traditional African epistemologies and cultural systems (Asante, 1990, 2003; Asante & Mazama, 2005; Carruthers, 1999; Diop, 1974; Hilliard, 1998). Anti-imperialism refers to combating the land and human theft and imposition of cultural assimilation perpetuated by anti-African countries (Burden-Stelly & Horne, 2020).[15] Similar to self-determination being the resolution for anti-colonialism, revolutionary transformation is the goal of anti-imperialism. Revolutions such as those that occurred in Ethiopia, Haiti, Algeria, Ghana, Cuba, South Africa, and other African countries during the twentieth century are examples of revolutionary transformations, albeit each of these examples remain in constant evolution with ebbs and flows (Horne, 2014b; James, 2012).

Anti-capitalism refers to the weakening and eventual elimination of an exploitative economic system that relegates the means of production and the majority of wealth assets therein to a numerical minority group of people and corporations across and within societies (Burden-Stelly & Horne, 2020).[16] Black internationalists adopt a more egalitarian economic philosophy grounded in socialism. Countries such as Venezuela, the former Soviet Union, Cuba, Ecuador, Bolivia, and Tanzania had leaders who promoted socialism, albeit to varying extents (Brown-Vincent, 2020; Eaton, 2013; Lal, 2015). Former Ghanaian president Kwame Nkrumah is known for popularizing the concept of scientific socialism in the 1960s and highlighting its connection to traditional African social systems (Nkrumah, 1973). Hence, anti-capitalism and socialism are indeed grounded in African worldviews (Asante, 1990, 2003; Asante & Mazama, 2005; Carruthers, 1999; Diop, 1974; Hilliard, 1998; Nkrumah, 1973).

Anti-sexism refers to the eradication of patriarchy and the oppression of women and girls throughout the world (Burden-Stelly & Horne, 2020).[17] Radical humanism deconstructs harmful connotations associated with gender and sex differences and honors and protects the shared humanity among everyone in an effort to foster harmonious coexistence (Burden-Stelly & Horne, 2020). This approach does not adhere to socially constructed gender hierarchies that create power differentials, but rather seeks to maximize the abilities and contributions of all humans. In a similar vein, anti-war refers to the ending and prevention of destructive military actions that seek to promote imperialism, colonialism, and capitalism (Burden-Stelly & Horne, 2020). Black internationalists champion durable peace with civil diplomacy, healthy interdependence, environmental sustainability, and non-military conflict resolution as key components of global progress (Burden-Stelly & Horne, 2020).

The recognition of these intersecting forms of oppression as outlined by Burden-Stelly and Horne's (2020) conception of Black internationalism is distinct from previous race-centric social movements such as the Pan-Africanism movement of the early 1900s. Although the Pan-Africanism movement acknowledged issues related to economic imperialism and issues of sexism, interracial alliances were not as pronounced with this ideology as with Black internationalism. This contrast is not intended to suggest one approach was more effective than another, but rather to recognize the nuanced intersections and divergences among Black resistance efforts over time, space, and context.[18] Burden-Stelly and Horne explained the theoretical significance of this paradigm and its centrality on Black liberation as "a conceptual framework that illuminates ecumenical anti-capitalist modes of analysis, struggles for liberation, and efforts at worldmaking emerging from the local, national, and global conditions for African people. It centers political economy analysis; theorizes the international character of Blackness as a special condition of surplus value extraction; interrogates intra-racial class conflict and antagonism; insists upon the importance of culture in the history, progress, and self-emancipation of African descendants; and strives for the eradication of white supremacist capitalist imperialism" (p. 70).

Black internationalists view White supremacy, imperialism, and neocolonialism as the primary sources of Black oppression and see global capitalist hegemony, militarism, and anti-African violence as by-products of these overarching ideologies. As a radical praxis, Burden-Stelly and Horne (2020) posited Black internationalism was formed "to collectively overthrow systems of domination and collaboratively forge human-centered social relations across borders" (p. 71).

As it relates to sport, similar to the emergence of Black internationalism as a social movement, during the interwar period the increased visibility and internationalization of sport heightened the political tensions associated with these seemingly innocuous social activities (Arnaud, 1998). From the highly politicized 1936 Olympic Games in Berlin, Germany, to the suspension of the Olympic Games in 1916, 1940, and 1944 due to World Wars I and II to the Black athlete protests during the 1968 Olympics in Mexico City to the boycotting of the 1980 Olympic Games in Moscow by several countries during the Cold War, sporting spaces became synonymous with political contestation (Boykoff, 2016; Cooper, 2021; Edwards, 1969/2017). In contrast to the myth of the apolitical or disengaged athlete, Black sportspersons during the mid-twentieth century mirrored the heightened sociopolitical consciousness of the broader social movements surrounding them (Cooper, 2021; Edwards, 1969/2017). Although attention has been paid to high-profile Olympic protests and their international implications, in chapter 4 I highlight the core elements of Black internationalism and its embodiment and reification by Black sportspersons during the mid-twentieth through early twenty-first centuries with anti-apartheid, anti-war, and Black Lives Matter (BLM) movement efforts. Situating Black sporting resistance within the broader Black internationalism movement across the globe is one of the unique contributions of this text.

Sporting Resistance Typology

Dating back to antiquity, Black resistance against oppressive forces has been exhibited in a plethora of ways (Asante, 1990, 2003; Asante & Mazama, 2005;

Carruthers, 1999; Diop, 1974; Fanon, 1952/2008; Hilliard, 1998; James, 2012; Rodney, 1972; Williams, 1974/1987). For example, military revolts have been a vital means of resistance for liberation movements from Haiti to the United States to Algeria to Ethiopia to Cuba to South Africa, among other nation-states (Horne, 2015, 2020b; James, 2012). However, these efforts did not operate in isolation. In an effort to account for a diverse range of resistance efforts, the African American Resistance Typology (AART) was created (Cooper, 2021). The initial typology was grounded in research on African Americans in general and African American sportspersons more specifically, but the categories have applicability to groups across ethnicities. Consistent with the theme of this text and the work of international and critical African diasporic sport scholars (Gilroy, 1993; Joseph, 2017), the notion of ethnonational essentialism or absolutism is not upheld as permanent or fully encompassing of the nuanced experiences of people of African descent globally. Hence, within this text, the resistance typology is applied to the examination of Black sporting efforts across nation-state boundaries, which reflects the evolution and malleability of the framework from its initial formation.

The resistance typology includes the following eight components: 1) *agency*, 2) *pioneering*, 3) *advocacy*, 4) *hybrid*, 5) *activism*, 6) *social movements*, 7) *revolutions/social transformations*, and 8) *sustained cultural empowerment* (Cooper, 2021). Agency, pioneering, and advocacy are deemed as borderline activist actions whereby under certain conditions they reflect activism and in other instances they do not (Cooper, 2021; Cooper et al., 2019). My colleagues and I defined activism as "engagement in intentional actions that disrupt oppressive hegemonic systems by challenging a clearly defined opposition while simultaneously empowering individuals and groups disadvantaged by inequitable arrangements. In addition, activism includes expressing specific demands for social change and operate in tandem with broader social justice movements" (Cooper et al., 2019, pp. 154–155).

The distinction between borderline activist actions and activism is that the latter must include intentionality for a collective aim, a clear opposition, concrete disruption to a hegemonic status quo, expression of specific demands for change, and connection to a broader social movement (Cooper, 2021; Cooper et al., 2019; Cooper et al., 2020). This distinction is important to better understand how, when, why, and where social change manifests through highly disruptive actions and/or less disruptive actions. Since human systems, psychology, and social behaviors are complex, corresponding resistance efforts seeking to change these realities must also be multifaceted and not monolithic.

As a borderline activist action, agency refers to individual or group actions that seek to convey a culturally situated form of personal expression or disposition (Cooper, 2021). Agency is closely connected with individual idiosyncrasies and creativity. Agency is also akin to Sage's (1998) conception of infrapolitics.

Moreover, agentic resistance is particularly important for African people who have been subjected to enslavement, dehumanization, and subordination whereby their individual choice was, and in many instances remains, largely stripped from them literally via codified by law and physical oppression and figuratively through tactics such as psychological suppression. Thus, any acts of defiance against oppression are grounded in agentic resistance. As it relates to sporting spaces, agentic resistance is highly provocative and powerful when exhibited by Black sportspersons who possess mass appeal, such as Jack Johnson and Muhammad Ali. Agentic resistance in and through sport are highlighted in chapters 2–4 to signify the power of disrupting ideological hegemony in subtle as well as in more pronounced ways.

Related to the notion of challenging social norms, pioneering as a form of resistance refers to the action of breaking a barrier by becoming the first of one's identity or identities to achieve a specific accomplishment (Cooper, 2021). Historically, in sport as within the broader society, certain types and levels of success were reserved for those who were deemed innately superior and/or acceptable. Given the widespread acceptance and imposition of White racism, modern sport was designed to be a site where White dominance was validated in a highly public manner. Yet Black sportspersons have continually debunked the racist myth of White superiority by achieving feats that previously were deemed impossible based on their perceived biological, psychological, cognitive, and physiological characteristics (Ashe & Ramperstad, 1993; Edwards, 1973; Henderson, 1939; James, 1963; Sailes, 2010; Wiggins & Miller, 2003). In chapters 2–4, select instances of pioneering in international sporting spaces as modes of resistance are highlighted and contextualized within broader social movements across nation-state boundaries. Advocacy as resistance involves concerted actions centered on enhancing awareness of and support for social justice causes (Cooper, 2021). Due to the uniquely vulnerable nature of being a disposable commodity in the form of an athlete, many Black sportspersons have opted to engage in advocacy for social justice as opposed to activism since the latter is much more disruptive and riskier.[19] Even though advocacy does not involve the same level of risk as activism, in a world where shifting attitudes and behaviors through interpersonal relationships and less inciteful messaging is more accepted, this borderline activist action has proven to be a useful method of resistance in and through sport. A recent example of a benefit of advocacy through sport was the voter turnout for the 2020 U.S. presidential and congressional representative elections related to the post-2020 Women's National Basketball Association (WNBA) and (Men's) National Basketball Association (M)NBA More Than A Vote campaign (Anderson, 2023; Butler, DeMartini & Cooper, 2023).[20]

Hybrid resistance is the embodiment of multiple counter-hegemonic actions across time, space, and context (Cooper, 2021). Sport activists have traditionally been celebrated for a single action or mode of resistance. In contrast to this myopic reading of resistors and activists,[21] the concept of hybrid resistance enables scholars and other observers to examine how strategic forms of resistance are activated at different times in varied contexts to stimulate positive social change. Each of the Black sporting efforts highlighted throughout this book illustrates how hybrid resistance is essential for any successful social movement or revolution. A social movement refers to mobilized resistance over time usually spanning over a year (Cooper, 2021). As noted earlier in the chapter, there have been numerous social movements that have catalyzed Black resistance in and through sport. Building on the seminal works of previous critical sport scholars (Carrington, 2010; Edwards, 1969/2017; Hawkins, 2010; Hylton, 2008; James, 1963; Joseph, 2017; Smith, 2009), a contribution of this book is the contextualization of intergenerational resistance efforts in and through sport across international contexts.

Revolutions or social transformations refer to the complete upending of a previous oppressive social system and replacing it with a new system of collective empowerment for a group that has experienced oppression (Cooper, 2021). The presence of revolutions in sport and the role of sport in broader political revolutions has been largely overlooked with the notable exception of the research on the Black athlete revolt of the 1960s (Edwards, 1969/2017; Hartmann, 1996). As such, within this text, the connections between revolutions beyond and within sport and the international impact of Black sportspersons are emphasized. Sustained cultural empowerment involves the perpetual freedom and empowerment of African people globally (Cooper, 2021). Although this aspiration has not yet fully manifested, the pursuit of it remains core to Black existence and resistance intergenerationally, or what Robinson (1983/2000) coined as the Black radical tradition. The expression of this aim by Black sportspersons in concert with leaders who champion international solidarity for a world free of all forms of oppression is highlighted in chapters 2–4.

Sport Activism Typology

Along the same lines as the resistance typology, the African American sport activism typology (AASAT) was created to account for the nuance involved in activist actions that are exhibited across time, space, and context (Cooper, 2021; Cooper et al., 2019; Cooper et al., 2020). Given its application to Black sporting resistance among and beyond African American sportspersons, the framework will be referred to as *sport activism typology* to emphasize its resonance beyond a single ethnic group. The ten typology categories are *symbolic, scholarly, grassroots, mass mobilization, economic, legal, political, media, music* and *art*, and *military*. An eleventh type of activism added in the current text is *religious activism*. Each of these types of activism highlights the modality and central mode of disruption activated to achieve a specific social justice goal or set of goals. In previous research, my colleagues and I delineated *sports-based activism* from *societal-centric activism* to indicate how disruptive empowerment has been enacted to directly change sporting spaces and in other instances the sporting space or status is used as a platform to ignite specific changes in the broader society, hence the use of the phrase *in and through sport* (Cooper, 2021; Cooper et al., 2019). Throughout the book, both *sport-based* activism and *societal-centric* activism are highlighted in connection to international social movements.

Because the definition of activism was presented earlier, brief descriptions of each type of activism are provided in this section. Symbolic activism refers to the enactment of a public protest of a social injustice (Cooper et al., 2019). This type of activism is flexible in terms of being performed by an individual or group, but in either instance agitation on behalf of a collective group is demonstrated, which is consistent with one of the criteria of activism. Symbolic activism is highly visible and disruptive because its utility is contingent upon its ability to interrupt the normal operations of a public sphere and a presumably apolitical athletic event. The visibility and cultural significance of sport makes these spaces uniquely influential sites for symbolic activism. Scholarly activism refers to the challenging of ideological hegemony in academic and intellectual discourses and spaces (Cooper et al., 2019). Traditionally, oppression has been initiated and substantiated through miseducational practices whereby pseudoscientific and outright fallacious myths have been promulgated (Carruthers, 1999; Woodson, 1933/2010). Specific to sport research, racist myths about Black genetic inferiority and selective superiority have been widely circulated (Coakley, 2017; Edwards, 1973; Eizen & Sage, 2012; Sage, 1998) and thus the articulation and production of anti-racist and counter-hegemonic research is essential to any liberation struggle.

Grassroots activism refers to organized counter-hegemonic disruption with the intention of igniting substantive change at the local level (Cooper et al., 2019). The local level refers to a specific community, state, or province. In examination of Colin Kaepernick's Know Your Rights Camp (KYRC), Wallace (2022) conceptualized this effort as a radical grassroots tactic that reflects a twenty-first century embodiment of the Black radical sporting tradition. When the intended scope of the direct impact extends across multiple states, provinces, nations, and/or societies, then it is considered mass mobilization activism. Oftentimes, social movements begin as grassroots efforts and later expand to mass mobilization. The infusion of the diaspora, transnationalism, and internationalism concepts facilitate the application of both grassroots and mass mobilization activism in and through sport in chapters 2–4, thus connecting the local with the global. Economic activism involves intentional monetary divestment from hegemonic systems and/or intentional financial investment in liberatory/emancipatory and empowerment entities (Cooper et al., 2019). In a system of global White racist capitalism, disrupting economies through boycotts and/or strikes and other means of creating financial duress for oppressive entities is particularly powerful and essential for resistance efforts. Boycotts, strikes, sanctions, and divestment strategies are part and parcel of economic activism.

Legal activism refers to the use of judicial systems to redress past and ongoing harms related to oppressive regimes (Cooper et al., 2020). Changing laws, rules, and policies has been essential for abolishing slavery, securing reparations, and shifting governmental interventions for restorative justice (Horne, 2020a).[22] Within sport, increased access to opportunities across various levels of sport and corresponding financial compensation has been opened due to legal activism. Closely related, political/civic activism refers to the strategic challenging of hegemonic governing systems to ignite sustained positive social change for an oppressed group or groups (Cooper et al., 2020). The 1994 election of Nelson Mandela in post-apartheid South Africa is an example of political and civic activism. In order for political systems to change, both legal and political/civic activism are imperative.[23]

Media activism involves the use of print and digital technologies to upend oppressive systems (Cooper et al., 2020). Along with miseducation (Woodson, 1933/2010), propaganda, particularly the use of sportswashing (Boykoff, 2016, 2022; Sage, 1998), remains one of the most powerful tools of ideological hegemony. Boykoff (2022) defined sportswashing as a strategy used by political leaders whereby sport is propped up as tool to convey legitimacy while nationalism and prevailing socio-structural inequities are maintained. In response to these and related deceptive tactics, the use of media to disseminate counter-hegemonic messages has been invaluable for sport journalists, athletes, scholars, activists, and advocates. Music and art activism involves the use of song, dance, paintings, drawing, and performance to challenge oppressive systems (Cooper et al., 2020). The international influence of former standout athlete, actor, singer, and activist Paul Robeson is a notable example of how music and art have been used to convey politically empowering and mobilizing messages (Cooper, 2021; Horne, 2016; Robeson, 1958/1988). Military activism involves the use of physical violence and weapons to achieve liberation and empowerment aims (Cooper et al., 2020). All African liberation efforts involve military activism (Fanon, 1961/2004; James, 2012), and in numerous instances Black sportspersons have leveraged their literal and/or figurative support for military activism or opposition to oppressive militarism, colonialism, imperialism, nationalism, and patriotism (Ali & Durham, 1975; Cooper, 2021). Religious activism refers to the challenging of oppressive religious practices that cause physical and/or psychological harm to those who belong to another religion or spiritual system. As highlighted in chapters 2 and 4, Muhammad Ali's profession of Islam was supported internationally by Muslim countries and other groups who had been subjected to religious persecution (Ali & Durham, 1975; Marqusee, 1995; Saeed, 2002).

Summary

Within this chapter, I highlighted the unique contributions of this text, which include the infusion of the diaspora, transnationalism, and Black internationalism concepts in the Black sporting resistance framework (BSRF). In concert with James (1963), Carrington (2010), Mwaniki (2017), and Joseph (2017), I seek to examine Black sporting experiences and impacts beyond nation-state boundaries. However, the current text centralizes different types of resistance and activism exhibited largely across the Black Atlantic (Gilroy, 1993), but also extending into the Black world more broadly across the Pacific regions. Similar to Horne (2015, 2018a, 2020a), I situate Black liberation efforts within an international lens and highlight strategic alliances and connections that contribute to progressive aims. My project focuses on sport whereas Horne's (2015, 2018a, 2020a) research has largely focused on political, social, military, and economic resistance beyond sport.[24] The presentation of select Black international social movements also informs the foundation and understanding of the BSRF. The components of diaspora, transnationalism, and internationalism in concert with the resistance and sport activism typologies provide an expansive analytic framework to understand the role of Black sportspersons' engagement in racially empowering social change efforts within and beyond sport across international contexts.

2
A Collective Consciousness

●●●●●●●●●●●●●●●●●●●●●

African (Black) Diaspora Sporting Resistance

> The "community" or the networks of affiliation constructed by practice are not reducible to race... but are to be understood in terms of the possibilities of resistance conditioned by relations of power and the very purposeful and self-conscious effort to build community.
> (Hartman, 1997, p. 59)

Diasporic scholars have posited that the concept of diaspora was developed to refer to groups who experience forced dispersal as a result of a traumatic event (Bauböck & Faist, 2010; Bruneau, 2010; Cohen, 1997; Faist, 2000). In ancient times, African tribes were largely delineated based on familial and regional ties (Asante, 1990, 2003; Asante & Mazama, 2005; Diop, 1974; Hilliard, 1998; Rodney, 1972; Williams, 1974/1987). Although there were similarities across various African tribes on the continent, the modern concept of African diaspora or Pan-Africanism had not yet manifested. Interactions between various African tribes ranged from harmonious coexistence/interdependence to contentious competition. The latter reality has been cited as one of the primary factors contributing to the stealth execution of the European transatlantic atrocity across Africa, widely known as the *maafa* among Africans (Rodney 1972; Williams, 1974/1987). Because Europeans often categorized African tribes as monolithically subhuman, the African diaspora was birthed out of the intergenerational *maafa*, which remains among the most egregious world-changing series of events in human history (Asante, 1990, 2003; Asante & Mazama, 2005; Diop, 1974; Hilliard, 1998; Rodney 1972; Williams, 1974/1987). In addition to possessing similar spiritual systems and cultural practices, the collective identity among African tribes was largely influenced through their shared experience with European colonization, and thus they had a common enemy in European colonizers.

As with all diasporic groups, collective identity via cultural symbols has been integral to the connectivity of African people across geographical regions. Cultural symbols have ranged from language to music to flags to spiritual and religious systems to political ideologies to real and imagined homelands (Patterson & Kelley, 2000).[1] These symbols signified African humanity, ingenuity, community, creativity, adaptability, and perseverance. In colonial societies, the creation of White saviors was achieved through forced psychological and social conditioning (Carruthers, 1999; James, 2012; Robinson, 1983/2000). Black revolutionaries have been demonized because they represent a psychological and spiritual jolt to the oppressed. Their mere existence signifies the possibility of liberation and the creation of a permanent decolonial habitus. The intergenerational existence and resonance of these cultural symbols have been an invaluable source of resistance against oppressive forces.

Historically, prominent athletes and sporting achievements served as cultural iconic symbols for political aims. Dating back to the ancient Greek Olympics, athletes represented ideological outposts for different nation-states and cultures (Coakley, 2017; Eitzen & Sage, 2007). When describing the sociohistorical significance of cultural icons, Ganguly and Thomas (2004) explained that "iconographic narratives that trace and explore both the evolution and appropriation of particular icons help us mark key moments in the cultural politics of communities, nations and global public spheres" (p. 1). Icons communicate cultural meanings, and in the case of Black people these individuals and groups often represent resistance to coloniality (Carrington, 2010).[2] Beyond sport participation being a leisure activity or mere entertainment for the masses, Black athletes, particularly in interracial contests, have competed under distinct historical and sociopolitical contexts. As such, the interplay between these ecological systems create a context whereby African (Black) diasporic athletes' feats were de facto associations with the aims of the Black world in confronting neocolonial realities. Scholars have noted how the expansion of modern sport coincided with worldwide European imperialism and colonialism (Carrington, 2010; Danylchuk, 2012; James, 1963; Mwaniki, 2017). As opposed to centering the colonial perspective, one goal of the current text is to explore how sporting spaces, icons, and practices have served as sites for African (Black) resistance against anti-Black oppressive forces. More specifically, this text situates Black sporting resistance within the context of the Black radical tradition referenced in the introduction whereby "a collective consciousness ... [and a] shared sense of obligation ... preserve the collective being, the ontological totality" (Robinson, 1983/2020, p. 171). This multilevel analysis involves a critical examination of the interplay between the emergence of the African diaspora, modern sporting practices, and Black sporting resistance during the colonial and neocolonial eras. Within this chapter, I examine how diasporic concepts such as cultural distinctiveness/collective identity, race and ethnicity, entrepreneurship, geosocial displacement, social oppression and endurance, resistance, and struggle have been manifested in and through sport (Bauböck & Faist, 2010; Bruneau, 2004, 2010; Davies, 2008; Faist, 2010; Gilroy, 1993; Hamilton, 1995).

Vicarious Achievement and African Diasporic Empowerment through Boxing

One of the most popular global sports between the mid-nineteenth and mid-twentieth centuries was boxing. This pugilist sport was violent and represented the ultimate physical expression of dominant masculinity. Boxing matches were and remain sites where racial ideologies are reproduced and contested (Carrington, 2010; Marqusee, 1995). Using his *sporting Black diaspora* theory, Carrington (2010) surmised the racial implications of boxing in postcolonial/neocolonial contexts: "The moment and act of physical struggle creates the conditions from which a post-slave consciousness, that is more fully and complexly human, can emerge.... We might better understand now how the role of the boxer (and therefore the black athlete) has come to be seen as a revolutionary agent of resistance to the most total forms of racial domination and white supremacy" (p. 91).

This analysis centers the perspective of Black spectators as opposed to the Black boxers themselves—hence, the diasporic effect. During the early to mid-twentieth century, interracial matches generated mass viewership and interest because the pugilists of each race were proverbial bearers of the collective fate of their respective racial groups, regardless of their personal intentions. In fact, several of these pugilists did not self-select into being cultural icons or representatives of their race, but nonetheless they understood their unique positionality as high-profile athletes in a highly racialized society (Cooper, 2021). Moreover, in accordance with Carrington (2010), I argue that Black pugilists of this era represented to the Black masses an elevation of Black people from what Gilroy (1993) referred to as being infrahuman to being full human with the freedom to defend oneself and express a full range of one's emotions.[3] The freedom of movement, domination of the White man, and sense of pride exhibited by Black pugilists created a metaphysical, psychological, and spiritual feeling of redemption and joy among all Black spectators who had been subjected to inhumane treatment. Stated differently, in victory, members of the victor's race experienced shared vicarious achievement. In defeat, members of the loser's race internalized a deep sense of deflation, subordination, and fear power usurpation in the broader society. Given the internationalization of boxing, the outcomes of these matches impacted local, national, and global perceptions of real or imagined/perceived power relations (Ganguly & Thomas, 2004). Hence, accomplished pugilists were inextricably connected to their race, the politics of their nation-states, and the broader international implications of their performances.

Among the most prominent examples of Black diasporic sporting resistance was Jack Johnson, the first Black heavyweight champion of the world. Johnson's unprecedented victories debunked racist myths that lionized White superiority. Johnson is widely celebrated as the first internationally iconic Black athlete (Carrington, 2010; Edwards, 1969/2017; Johnson, 1927; Marqusee, 1995; Wiggins, 2018; Wiggins & Miller, 2003). Johnson's distinct social and political position can be described as cultural iconography. Black athletes during the early to mid-twentieth century served as symbolic icons for Black empowerment. More specifically, the Black athletic body represented Black power via muscles, strength, fitness, physique, agility, skillful movements, dedicated training, and unflappable confidence. These attributes reflected deeply held aspirations and beliefs among Black people who were seeking to express their humanity in a colonized world that imposed inhumane conditions on them. Black athleticism constitutes a distinct form of cultural iconography that can align with Black Power and broader social movements across time, space, and context due to its combination of contested nature, action-packed improvisation, high public visibility, sensory stimulation, and storyline narratives.

It is also worth noting that Johnson's ascension as a Black pugilist occurred during the post–Haitian revolution era and post–U.S. emancipation era, yet prior to the proliferation of African nation-state independence from colonial rule on the continent.[4] During this period, Black people were viewed as subhuman savages who were incapable of competing with Whites in any human endeavor.[5] The Haitian revolution was viewed as an anomaly and the abolition of slavery in the United States was highly contested by settler colonizers rather than being viewed universally as evidence of Black humanity and resolve in the face of injustice or as a progressive step forward for all humanity (Horne, 2005, 2014a, 2015). Therefore, when Johnson or any other Negro boxer was scheduled to fight a White boxer, the expectation was the latter would demonstrate unequivocally the superiority of the White European race and thus these victories would serve as evidence for why Whites were divinely chosen to dominate "weaker" races such as Black people.[6]

Much to the chagrin of White spectators, Johnson's unabashed physical domination, skillful maneuvering in the ring, and impressive stamina against White opponents in international venues irrevocably fractured the myth of White superiority that was promulgated through popular pseudoscientific publications (Carrington, 2010; Cooper, 2021; Johnson, 1927). For example, on December 26, 1908, Johnson defeated Canadian boxer Tommy Burns in Sydney, Australia, to become the first Black heavyweight champion of the world in front of thousands of onlookers (Johnson, 1927). Within the broader social context of the European imperialism taking place during the early twentieth century, Erenberg (2006) articulated the psychosocial and political impact of Johnson's victory against Burns: "With physical superiority considered a sign of racial supremacy, most whites saw Johnson's crown as a threat to Caucasian racial and national prestige. . . . In an era of Social Darwinism, it was assumed that the strongest male individual represented the best race. If a black man won, then the white race lost" (p. 34).

The fact that a Black American of enslaved lineage defeated a White Canadian in Australia sent shockwaves through a world that had been wrought with colonial fallacies for over four centuries. It is precisely the dialectical relationship between Black athletes' presence and achievements in contestation with hegemonic racist stereotypes in public spaces that underscores the power of their *agentic participatory resistance* and particularly their pioneering resistance.[7] Stated differently, I argue the psychological rupturing of taken-for-granted norms associated with racist myths is rooted in contradictory tensions between perceived beliefs and observable facts. It is the interplay of tensions and contradictions that result in social change over time, space, and context. On July 4, 1910, Johnson shattered any doubts that a Black man could be the best fighter in the world when he soundly defeated White American boxer Jim Jeffries in Reno, Nevada (Johnson, 1927). White-incited race riots broke out across the United States after Johnson's defeat of Jeffries. The riots resulted in numerous deaths in Georgia, New York, Washington, D.C., and Texas (Johnson, 1927). The international impact of this fight was evident in the fact that several nation-states, including the United States and United Kingdom, banned the filming and broadcasting of interracial fights (Erenberg, 2006; Horne, 2020b).

The ideological blow to assertions of White superiority and concurrent psychological jolt to Black people globally underscored how Black athletic pioneering accomplishments, as a form of resistance, fulfill a distinct role in African diasporic efforts. For example, Johnson's victory over Burns in 1908 was celebrated by Aboriginal groups in Australia, Pacific Islanders, South Africans, West Indians (later known as Caribbeans), and African Americans (Johnson,

1927; Marqusee, 1995; Maynard, 2005). Throughout the history of the African diaspora, connections with various diasporic groups, particularly those who have been victimized by European colonization, have been established due to mutual interests (Cohen, 1997; James, 2012). In other words, when diasporic groups share a common adversary or system of domination, then symbols of liberation are also often shared.[8] I refer to this phenomenon as *inter-diasporic alliances*; sporting resistance historically has played an integral role in such alliances. For example, throughout his career, Johnson traveled to England, Spain, Russia, Germany, Australia, Cuba, and Mexico to not only showcase his athletic acumen but also to foster *inter-diasporic alliances* with oppressed people globally (Horne, 2005; Maynard, 2005). Prior to his fight in Australia against Burns, Johnson established relationships with Aboriginal Australian activists such as Fred Maynard and members of the Coloured Progressive Association of New South Wales and the Australian Aboriginal Progressive Association (AAPA) (Maynard, 2005). The AAPA used the same motto as Marcus Garvey's Universal Negro Improvement Association (UNIA): "One God, One Aim, One Destiny" (Maynard, 2005). This shared motto illustrated the mutual interests of decolonization and self-determination among these diasporic groups. Maynard (2005) explains the diasporic significance of Johnson's arrival and engagement with the Aboriginal people in Australia: "Certainly the coming of Johnson to Australia gave Aboriginal people an identifiable black icon of great celebrity to cheer, and something to aspire to" (p. 4). Later in 1919, while in exile in Mexico, Johnson was befriended by a group of Mexican revolutionaries called the Carrancistas (also known as the Constitutionalists), led by Venustiano Carranza and Álvaro Obregón (Horne, 2005). Given the institution of the color line globally, Johnson resonated and connected with oppressed groups across the world. Hence, Johnson's life as a pugilist and agitator reflected his Black sporting resistance inside and outside of the ring. As a pioneer and agentic disruptor in the ring, Johnson symbolized Black prowess against White terror. As an advocate and inter-diasporic ally, Johnson embodied resistance against global European imperialism and colonialism.

Moreover, the international resonance of Johnson meant that his importance transcended nation-state boundaries and connected with anti-colonial efforts in every corner of the globe. For example, Marcus Garvey, the leader of the largest mass movement of African people in world history and founder of the UNIA, cited Johnson's victories as evidence of the inevitable manifestation of a global Pan-African revolution (Horne, 2005). Garvey's international reach with his publication *The Negro World* further illustrated Johnson's diasporic reverberation through his sporting resistance. At its peak, *The Negro World* reached over 200,000 people worldwide (Martin, 1986). In the 1920s, the UNIA established 41 chapters worldwide (Maynard, 2005). The UNIA connected African Americans, continental Africans, West

Indians, Canadians, Aboriginal Australians, and South and Central Americans (Levine, 1993; Maynard, 2005).[9]

Although Johnson did not set out to represent his race or amplify international Black liberation movements,[10] as a cultural icon with global visibility the aspirations and dreams of African people and anti-colonial groups were mapped onto him and his achievements. Concomitant Black social movements during Johnson's boxing career included the Pan-Africanism movement, Black Nationalism movement, New Negro movement, and the first wave of Black athlete activism (Cooper, 2021; Edwards, 2016a). Rather than embodying characteristics of an activist, Johnson exhibited agentic resistance whereby his personal motivations, individual disposition, and athletic accomplishments were viewed as threats to the White social order.[11] These threats largely aligned with the sentiments of broader Black social movements even though Johnson did not view himself as a vanguard for domestic or international Black liberation efforts (Johnson, 1927). Furthermore, it is important to note that African (Black) diasporic identities do not require an explicit commitment to a specific political ideology. Rather, diasporic identities emerge from shared experiences with distinct societal conditions (Cohen, 1997; Faist, 2010; Patterson & Kelly, 2000). In the case of Johnson, a descendant of African people who were enslaved in the United States,[12] his connections to being viewed and treated as an undesirable brute by White society enabled his agentic resistance to be associated with broader Black liberation projects that sought to upend White racist oppression in all its manifestations. In other words, the purported and internalized belief was and remains that if a Black man can become heavyweight boxing champion of the world and dominate the image of White patriarchy in an indisputable manner, then African people globally could break the chains of colonialism and exhibit self-determination politically, economically, socially, culturally, and spiritually.

Another cultural iconic pugilist during the twentieth century was Joe "the Brown Bomber" Louis. As an African American boxer who emerged during the interwar years (1919–1939), Louis's athletic career was associated with both the domestic New Negro and pre–Civil Rights movements as well as the international anti-fascist movement. Scholars such as Munro (2008) and Horne (2020b) surmise that it was during the post–World War I era when African American contempt for racist policies and norms heightened the internationalization of their efforts, which coincided with shifts in global forces and conflicts involving fascists versus anti-fascists and communists versus capitalists.[13] In 1935, Italy was preparing to invade Ethiopia. As noted earlier, Ethiopia has been viewed as a diasporic symbol of African unity (Cohen, 1997; Horne, 2005; James, 2012; Munro, 2008; Patterson & Kelley, 2000). Ethiopia was the only African country that was not colonized by Europeans and, with Italy's impending invasion, Africans worldwide rallied to support Ethiopian independence (Horne, 2005; James, 2012; Patterson & Kelley, 2000). As a result, Ethiopia was a cultural icon for Africans across the globe who were resisting colonialization.

Concurrently, interracial contests on international stages carried a heightened meaning for African Americans in connection with their fellow Africans across the globe who were also facing the imminent threats of lingering colonialism, imperialism, fascism, anti-Black racism, and racial capitalism. In 1935, Joe Louis's bout versus Argentinian Primo Carnera at Yankee Stadium in New York was touted as one of the most anticipated fights in boxing history (Cooke, 2014; Louis et al., 1978). Although neither Louis nor Carnera were citizens of Ethiopia or Italy, their racial identities were proxies for the two countries, particularly the former. When Louis defeated Carnera in front of an international audience, African supporters of Ethiopia celebrated his victory as emblematic of their struggle (Cooke, 2014). An example of this international support occurred when Marcus Garvey paused the UNIA meetings to allow attendees to listen to the fight (Martin, 1986). Garvey was quoted as saying the future of the African race lay on the shoulders of Louis (Martin, 1986). Albeit an embellished account, the underlying meaning was that Louis's performance in the ring was meaningful for Black liberation efforts worldwide. The UNIA was engaged in serious political organizing to upend European colonialism, and the significance of their meetings being halted to show their support for Louis underscored the impact of Black sporting resistance as a part of the broader Black freedom struggle during the early to mid-twentieth century.

The association between Louis and anti-fascism was heightened with his legendary bouts against German boxer Max Schmeling in 1936 and 1938 (Henderson, 1939; Louis et al., 1978). Given the global politics surrounding the interwar period, Louis and Schmeling were inextricably linked to the racial clash between purported Nordic superiority and African resistance. Regarding their respective nation-states, Schmeling was perceived as representing the Aryan-led National Socialist party in Germany, whereas Louis was viewed as a symbol of American democracy and nationalism as well as the African freedom struggle, albeit the latter two were not inherently synonymous (Cooper, 2021; Erenberg, 2006; Louis et al., 1978). The year 1936 was a turning point for Black sporting resistance in terms of its impact on international racial justice movements. Adolf Hitler was the dictator of Germany and promoted the ideology of Aryan supremacy. Hitler had spearheaded the atrocious Jewish Holocaust starting in 1933 and described all races other than Aryans as savages and subhuman. The popularity of his militaristic and propagandistic efforts was evident among racist and fascist regimes throughout Europe (Erenberg, 2006).

Thus, when Schmeling soundly defeated Louis in the 12-round bout in 1936, it was viewed as a resounding victory for White supremacy, specifically Aryan superiority. It was not only the outcome of the fight that resonated with viewers, but the way Schmeling dominated Louis for a majority of the match. As Carrington (2010) noted, boxing represents a space where dominant masculinity is exercised and political power is reified. Schmeling's domination of Louis was interpreted as the inevitable success of Nazism and fascism more broadly. Internationally, Africans and Jews were deflated because a Louis victory would have signified that Hitler's views were inherently flawed (Louis et al., 1978). However, a short two months after Louis's loss, a group of African Americans including renowned track and field star Jesse Owens achieved unprecedented success at the 1936 Olympics in Berlin, Germany.[14] Headlined by Owens's four gold medals, the African American victories sent shockwaves through the world, especially since the Olympics were held in the German capital in front of Hitler. If there was any group that had an advantage by competing within their native country, it would have been the Germans, so when the African American Olympians demonstrated their prowess it was a major blow to racism in the United States and internationally. Domestically, groups such as the National Association for the Advancement of Colored People (NAACP) leveraged the public visibility of African American sport achievements to amplify support for the nascent Civil Rights movement (Cooper, 2021). Internationally, Pan-African organizations such as the UNIA used these victories as reference points to galvanize anti-colonial, anti-imperial, and anti-fascist alliances across the world (Erenberg, 2006). Simultaneously, U.S. nationalists were using the victories for their own agendas, which involved propagandizing American capitalism and "democracy" as the panacea for racial integration (Cooper, 2021). Hence, African American sporting success in international spaces illuminated the dialectical tensions between nationalism movements and other concomitant political movements.[15]

Two years after their famous bout, in 1938, Schmeling and Louis agreed to a rematch at Yankee Stadium in New York ("Joe Louis knocks out Max Schmeling," 1938; Louis et al., 1978). This time, Louis entered the fight as the heavyweight champion of the world and with increased confidence in his ability to defeat his nemesis. In a historic performance, Louis defeated Schmeling by knockout within two minutes and four seconds of the first round in front of 80,000 spectators (Dawson, 1938).[16] It was described as one of the most lucrative boxing matches in history up to that point, with a reported $900,000 in paid receipts (Dawson, 1938). The significance of the fight was reflected in some of the notable attendees, including a member of U.S. president Franklin Delano Roosevelt's cabinet as well as governors and senators of several states (Dawson, 1938). The global coverage of the 1938 fight further illustrated the far-reaching, including diasporic, implications of this match. The fight was broadcasted in English, German, Spanish, and Portuguese worldwide and it was reported that 70 million radio listeners tuned in (Dawson, 1938; Erenberg, 2006). Celebrations and media coverage of Louis's victory over Schmeling took place across the Black world in places such as Panama, Nigeria, and South Africa (Erenberg, 2006). Black international luminaries such as Marcus Garvey of UNIA, C.L.R. James of the Independent Labor Party, William L. Patterson of the American Communist Party, Paul Robeson of the Council of African Affairs (CAA), renowned novelist and intellectual Richard Wright, and Mary McLeod Bethune of the National Council of Negro Women (NCNW) expressed their support for Louis and emphasized the role his success in the ring played in the broader struggle for the African diaspora and Black liberation (Cooper, 2021; Erenberg, 2006; Louis et al., 1978). When reflecting on the rematch, Erenberg (2006) described Louis's significance to African people globally when he referred to him as a "Pan-African hero fighting against colonial oppression" (p. 154). In addition to Pan-African support, Louis also received support from the Jewish community for defeating Hitler's prized fighter. For example, the famous Black-owned *Chicago Defender* newspaper reprinted the *Jewish Daily Courier*'s tribute to the undisputed heavyweight champion (Erenberg, 2006). The Jewish support for Louis was yet another example of how Black sporting resistance can foster inter-diasporic alliances.

Aside from being Black males, boxers, and African diasporic symbols, Johnson and Louis shared another commonality. Both embodied what I describe as agentic resistance. *Agency* refers to "the use of personal choice and/or group actions to express a sense of individuality and/or sociocultural disposition within a specific context" (Cooper, 2021, p. 76). *Resistance* is defined as "intentional and/or unintentional actions by individuals, groups, organizations, and/or institutions that challenge oppressive systems and ideological hegemony" (Cooper, 2021, p. 7). The primary difference between agency as resistance as opposed to being a form of activism lies in the fact that in the case of the latter term, certain criteria must be met. My colleagues and I posited that activism involves the enactment of five criteria: 1) there is explicit intent from the actor or actors to achieve collective goal, 2) action must involve a direct encounter with an oppositional force, 3) action must create concrete disruption to the status quo, 4) specific demands for social change are articulated, and 5) connection to a broader social movement is evident (Cooper, 2021; Cooper et al., 2019). Regarding Black pugilists of the early twentieth century, many of them, including Johnson and Louis, did not identify as activists or express interest in serving as representatives of their race, nor did they communicate collective goals for their sporting achievements (Johnson, 1927; Louis et al., 1978). In his study of African migrant professional athletes, Mwaniki (2017) explained the paradox facing high-profile Black athletes in terms of their vulnerability and hesitancy with being activists: "Diasporic African athletes, by their mere presence, do work against nationalist understandings of spatial boundaries and rooted belonging, but the nature of sport, celebrity, and media often prevents athletes from being politically resistive figures" (p. 183).

It is important to note that both Johnson and Louis, by virtue of societal conditions, understood their roles as representatives and symbols of hope for African Americans and oppressed people broadly, albeit not in the wholesale manner like Muhammad Ali. The point being made here is that neither of them intended to pursue the role of being race men or leaders as boxers. Thus, I view them both as resistors and advocates rather than activists (Cooper, 2021). Notwithstanding, the broader sociopolitical and sociohistorical context in which they lived created a situation where they and their sporting performances were thrust into the role of serving as ideological symbols for the African diasporic freedom struggles against White supremacy and colonialism.[17] Hence, Black athletes who are viewed as African diasporic icons often engage in agentic resistance or what I refer to as *stealth racial empowerment* (also referred to as *stealth diasporic sporting resistance*) whereby they may not self-identify as activists, but nonetheless they engage in actions that advance the causes of their race or are used by activist groups for counter-hegemonic purposes.[18]

This analytical point is important to emphasize because it underscores how African diasporic resistance does not inherently involve intentionality for disruption by the resistor, but rather it is predicated on cultural distinctiveness/collective identity, geosocial displacement, social oppression, and struggle (Bauböck & Faist, 2010; Bruneau, 2004, 2010; Davies, 2008; Faist, 2010; Gilroy, 1993; Hamilton, 1995). Louis exhibited *stealth racial empowerment* through his nonconfrontational resistance to prevailing racial stereotypes inside and outside of the ring. Relatedly, Heywood and Dworkin (2003) explained how stealth feminism manifests itself through everyday actions by feminists: "Through their work on women's sports issues, every day feminists are advancing their causes in a kind of stealth feminism that draws attention to key feminist issues and goals without provoking kneejerk social stigmas attached to the word feminist, which has been so maligned and discredited in the popular imagination" (p. 51). In a related vein, Louis's success in the ring, mild-mannered disposition, and social networking with Black community members and leaders enabled him to advance the causes of African Americans and Pan-Africanists without explicitly describing himself as an activist or a Pan-Africanist. The labels of activist or Pan-Africanist were viewed as divisive by mainstream Whites as well as by some segments of Black people in the United States, such as those who either supported ongoing segregation or gradual assimilation approaches to racial integration.

Moreover, similar to how the second and third waves of feminism needed female athletes to advance their causes (Heywood & Dworkin, 2003), the New Negro, nascent Civil Rights, Pan-Africanism, Black Nationalism, and anti-colonial movements not only wanted Louis to be successful to demystify the notion of White superiority, but also to psychologically serve as a catalyst for Black collective self-esteem in the midst of perpetual oppression. Famous

African American poet Maya Angelou poignantly captured the African diasporic sentiments associated with Louis's bouts with White opponents:

> My race groaned. It was our people falling. It was another lynching, yet another Black man hanging on a tree. One more woman ambushed and raped. A Black boy whipped and maimed. It was hounds on the trail of a man running through slimy swamps. It was a white woman slapping her maid for being forgetful.... This might be the end of the world. If Joe lost we were back in slavery and beyond help. It would all be true, the accusations that we were lower types of human beings. Only higher than apes. True that we were stupid and ugly and lazy and dirty and, unlucky and worst of all, that God Himself hated us and ordained us to be hewers of wood and drawers of water, forever and ever, world without end.... Champion of the world. A Black boy. Some Black mother's son. He was the strongest man in the world. (Angelou, 1969/2009, p. 113)

In a world where Black expression was highly sanctioned and thus real emotions had to be perpetually suppressed, Black boxers represented the hopes, dreams, and lifelines for Black people who believed that their humanity mattered, and their previous and current oppression would eventually come to an end. The relationship between sporting resistors and broader social movements is reciprocal. There is no measurable value one can place on the diasporic power and impact of cultural icons such as the Black boxers of the twentieth century.

Following Johnson and Louis, the greatest Black athlete activist in modern times, Muhammad Ali, emerged. Departing from the *stealth racial empowerment* approaches embodied by his predecessors, Ali reflected Black sporting activism in and through sport. It is important to contextualize the period in which Ali's career ascended to understand why his global influence was so powerful. One, Ali emerged during the height of the Civil Rights and Black Power movements in the United States in the 1960s and 1970s. An iconic axiological example of Ali's Black sporting resistance is when he famously said he threw his Olympic gold medal into the Ohio River to express his disdain for anti-Black racism in the United States despite his athletic fame (Ali & Durham, 1975).[19] International attention was shifted to injustices against African Americans due to the effectiveness of grassroots, mass mobilization, media, political, and legal activism (Cobb, 2016; Cooper, 2021; Hine et al., 2006). Ali's association with the spirit of the Black Power movement further internationalized his own influence. The Black Power movement in the United States influenced activists in countries such as the United Kingdom, South Africa, and India (Ali & Durham, 1975). For example, in 1972 in Bombay, India, the Dalit Panthers of India adopted their name to signify their solidarity with the Black Panther Party in the United States (Prashad, 2000; Rajshekar, 1995). As noted earlier, international offspring of the Black Panther Party included the Chicano Brown Berets, Puerto Rican Young Lord Party, Asian American Hardcore, Yellow Brotherhood, American Indian Movement, Polynesian Panther Party, the Sephardic Black Panthers in Israel, and Dalit Black Panthers in India (Newton, 1973; Ogbar, 2020). Hence, similar to Black Power activists who were internationalizing their resistance efforts, Ali was using his platform through sport to champion the same causes. Saeed (2002) described the diasporic impact of the Black Power movement and its supporters: "In some respects it could be argued that Black Power created a global 'imagined community'" (p. 65). In addition, African liberation efforts on the continent and throughout the Caribbean region were occurring at a rapid rate during the mid-twentieth century (Farred, 1995; James, 2012).[20] In fact, a majority of the African countries secured their independence from European colonial rule between 1847 and 1965 (James, 2012; Wallerstein, 1961/1967/2005). Thus, the appetite for anti-colonial symbols and confrontation with White supremacy was arguably at an all-time high during the 1960s.

Ali's hybrid activism amplified *inter-diasporic alliances* for multiple reasons, including his unapologetic embrace of his African identity, Muslim identity, and anti-U.S. militarism and imperialism stances. From growing up in a predominantly Black neighborhood in Louisville, Kentucky, to ascending to the highest heights of boxing as an Olympic gold medalist in 1960 and later as a heavyweight champion in 1964, Ali became a cultural icon for African Americans (Ali & Durham, 1975). However, it was not until later in his career, when he traveled to meet with several African heads of state such as Kwame Nkrumah of Ghana and Abdel Nasser of Egypt and he intentionally scheduled a fight in Kinshasha, Zaire (now the Democratic Republic of Congo), during the African independence era that his diasporic influence extended beyond the United States (Farred, 1995).[21] Ali's meetings with these African heads of state also reflected his connections to his mentor Malcolm X. On July 17, 1964, Malcolm X addressed the First Ordinary Assembly of Heads of State and Governments at the Organization of African Unity (OAU) in Cairo, Egypt (Blackman, 2012). This trip occurred after Malcolm X had defected from the Nation of Islam (NOI), and the purpose of this trip was to internationalize the plight of African Americans as a violation of human rights and secure the support of African countries to bring this issue to the United Nations in the form of a petition (Ali & Durham, 1975; Blackman, 2012).

One of the primary reasons African leaders were supportive of Ali was because he shifted his politics from being a passive assimilationist of American propaganda during his late teenage years to being one of its most vocal critics during his adult years (Ali & Durham, 1975).[22] After his religious conversion and alignment with the NOI, Ali would routinely criticize the U.S. government and other racist governmental entities. Given the public visibility of these interviews, I argue Ali embodied symbolic, political, and military activism. As symbolic activism, Ali disrupted the status quo of athlete interviews by not only infusing politics into the commentary but by controlling the narrative and highlighting the connection between his African and Muslim identities with the broader Black Power, anti-colonial, and anti-imperial social movements. Ali's interviews became iconic because oppressed people worldwide would look to him as their spokesperson. In other words, symbolic activism is not limited to a single performative gesture such as raising one's fist or taking a knee during a sporting event, but it involves a publicly disruptive action that articulates a clarion call for freedom and radical change. In terms of political activism, Ali did not mince his words when identifying the source of tyranny against African Americans in the United States and Black people worldwide, and this enemy was the U.S. government and other Western nations seeking to dominate African, Asian, and Indigenous countries. A clear indication of the effectiveness of his political activism was his subsequent monitoring and targeting by the Federal Bureau of Investigation (FBI) and other state entities locally, nationally, and internationally (Ali & Durham, 1975). In addition, his military activism was reflected in his direct opposition to the Vietnam War, including his refusal to serve in the U.S. Army upon being drafted in 1967. Hence, Ali's hybrid activism differentiated him as a Black sporting resistor from his African diasporic pugilist predecessors.

Furthermore, Ali's anti-colonial stance, in concert with his predecessor Malcolm X, signaled to the African diaspora and their inter-diasporic allies that he was in alignment with their efforts. He astutely characterized groups based on either their support for colonialism or anti-colonialism, which enabled him to connect with oppressed groups beyond the United States and those who identified as Black (Farred, 1995). In other words, he emphasized his racial and political identities at the expense, and in spite, of his national citizenship identity. Thus, beyond simply embracing the Black Atlantic (Gilroy, 1993), Ali embraced his African diasporic and anti-colonial identities. Ali also intentionally participated in high-profile fights in Asia in places such as Manila, Philippines; Jakarta, Indonesia; and Kuala Lumpur, Malaysia (Ali & Durham, 1975). The intentionality of traveling outside of the United States for high-revenue fights reflected his anti-U.S. politics. This method of agentic activism should not be overlooked or minimized. Ali's courage and commitment to establishing and strengthening international ties associated with anti-colonial groups is an important form of resistance in a world that seeks to distort transnational connections via nationalistic propaganda and other restrictive means. Relatedly, Farred (1995) argued that Ali's connections to the Third World were strengthened by his willingness to fight these bouts in Africa and Asia, which coincided with the heightened international popularity of these matches. Along the same lines, Saeed (2002) described how when his South Asian family was living in

Scotland they rooted for Ali because of his unwavering commitment to Islam and unapologetic critiques of colonial practices.[23] In an analysis of non-White British immigrants, Marqusee (1995) noted how these groups looked to Black America for role models: "For these communities, especially South-Asian communities, the concept of Black Power that Ali clearly embodied was never just about blackness or pan-Africanism" (p. 63). These sentiments reiterate the power of Black sporting resistance as a tool for strengthening inter-diasporic alliances, connectivity, and anti-colonial collective identity.

Moreover, when he traveled to these countries Ali was revered because they viewed him as a champion for the oppressed rather than a representative of United States–imposed imperialism. For example, on October 30, 1974, in Kinshasa, Zaire, Ali entered the ring with a resounding chant of *"Ali Bomaye"* (Ali, kill him!) from the native Zairians (Ali & Durham, 1975). Before the fight, he expressed interest in wanting to wear the Zairian flag, which represented the OAU (Marqusee, 2017). It is customary for boxers to wear the flags of their native countries in the ring; it is less common for them to wear the flags of another country. Ali's understanding of and respect for Zairian freedom fighters and the OAU illustrated his African diasporic identity and commitment. The Zairian support for Ali and concomitant disdain for George Foreman had less to do with the latter's racial identity, but rather the notion that each boxer embodied the political postures of the era: pro-African independence and Third World liberation versus pro-U.S. nationalism and Western imperialism. Although Foreman was not a White opponent as with Johnson's and Louis's adversaries in the early 1900s, he represented the new U.S. symbol of nationalism, which was not well received by Africans across the diaspora and on the continent.

Furthermore, Ali's international coalition building mirrored the efforts of African American activists of the New Negro era such as W.E.B. Du Bois, Paul Robeson, and William L. Patterson (Horne, 1985, 1994/2020, 2013a). These racial justice champions were pursuing what Horne (1985, 1994/2020, 2013a) describes as *internationalizing the struggle* for Black freedom and global human rights, which granted them inter-diasporic influence. When Ali regained his heavyweight title, he received congratulatory notes from Ghanian president and Pan-African leader Kwame Nkrumah, Algerian prime minister Ben Bella, French president Charles de Gaulle, Egyptian president Gamal Abdel Nasser, Haitian president Francois Duvalier, Saudi Arabian king Faisal Abdel Aziz, Pakistani president Zulfikar Ali Bhutto, Irish prime minister Jack Lynch, Libyan president Muammar al-Qaddafi, and Ugandan president Idi Amin (Ali & Durham, 1975; Marqusee, 2017). Suffice it to say, Ali was the consummate Pan-African sporting icon in the mid-twentieth century.

Another integral aspect of Ali's African diasporic appeal was his religious identification and resonance. On February 28, 1964, Cassius Marcellus Clay shared with the world that he was changing his name to Muhammad Ali and becoming a member of the NOI (Ali & Durham, 1975). Ali indicated that Clay was a name associated with African bondage whereas Ali was an Arabic name connected to his African roots.[24] Farred's (1995) analysis captures the political and intercultural significance of Ali's name change: "The name Muhammad Ali can stand, metaphorically, for those same anti-colonial struggles in Africa and Asia... struggled for the recognition of history, culture and material depravity of an oppressed community... the anti-colonial movements battle to fundamentally reorganize the political landscape of a society" (p. 43).

Ali's conversion to Islam internationalized his identity and struggle with Muslim people worldwide who had suffered from European colonialism including from masquerading Christians.[25] For example, Ali's first fight against Floyd Patterson in 1965 in Las Vegas, Nevada, was promoted as "Islam vs. Christianity" (Saeed, 2002, p. 59). This framing of religious conflict between two African American boxers was particularly telling given the historical foundations of religious conflict that preceded global colonization via the transatlantic atrocity (Horne, 2014a). Muslims across the globe have suffered religious persecution and thus they have been an oppressed group who have sought freedom and redemption against colonial and imperial forces for generations.[26] Religions have historically served as proxies for imperial and settler colonial domination (Horne, 2014a, 2018a, 2020b). For example, Mwaniki (2017) articulated how religions such as Islam have been racialized over time whereby those who identify with the belief system were subjected to the same racial terror imposed upon groups based on skin color and culture.[27] Religious conflict is an international affair; countries have fought for sovereignty, legitimacy, power, and resources along religious lines for centuries. Relatedly, the enslavement of Africans by Europeans was justified through the insidious manipulation of Christian scriptures, hence my reference to these groups as masquerading Christians as opposed to true followers and disciples of Jesus Christ. Both Ali's joining the NOI and his unapologetic expression of the NOI's Black Nationalist message illustrated his activation of religious activism and participation in mass mobilization activism.[28] This transition and his subsequent commitment to the struggle was influenced by (and similarly he influenced) the broader Black Power and Black Nationalist movements across national boundaries.

By embracing and emphasizing his Black and Muslim identities Ali distanced himself from the U.S. colonial identity that was associated with his national citizenship. This identity shift underscores Gilroy's (1993) critique of nation-state boundaries and citizenship and accentuates the influence of hybridity and transnational connections. In reference to Ali's global impact as a postcolonial diasporic figure, Farred (1995) noted that "Ali's foregrounding of his blackness allowed him to make a racially essential connection with the decolonized world; his oppositionality to the US government cemented the radical aspects of those ties; and his faith in Islam enabled him to speak empathetically to Muslim constituencies in newly independent societies" (p. 41).

An example of his international resonance as a Muslim was reflected in the fact that his fight in 1973 in Jakarta, Indonesia, was welcomed by the Muslim country. Ali's appeal to Muslim states such as Libya, Kuwait, Indonesia, Malaysia, Thailand, Lebanon, Iran, Saudi Arabia, Pakistan, Syria, Egypt, Turkey, and numerous newly independent African nations illuminated his inter-diasporic appeal (Ali & Durham, 1975; Marqusee, 2017; Saeed, 2002). Likewise, Marqusee (1995) described how British-Asians supported Ali largely because of his Muslim identity.[29] The public visibility of boxing during the mid-twentieth century combined with Ali's conversion to Islam and his outright condemnation of the Vietnam War elevated his popularity among Muslim countries that had experienced masquerade Christian imperialism (Saeed, 2002). Despite the fact that Islam is a religion with multiple sects,[30] Ali's popularity revealed how Blackness and Muslim identity, specifically *Ummah*,[31] can create real and imagined communities.

One aim of this text is to highlight the interplay between broader sociopolitical, cultural, economic, and international movements and concurrent actions of and meanings attributed to Black sportspersons within and beyond the athletic milieu. In some cases the relationships are direct, as with Ali and his membership in the NOI, and in other instances are less direct, as in the informal advocacy and mutual respect between Johnson and the Australian Aboriginal Progressive Association (AAPA) or Louis and the American Communist Party (ACP) (Horne, 2020a; Marqusee, 1995, 2017). As it relates to these relationships, convergent interests lead to what I describe as *inter-diasporic alliances*. With Johnson, Louis, and Ali, inter-diasporic alliances were forged within and beyond the sphere of Pan-Africanism and Black Nationalism. For Johnson, his alliances included African Americans, Aboriginals of Australia, and Carrancistas of Mexico. With Louis, his alliances included pro-Ethiopian and African independence advocates, proponents of anti-Nazism, and anti-fascists. With Ali, his alliances included Black Power supporters, anti-war activists, anti-colonialists, and Muslims across the globe. I argue the existence of these *inter-diasporic alliances* is a precursor to the adoption of shared symbols as in the case of Black athletes as cultural icons who represent the aspirations of not only their own racial and ethnic groups, but also various oppressed groups who share a common adversary.

Hence, the current analysis explains how and why Black sporting resistance, ranging from agentic resistance and stealth racial empowerment with Johnson and Louis to symbolic, political, military, religious, and mass mobilization activism with Ali, serves as an integral part of broader social justice movements. Rather than solely serving as a direct militaristic, legal, grassroots, or scholarly function for political movements, African diasporic sporting resistance contributes a vital form of psychological empowerment via vicarious achievement and provides evidence of the radical possibility for the liberation of oppressed people worldwide. To that end, African (Black) diasporic sporting resistance serves as a counternarrative/reality to the ideological hegemony that propagates normalized oppression. If Black athletes can defy White superiority in sporting spaces, then it becomes more difficult to rationalize racist myths, and more importantly it inspires activists, advocates, and global citizens to optimize their spheres of influence to champion radical humanism. As Garvey stated of Joe Louis, he served his race well by being the best pugilist and representative of the race he could be (Martin, 1986). The sporting resistance of Johnson, Louis, and Ali during the twentieth century constituted valuable disruptions to the status quo and amplified Black and inter-diasporic social movements across the world by serving as rallying cries for transformative change at the local, national, and international levels.

Fútbol, Representational Politics, and African Diasporic Sporting Resistance

Historically, African sporting opportunities were confined to settings where representation in key decision-making positions reflected the athletes (Yehudah, 2020).[32] However, when Europeans controlled the sporting spaces, African participation was contingent upon the political aims of the former (Maguire, 1999; Sage, 1998; Coakley, 2017). Despite these unfavorable conditions, Black athletes on the continent and across the diaspora used sport as a platform to exhibit their humanity, skillfulness, and resolve. Beyond boxing, Black sport participation has been inextricably connected to the racial, cultural, social, and political groups that Black sportspersons represented. In other words, revisiting the theme presented in the introduction, sport is always political with racial, cultural, social, and economic implications. Within this section, I will highlight select instances where Black representation in fútbol reflected African diasporic sporting resistance.

The most popular sport in the world is fútbol. The most widely known international leagues and events are the European Premier Leagues and the Fédération Internationale de Football Association (FIFA) World Cup (Doidge, 2016; Kassimeris, 2007). As a by-product of African underdevelopment by European colonizers (Rodney, 1972), the infrastructure of several African institutions including sport organizations has yet to reach the level of international visibility and prestige as their European counterparts. Consequently, the best African players on the continent and throughout the diaspora are often recruited by European teams and paid lucrative salaries for their services (Darby et al., 2007). Previous scholarship has focused on the labor exploitation associated with this relationship. For example, Magee and Sugden (2002) introduced a typology of football labor migration based on different groups of players who participated in the English Premier League under varied conditions and motivations. The typology included the following six categories: a) *settler*, b) *ambitionist*, c) *exile*, d) *nomadic cosmopolitan*, e) *expelled*, and f) *mercenary*. The authors argued that premier leagues are supported by foreign investment via international talent extraction. In their analysis, they offered the following conclusion regarding the migration of players from country to country for labor purposes: "The globalization of football and its labor migrants can only be considered as part of a multifaceted and multidirectional process" (Magee & Sugden, 2002, p. 421).

In a similar vein, Wallerstein's (1974) world systems theory posits that global economies are structured based on the core, semi-periphery, and periphery countries. The core represents the colonizing and imperial countries. The semi-periphery represents the countries that serve as intermediaries between core and periphery countries. The periphery countries are those that are underdeveloped and exploited by the core and semi-periphery countries for resources. Along the same lines, Fanon's (1961/2004) internal colonization theory posits that European colonizing countries seek to exploit African countries for land, human, material, cultural, and economic resources for imperialist aims. Collectively, the contributions of these scholars have provided useful insights into understanding the relationship between the colonized and colonizers. These approaches have garnered significant attention in scholarly inquiries regarding Black sport participation (Hawkins, 2010; James, 1963; Smith, 2009).

However, within the current analysis, I approach these relationships from a different perspective. I centralize the resistance efforts embodied by African sportspersons who have been subjected to oppression rather than emphasizing their disadvantageous position or the economic logics that inform their migration patterns. Although colonial power wielding and exploitation are important within my analysis as well, it does not consume the central focus in terms of understanding Black sportspersons and their actions. In the sport of fútbol, Europeans have historically viewed themselves as superior to Africans. Thus, when Brazil won their first of its five World Cups in 1958 with a roster composed of numerous Afro-Brazilians, this accomplishment served as victory for the African diaspora. The most notable player on the 1958 Brazilian World Cup championship team was as Afro-Brazilian named Edson Arantes do Nascimento, more commonly known as Pelé. He became the youngest player in World Cup history to score a goal, record a hat trick, and be a member of a championship-winning team. Although there had been African diasporic superstars prior to Pelé's ascension, Davis (2009) described his uniqueness in being "the first international black/African sporting icon in a mass-based team sport" (p. 128). As a young phenom, Pelé amazed the world with his skillful maneuvering and deft ball placement. He was also a member of the 1962 and 1970 World Cup championship teams, which made him the first player to win three World Cups. His *pioneering* success symbolized Black athletic excellence in the coveted game of fútbol and inspired scores of future African diasporic and continental footballers.

The history of Afro-Brazilians and their connection to African diasporic resistance efforts amplified the popularity of Pelé. He remains arguably the greatest fútbol player in world history. Beyond his undeniable talent on the pitch, among the most compelling aspects of Pelé's game was the creative style in which he and his fellow Afro-Brazilians played the game. In contrast to European styles of play, Andrews and colleagues (2016) described the resistance embedded in the distinct form of fútbol embodied by Afro-Brazilians called *brasilidade*:

> A sense of Brazilian identity through *futebol* was initially provoked in opposition to the English originators of the sport in its modern form; subsequently against the social elites who dominated the early decades of the game in Brazil.... In a similar vein to other expressions of Brazilian corporal populism (i.e., *capoeira*, *samba*, and *carnival*), *futebol's* oppositionality has thus been rooted in a vernacular resistance against the perceived authority variously expressed through Anglo, social elite, and latterly European ways of both administering and playing the game. (p. 424)

The authors' reference to capoeira, samba, and carnival indicate that their use of term *Brazilian* is a proxy for an Afro-Brazilian-influenced or hybridized culture that is oppositional to European aristocracy. Contextualizing Pelé's influence within the ecological systems in which he existed, Foster (2003) surmised that his "'Dionysian' virtuosity" was emblematic of an egalitarian way of life that challenged the postwar British social order (p. 74). Brazil's World Cup victories in 1958, 1962, and 1970 added international legitimacy to the African diasporic Dionysian, creative, and spontaneous style of play compared to the Apollonian, tactical, and rigid style associated with European teams (Andrews et al., 2016; Foster, 2003).

It is here that I emphasize the dialectical relationship between the discourse framing of an African diasporic Dionysian style of play and a European Apollonian style of play. The inherent contradictions associated with the success of a presumably inferior style of play ruptured the myth of European supremacy in fútbol as well as within the broader promulgation of purported human hierarchies. Stated differently, Afro-Brazilian achievements on the fútbol pitch constituted and still constitute Black sporting resistance through a collective manifestation of a counter-epistemological, counter-ontological, and counter-axiological mode of existence against neocoloniality. It is precisely the tension that arises between the contradictions of *good versus evil*, *human versus subhuman*, *worthy versus unworthy*, and *capable versus incapable* that make sporting spaces, particularly interracial contests, powerful sites of resistance, reimagination, and reorientation from a local to a global milieu. The diasporic effect of *brasilidade* in fútbol that emerged in the mid-twentieth century was evident in the celebration of Brazilian success across African Black enclaves in places ranging from Salvador, Brazil, to Cape Town, South Africa, to Washington, D.C., to Paris, France, to London, United Kingdom to Hamilton, Bermuda and other locations across the Caribbean region, the Americas, and the Pacific region. From my analysis, I assert that stealth racial empowerment through distinctive performances serves as an essential component of African (Black) diasporic sporting resistance. The confluence of public visibility, symbolic representation, vicarious achievement, and culturally familiar and empowering expressions result in explicit (seen and expressed) and implicit (felt and understood) diasporic hubris. In accordance with James (1963), I argue the manner in which African diasporic people participate in sports cannot be overstated; hence, Black sporting resistance signifies victory in and of itself through the cultural preservation of the ontological totality (Robinson, 1983/2000) and thus any other forms of gratification are ancillary benefits.

Moreover, similar to Jack Johnson and Joe Louis, Pelé did not seek to become a representative for African people worldwide (da Silva, 2014), but his athletic success in the world's most popular sport generated pride across the diaspora in a period when the Pan-Africanism, Négritude, Black Power, Civil Rights, Black Freedom, and African independence movements were influencing the broader global sociopolitical context (Green, 1982; Ogbar, 2020; Singh, 2004). Within Brazil, the Afonso Arinos Law, which outlawed discrimination against Black people, was passed in 1951 (da Silva, 2014). Pelé's success on the national team in 1958 was viewed as evidence that anti-discrimination laws and racial integration formed a path toward social harmony in the post–World War II era. In her analysis of the racial discourse around the 1958 Brazilian World Cup journey, da Silva (2014) highlighted how throughout his career, Pelé embodied a liberalist view of combating racism whereby he expressed that good character and self-discipline would reduce racial discrimination more than direct confrontation of racist beliefs and systems such as via protests. Given the prevailing ideologies of the era and context, this liberalist view was supported by Black social movements in Brazil in the 1950s and thus Pelé was propped up as a symbol for Black liberation nationally and internationally based on his athletic success as an African diasporic person who shared a collective identity with Africans worldwide (da Silva, 2014).[33]

However, Pelé's symbolic representation was not only utilized by Black activists, but also by the Brazilian government for their own purposes. In the postwar era, the Brazilian government was promoting an ethos of multiracial nationality (Foster, 2003), which mirrors what sociologist Eduardo Bonilla-Silva (2018) describes as color blindness or color-blind racism. When describing how Pelé was used by political leaders during the mid-twentieth century, Foster (2003) offered the following interpretation of his own complicity in these efforts:

> Pelé himself was shamelessly used by the football establishment, itself an arm of the military regime as of 1970, to endorse its doctrines, embody its values and to rally national pride—not that he needed much persuasion. A vociferous patriot and an instinctual proponent of Brazilian values, Pelé counselled that poor blacks should in no way aspire to the success and the trappings of wealth he enjoyed, for God Himself had made his poor, black brothers poor and black, just as He had given Pelé unmatched athletic prowess so as to bring joy to those less fortunate. (p. 84)

One of the limitations of African diasporic sporting resistance is that when the agency of the Black athlete or team is not grounded in an activist foundation, their representation is susceptible to being interpreted, manipulated, and co-opted by various groups for different purposes. In the case of Pelé, his identity and achievements were simultaneously being used to advance Brazilian color-blind integrationist and nationalist aims while also being used by Black Power activists locally and internationally who championed race-conscious remedies for centuries of neocolonial policies and practices (da Silva, 2014; Davis, 2009; Foster, 2003).

The aforementioned nuance is important to acknowledge because previous analyses of what I describe as stealth racial empowerment has often been erroneously categorized as activism while minimizing the personal intentions or political orientation of the athlete whose sporting success resonated with the African diaspora (Wiggins, 2018; Zirin, 2008). More specifically, I purport that African diasporic sporting resistance has primarily involved non-sport activist groups' strategic use of Black athletes' achievements to advance their political agendas with little to no regard for the former's political orientation or intentions. In other words, vicarious achievement and racial collective identity superseded the misalignment of political philosophies between sportsperson and broader social movements because in a system of White neocolonialism, any sources of Black empowerment are considered valuable and utilized for racial progress.

Rather than engaging in symbolic and political activism, many African diasporic athletes' actions are often more reflective of agentic and pioneering resistance or what my colleagues and I refer to as borderline/contingent activist actions.[34] As noted earlier, activism involves *intentional* engagement in a disruptive counter-hegemonic action with explicit aims for advancing the plight of an oppressed group or multiple oppressed groups (Cooper et al., 2019). Even though all forms of resistance create a level of disruption, each form of resistance does not inherently include the intention of the actor to advance the cause of a collective group in concert with a broader social movement. In many instances, agentic actors are striving to achieve personal goals regardless of or with little regard for the broader political implications of their representation and performances. Athletes in general are indoctrinated into the belief that sports and politics should not be intertwined and the best way to advance social relations is through colorblindness, apolitical postures, and focusing on winning by adhering to the sport ethic (Boykoff, 2016; Coakley, 2017; Cooper, 2019, 2021; Eitzen & Sage, 2017; Foster, 2003; Mwaniki, 2017). Thus, athletes including Black athletes have been financially and socially rewarded for distancing themselves from revolutionary or radical political orientations and acquiescing with the hegemonic status quo including neocolonial governments.

Moreover, as it relates to Black athletes, particularly pioneers in interracial sporting spaces, they have been viewed as de facto representatives of their race, hence their distinct appeal to the African diaspora in a world that remains embedded in the vicissitudes of White neocolonialism and anti-Blackness. As stated earlier, diasporic sporting appeal does not require intentionality or endorsement on behalf of a Black athlete or team. It only requires the perception of collective identity, an imagined community, and the malleable use of sporting achievements for specific political goals. In modern-day fútbol, it is not uncommon to see the top players across the European Premier Leagues and European powerhouses such as France and Netherlands to be of African ancestry.[35] From George Weah (a Liberian who played in Liberia, Cameroon, Monaco, France, and England) to Abedi Pele (a Ghanian who played in Ghana, Qatar, Switzerland, Benin, France, Italy, Germany, and United Arab Emirates) to Didier Drogba (a Ivorian played in Côte d'Ivoire, France, England, China, Turkey, Canada, and the United States) to Samuel Eto'o (a Cameroonian who played in Cameroon, Spain, Italy, Russia, England, Turkey, and Qatar) to Jay-Jay Okocha (a Nigerian who played in Nigeria, Germany, Turkey, France, Qatar, and England) to Yaya Touré (a Ivorian who played in Côte d'Ivoire, Belgium, Ukraine, Greece, Spain, England, and China) to Micheal Essien (a Ghanian who played in Ghana, Belgium, Ukraine, Greece, France, Spain, England, and China) to Kylian Mbappé (a Frenchman with Cameroonian and Algerian roots who plays in France), Africans have left an indelible mark on the world's greatest game. These athletes are celebrated in their homelands as national representatives and even more so as African diasporic champions for their accomplishments in the *white man's game* (Acheampong et al., 2019). Hence, as noted by previous critical sport scholars, the cultural and racial ties extend beyond nation-state citizenship (Carrington, 2010; James, 1963; Joseph, 2017; Mwaniki, 2017).

The fact that the ancestral lineage of these African players is connected to homelands that were previously colonized by European countries further reflects the intergenerational resistance of African people in sport and beyond. In other words, although European colonization was created to dominate and exploit African people in perpetuity, the success of these players demonstrates that the myth of European superiority is flawed and it simultaneously shows the brilliance and resolve of African people in spite of neocolonial circumstances.[36] Recursively, Mwaniki (2017) explained how African players such as Drogba and Benoît Assou-Ekotto, who grew up in European countries with African familial roots, chose to represent their African homelands because they feel a sense of belonging and meaning in these contexts whereas in Europe, regardless of citizenship and athletic status, they persistently feel as if they are outsiders, foreigners, or the Other. The embracement of hybridity by these African diasporic athletes, in contrast to simplistic national allegiances, reflects what Mwaniki (2017) described as "resistive transnational identities" (p. 157). Therefore, the African diasporic effect through sport is not unilateral, but rather multidimensional whereby the histories and contemporary realities of the African continent, African countries, and specific African communities and families intersect with and influence African diasporic athletes' sense of identity, culture, belonging, and purpose and vice versa. As with all forms of Black sporting resistance, the personal is always inextricably bound to the historical and contemporary collective diasporic identity.

Furthermore, the sacrifices of their ancestors also contributed to African athletes' subsequent success, and whether they directly represent their native homelands or a colonizing country, their Black racial identity and African familial and cultural lineage is as undeniable as their talents. This recognition of African talent, albeit a primary source of White racial capitalism, is also a constant reminder that African people have never been subhuman, contrary to the promulgation of racist tropes. This analysis does not negate the commodification component of their professional athletic status, but instead of solely focusing on this aspect of the arrangement, I posit that these sportspersons' identities, experiences, and impacts can and often do transcend one aspect of their condition. Hence, I describe their representation and success in non-African settings as *stealth migrant sporting resistance*, with an emphasis on their displacement or migration status in a land where they reside and/or work while maintaining diasporic resonance with their homelands and racial groups beyond their national citizenship or ethnicity.

Related to representing native countries, Black sporting resistance via representational politics does not only occur when African players migrate to participate and excel in European leagues or for European countries in international competition, but also and more importantly when they decide to represent their native countries. Players such as Didier Drogba of Côte d'Ivoire and Jay-Jay Ochoa of Nigeria opted to play for their national teams rather than represent another country. I refer to this phenomenon as *native homeland sporting resistance*. This type of resistance is akin to grassroots and mass mobilization activism except it does not inherently involve the same level of direct political confrontation as the latter two forms of resistance. When explaining the paradox and opportunity facing African diasporic athletes with this decision, Mwaniki (2017) captured the significance of those who choose to represent their native African countries: "Athletes... who have choices to make about which countries they represent internationally, challenge hegemonic notions of race and nationalism and national coherence" (p. 143). The success of African teams in international competitions, such as the Nigerian men's soccer that claimed the gold medal at the 1996 Olympics in Atlanta, Georgia, are celebrated across the diaspora because the African teams signify continental and diasporic pride in a neocolonial world where Blackness continues to be deemed inferior due to the ongoing effects of European imperialism.

Native homeland sporting resistance has also been exhibited through megaevents in African countries. In 1965, the Association of National Olympic Committees of Africa (ANOCA), National Olympic Committees of Africa (NOCs), African Sports Confederation (AOCs), and International Olympic Committee (IOC) coalesced to create the historic All-Africa Games in Brazzaville, Congo (FEI, 2022).[37] These multisport continental events are held every four years for countries that are members of the Supreme Council for Sport in Africa (SCSA) and constitute a form of organizational activism via mass mobilization. The unification of Africa countries and sport organizations for continental progress economically and socio-culturally reflects the power of Pan-Africanism. As of 2019, a total of twelve All-Africa Games had been hosted in Congo, Nigeria, Algeria, Kenya, Egypt, Zimbabwe, South Africa, Mozambique, and Morocco. The establishment of an All-African sporting event signifies African diasporic sporting resistance by generating economic, social, and cultural benefits by and for African countries. The participation of different African countries and the rotating host site underscores the collaborative spirit among African nations and their respective ministries of sport in the postcolonial era. The continental partnerships with these sport events reflect African diasporic sporting resistance through collective identity in organization and event formation, endurement in a postcolonial era, and entrepreneurship. Hence, the ethos of the broader Pan-Africanism movement, particularly selfdetermination, was prevalent in sporting spaces during the mid- to late twentieth century and remains active in the early twenty-first century.

It is also worth noting these games were created in the mid-twentieth century when African independence efforts were at an all-time high. Between 1956 and 1965, over 30 African countries had won their independence from European colonizing countries (Wallerstein, 1961/1967/2005). Two years prior to the establishment of the All-Africa Games, the OAU was established in 1963 in Addis Ababa, Ethiopia (Harris, 1994).[38] It is not a coincidence that this continental unification effort was founded in the same country that symbolized the African diasporic homeland (Patterson & Kelley, 2000). According to Harris (1994), the basis of the OAU was Pan-Africanism. Despite the reality of numerous intra- and international ideological differences and challenges, this Pan-African effort during the height of African decolonization from Europe was symbolic of the growth of diasporic processes and partnerships across the continent. The parallel processes of decolonization, self-determination, and self-governance for African nations and their sport governing bodies exemplifies the diasporic spirit of the All-Africa Games. The popularity of African athletes in Olympic competition also increased during the mid-twentieth century, particularly in track and field events (Mwaniki, 2017). In these instances, the success of African athletes served as an ideological and political symbol for newly independent African nations who had shed the proverbial chains of colonial rule (Bass, 2002). In other words, African sport organizations mirrored self-determination efforts in the African societies from which they emerged. Another high point of African sporting resistance and self-determination occurred in 2010 with the FIFA World Cup in South Africa.[39] It was the first time the international mega-event was hosted on African soil. The event was heralded as a success and highlighted the progress of the post-apartheid South Africa, which was a part of the vision of the revolutionary and former president Nelson Mandela.

Capoeira as Intergenerational African Diasporic Sporting Resistance

Throughout generations, African people have expressed their creativity and ingenuity in all forms of human life (Asante, 1990, 2003; Asante & Mazama, 2005; Carruthers, 1999; Diop, 1974; Hilliard, 1998; Rodney, 1972; Williams, 1974/1987). Africana studies scholars have documented various forms of music, dance, and acrobatics that African people engaged in as a part of their spiritual systems and cultural rituals (Asante & Mazama, 2005; Hilliard, 1998). One martial arts form that emerged in Angola during the sixteenth century was capoeira (Aula, 2017; Joseph, 2012b; Lindsay, 2019).[40] This distinct form of physical activity was described as a manifestation of resistance against slavery (Assunção, 2005). Capoeira from its creation served multiple purposes ranging from revolutionary violence to personal development. For example, Lindsay (2019) explained how *capoeira Angola* was founded upon the principle of self-control and designed to foster harmonious conflict resolution without physical harm unless facing an imminent threat. Unnecessary aggression in *capoeira Angola* was condemned and frowned upon (Dossar, 1992).[41] However, capoeira was also utilized as a source of training for battle against European oppressors,[42] and it was enacted as a weapon to secure

African liberation in places such as Angola and Brazil (Dossar, 1992; Lindsay, 2019). Benefits associated with capoeira included mental and physical training for participants to combat their enemies, the development of self-control, celebration of communal harmony, and the honoring of ancestors. Symbolically, the acrobatic movements represented escaping the entanglement and restrictions of slavery, and the modern-day performance of capoeira serves as a release from the oppressive realities imposed upon African people (Joseph, 2012b). Freedom of bodily movement and creative expression are among the highest desires of any human being and especially for people who have been subjected to enslavement.

More specifically, in the face of European colonization, the sustainment of ancient African spiritual systems, rituals, and practices constitutes *collective cultural resistance*. Similar to agentic resistance, *collective cultural resistance* involves the enactment of counter-hegemonic epistemological, axiological, and/or ontological forms of expression grounded African ecosystems. However, *collective cultural resistance* is different from agentic resistance because it inherently involves a group of people whereas the latter often refers to efforts centered on individual actions. The variations of capoeira also reflect the hybridity of the practice whereby the meaning is shaped by the participants and distinct cultural contexts. Moreover, as a result of transnational migration and flows of people, ideas, and customs over time, space, and context, hybridized environments contribute to the morphing of diverse cultural practices such as capoeira. Regarding the evolution of *capoeira Angola*, Dossar (1992) described how the historical foundations reached beyond the continent: "The resilience of African based culture, its ability to survive the exterminating pressures of European cultural hegemony in the New World, and the ability of African culture in the Americas to continually create and reconstruct itself in spite of racism and oppression point to future resurfacing of African based cultural traits. Capoeira angola, dancing between two worlds, is but one tool African descendants are using to reclaim African based culture" (p. 9).

Over time, capoeira spread from Angola to other parts of the world such as Brazil (Aula, 2017; Lindsay, 2019), Russia (Lipiäinen, 2015), Canada (Joseph, 2008, 2012), England, New Zealand, and other countries (Delamont & Stephens, 2008; Delamont et al., 2017). From a multisite ethnographic study of capoeira, Aula (2017) offered the following description of the martial arts form: "the multimodal practice of capoeira forms a 'translocal culture' uniting practitioners in diverse localities and connecting them to a transnationally formed, diasporic Afro-Brazilian heritage, deviating from a modern colonial framework" (p. 68). The author also posited that capoeira participants worldwide create imagined communities and situate themselves within Brazil and Angola via the art form (Aula, 2017). It is also worth noting that Brazil comprises the largest number and concentration of African diasporic peoples in the world outside of the continent because a majority of those who were transported via the *maafa* were displaced to this region. Hence, the depth of African collective memory in Brazil, particularly northeastern Brazil in areas such as Salvador, Bahia, is expansive and evident in a multitude of cultural practices such as capoeira and among other spiritual, religious, and social customs.

More specific to the African diaspora, Joseph (2012b) explained how the transmission of language, music, art, and even sports such as capoeira help to "connect distinct nation-states and broad historical and contemporary diasporas" (p. 1078). As a result of the transatlantic atrocity, Africans from the Angolan region who were enslaved and transported to the Americas would also bring with them memories and practices of their homelands. Consequently, capoeira spread to colonized countries such as Haiti, Cuba, and Brazil (Dossar, 1992). Between the sixteenth and nineteenth centuries, capoeira embodied what scholars describe as Black cultural formations and served as a means of survival and adaptability in displaced settled lands (Abdel Shehid, 2005; Farred, 2022; James, 1963). It is at this point when capoeira transitioned from a local cultural practice in Angola to being a diasporic practice with an international influence. For example, Joseph (2012b) outlined the core aspects of capoeira as it is practiced in Brazil:

> Capoeira is a physical *jogo* (game), performed by two people in a *roda* (a circle of participants). After crouching at the bottom, or "foot" of the lead instrument, the berimbau, two players enter the *roda* and intertwine their bodies using swaying dance steps called *ginga*; improvise strikes with their head, hands, and feet; and force spontaneous, acrobatic escapes. Those standing around the *roda* clap, sing songs that use Portuguese and African words, and play Afro-Brazilian musical instruments to send messages to the players and dictate the pace of the *jogo*. (p. 1079)

Similar to other aspects of African culture that were morphed across time, space, and context, capoeira became a creolized cultural practice whereby different nuances were embedded by participants based on their lived experiences and local context (Gilroy, 1993; Joseph, 2012b). Despite the adapted versions of capoeira, original characteristics of the cultural practice have sustained over time, including the importance of oral history, storytelling, and an emphasis on the liberation of the oppressed.

Brazil capoeira is internationally recognized as a sport (Assunção, 2005; Dossar, 1992; Talmon-Chvaicer, 2008; Taylor, 2007). During the transatlantic atrocity, 3.5 million Africans were displaced to Brazil (Dossar, 1992). Between the sixteenth and nineteenth centuries, Assunção (2005) explained how capoeira evolved from a leisure activity with spiritual underpinnings for Africans who were oppressed in Salvador, Bahia, to later being criminalized by the

Brazilian government in the late nineteenth and early twentieth centuries. The Afro-Brazilian religion of Candomblé, which has roots with the Yoruba cosmology and tradition in West Africa, was connected to Afro-Brazilian capoeira (Joseph, 2012b). The following description typifies the revolutionary power of capoeira during the period spanning the sixteenth to nineteenth centuries:

> The games, dances, and foot fighting confined within Brazil's slave system, combined with the Africans' desire for liberation became a deadly form of self defense.... In colonial Brazil, capoeira was seen as a threat to the plantation system, because of this its teaching was banned. As a result, capoeira was put to music and disguised as a dance. Capoeira as dance and fight entered the 20th century rooted in the basic human right of freedom. As a self-defense system born of African traditions, capoeira angola presents a holistic system incorporating aspects of African based dance with cosmology, and physical training—it is a system of human development. (Dossar, 1992, p. 6)

A common feature of African resistance efforts is the presence of neocolonial backlash in the form of sanctioning, surveillance, and criminalization. Hegemonic groups understand that any mode of African self-determination and empowerment can and often does become fertile ground for revolutionary mobilization. Hence, *collective cultural resistance* is a powerful weapon for African liberation that can be activated in concert with other methods of activism.

One of the first Brazilian capoeira academies was established in 1932 by Manoel dos Reis Machado, the founder of *capoeira regional* (Dossar, 1992). This form of capoeira is distinct because it includes a blend of techniques from multiple martial art forms. For example, Dossar (1992) explained notable differences with capoeira regional, which include "a larger number of striking techniques, a faster pace, more up-right attacks, and does not stress the use of malicia (a performative act of feinting)" (p. 6). In 1941, Vicente Ferreira Pastinha created an Angola school of capoeira to preserve the sport's African roots.[43] An important distinction between *capoeira Angola* and other versions of the cultural practice is the former prioritizes communal strength and development over competition.[44] In typical African diasporic form, Joseph (2012b) explicated how *Angoleiros* sought to retain an imagined memory of their ancestors' homeland: "For angoleiros, the symbols, rituals, song lyrics and physical movements of angola represent the way (they imagine) capoeira was played 'hundreds of years ago,' that is, embedded in 'African culture' including cosmology, aesthetics and history" (p. 1084).

Along with the intentional inclusion of the birthplace of the art form in the title, *Angoleiros* are also serious about retaining the symbolic rituals and meanings of the expression. As an extension of *capoeira Angola, capoeira contemporânea* was created. *Capoeira contemporânea* emerged as a regional and hybrid westernized version of the cultural practice that emphasized competition between opponents and established more formal rules to restrict certain movements (Assunção, 2005; Delamont et al., 2017; Joseph, 2012b). Despite the evolution of the cultural practice, it is worth noting that capoeira scholars have highlighted how the core traditions have been retained across geographical spaces; the primary distinctions are between unique Brazilian features compared to those who practice it in North America, New Zealand, and across Europe.[45]

In an ethnographic study of capoeira in Toronto, Canada, Joseph (2012b) explored how Canadians learned and embodied capoeira. Using Gilroy's (1993) conception of the Black Atlantic, Joseph (2012b) offered the following analysis of the Canadian capoeira participants she observed: "Some capoeriristas (capoeira adepts) understand their practice as a means to preserve 'African' heritage through symbols and embodiment of ancestral gestures (roots). Others use their corporeal gestures to display antiphony, innovations and transnational dialogues (routes)" (p. 1079). Akin to the original purpose of *capoeira Angola*, participants in the class learned that mastery of movements and performance was more important than striking an opponent to defeat them. From an educational standpoint, the participants used capoeira to engage with Aboriginals in Canada and multiculturalism politics. For example, in honor of Aboriginals in Canada, the students embroidered Aboriginal iconography on their uniforms to generate more awareness of their histories and current challenges (Joseph, 2012b). The classes would also involve a local Aboriginal elder performing a welcome ritual. Introducing Canadians to the history of capoeira empowered students to make connections to contemporary racial injustices (Joseph, 2012b). These findings highlight how engaging in African cultural practices such as capoeira can foster *inter-diasporic relationship building* and allyship via grassroots (i.e., local capoeira class) and scholarly activism (i.e., publication of ethnographic research) as well as through *collective cultural resistance* (i.e., intentional embodiment of African-centered practice among a group of people).

In a similar vein, Lindsay (2019) described his experience as an African American who learned about capoeira in the United States and later traveled to Brazil to learn from respected *Mestres*. From this experience, he created a capoeira program for Black males living in a metropolitan city in the midwestern United States. At the facility, he decorated the walls with Pan-African and Brazilian flags to honor the roots of the art form (Lindsay, 2019). The purpose of the capoeira program for Black males was "to equip their students with the tools necessary to resist White supremacy (racism) . . . [by administering] culturally responsive curricula and tools such as Capoeira to encourage social movements led by our youth with the intention to achieve justice for all oppressed people" (Lindsay, 2019, p. i). This mission is emblematic of scholarly and grassroots activism with its clear purpose of using a culturally grounded physical activity to disrupt and dismantle White supremacy. In addition to the routine class sessions, his class organized a school march to protest police brutality in the United States in January 2016, which illustrated their activation of symbolic activism. This hybrid resistance at the individual and collective levels reflects how sporting practices can infuse social justice education and cultivate self-efficacy among participants for activating their own resistance efforts.

Summary

This chapter explored the manifestation and impact of African (Black) diasporic sporting resistance. *African diaspora* refers to real and imagined communities of dispersed African people who share cultural and social experiences, particularly those related to encounters with anti-Black racism at the micro, meso, and macro levels. In the face of insurmountable conditions, African people globally have used their ingenuity and resources to engage in counter-hegemonic actions. African (Black) diasporic sporting resistance has been embodied through vicarious achievement with international boxing matches, representation and performances in international fútbol, and through capoeira in different geopolitical spaces. Concepts such as *agentic participatory sporting resistance, inter-diasporic alliances, stealth racial empowerment, collective cultural resistance, stealth migrant sporting resistance,* and *native homeland sporting resistance* were introduced as extensions to the sport activism and resistance typologies. In summary, African (Black) diasporic sporting resistance serves as an expansion of broader racial justice efforts that do not inherently require political alignment between the athlete and those who draw inspiration from their accomplishments, demeanor, and personal expressions. The primary requirements for African (Black) diasporic sporting resistance are perceived or imagined collective identity and the malleable use of the sportsperson(s) and their sporting achievements for the advancement of the psyche and/or cause of groups resisting oppressive forces. Thus, African (Black) diasporic sporting resistance may be symbolic in nature, but when activated in concert with other forms of resistance, the collective impact is powerful beyond measure.

3
They Lived on Their Own Terms

• • • • • • • • • • • • • • • • • • •

Black Transnationalism
Sporting Resistance

> The sense of black community expressed by "having a good time among our own color" depends upon acts of identification, restitution, and remembrance ... the networks of affiliation enacted by performance, sometimes referred to as the "community among ourselves," are defined by ... the connections forged in the context of disrupted affiliations, sociality amid the constant threat of separation, and shifting sets of identification particular to site, location, and action. (Hartman, 1997, p. 59)

The quote above is from Saidiya Hartman's (1997) seminal text *Scenes of Subjection: Terror, Slavery, and Self-Making in Nineteenth-Century America*, which explores the experiences of Africans who were enslaved in the United States. In her text, she interrogates how power is exercised by both the oppressors and the oppressed. One of the primary means of oppression wielded against Black people has been the control and surveillance of their bodies. More specifically, the movement of and by Black people historically has been restricted in every sense in neocolonial contexts. During slavery, Black people were subjected to conditions that communicated to them that they did not own their bodies. This reality meant all movement and actions must be approved by their oppressors and, more importantly, were compelled to serve the latter's desires—economically, politically, sexually, and psychosocially. Thus, control over one's body was and remains a highly valued aspect of freedom for Black people. For example, Wiggins (2018) noted how Africans who were enslaved on plantations in the southern United States cherished the fleeting moments away from their forced labor when they were allowed to dance, sing, and worship to reconnect with their African spiritual and cultural systems. Similarly, Carrington (2010) characterized Black people's freedom of movement as "embodied emancipation" (p. 50). Thus, in neocolonial environments, agentic bodily control and expression for Black people constitutes a political act of ontological resistance against imposed confinement and exploitation.

The history of Africans being transported against their will during the transatlantic atrocity has been widely documented. However, in concert with the purpose of this book, Black radical tradition scholars have emphasized an unintended consequence of transporting African people with the fallacious assumptions that these groups possessed no history or culture. Robinson (1983/2000) explained the deeper significance of Black resistance even during the *maafa*: "The transport of African labor to the mines and plantations of the Caribbean and subsequently what would be known as the Americas meant also the transfer of African ontological and cosmological systems; African presumptions of the organization and significance of the social structure; African codes embodying historical consciousness and social experience; and African ideological and behavior constructions for the resolution of the inevitable conflict between the actual and the normative" (p. 122).

Throughout this chapter, I highlight how Black transnationalism sporting resistance reifies the intergenerational epistemologies, axiology, and ontologies of African diasporic people across time, space, and context. Consistent with Robinson's (1983/2000) Black radical tradition and Horne's (1985, 1997, 2005, 2014a, 2014b, 2015, 2018a, 2018b, 2020a, 2020b) extensive scholarship, I focus on African diasporic resistance from those within a North American context, including African Americans and Caribbeans, while also highlighting their transnational connections and implications.[1] This embodiment contradicts and undermines Eurocentric distortions of African people, their cultures, and their ingenuity. In concert with Robinson (1983/2000)—albeit with a focus on sportspersons and organizations—I argue Black people not only enact their humanity through their resistance, but even more express their unique sense making (e.g., values, beliefs, customs), relational capacities (e.g., family and kinship bonds, interactions with community members and external groups), and creative adaptations (e.g., adjustments to climates, political economies, and social conditions) across different chronosystems through transnational formations.

Another aspect of movement that signified freedom for Black people was the ability to physically travel across state and national boundaries. For example, during the antebellum era in the United States, Black people in the South created networks among their race and with non-Black allies to establish routes to freedom in northern states and Canada, such as the case with establishment of the Underground Railroad (Franklin, 1947/1974). During these escape missions, the North Star metaphorically represented freedom from slavery and literally provided a navigational aid for enslaved Africans (Hine et al., 2006). In addition, throughout the nineteenth and twentieth centuries, Blacks who lived in the United States would also migrate to Africa as a part of the emigrationism movement and to select European countries such as France (Franklin, 1947/1974). Those who lived in the Caribbeans would migrate northward to the United States and Canada as well as to Europe for similar purposes (Franklin, 1947/1974; Horne, 2015, 2020a, 2020b; Joseph, 2017). As such, migration, or *movement by choice* as opposed to *movement by force* (as in the case with the transatlantic atrocity), constituted an embodiment of humanity and freedom that was denied to millions of Africans from the fifteenth to the early twentieth centuries.

During the twentieth century, when Black migrants were occupying new and foreign spaces either temporarily or permanently, they were able to recreate their native cultures through various cultural practices including through music, religious expression, business exchanges, familial and community gatherings, and educational engagements (Franklin, 1947/1974; Gilroy, 1993; Hine et al., 2006). In addition to these activities, another primary cultural practice that enabled Black migrants to create a sense of community was sport and physical activity. Carrington (2010) describes the importance of these cultural spaces for African diasporic people: "For black peoples throughout the African diaspora, such cosmopolitan formations and outer-national identifications operate as powerful counter-claims against nation state nationalisms and conservative mono-cultural ideologies, with their associated assimilationist drives. Such self-consciously selected identifications cut across national borders, reconfiguring what it means to be a national subject, providing transnational routes of identity formation.... These sporting identifications re-articulate ... new forms of black identity" (p. 55).

Because racial segregation was strictly enforced in settler colonial nation-states (Horne, 2020a, 2020b), the ethnic stratification in these environments facilitated Black transnational formations (Dahinden, 2010). By-products of these arrangements included the emergence of cooperative economics and cultural exchanges. More specifically, Black sport organizations as transnational communities embodied safe spaces, reciprocal relationships, and cultural distinctiveness (Faist, 2010; Gilroy, 1993).² Within this chapter, I highlight five Black transnational communities and their resistance actions amid racially oppressive conditions: a) West Indian cricket players and teams (James, 1963; Joseph, 2011, 2012a, 2014, 2017); b) Negro and Afro-Latino baseball players, teams, and leagues (Burgos, 2007, 2011; Lomax, 2003, 2014); c) the Colored Hockey League of the Maritimes (Fosty & Fosty, 2008); d) the Black Fives/Harlem Rens basketball team (Henderson, 1939; Rayl, 1996, 2017); and e) rodeo's Shadow Riders of the Subterranean Circuit (Cartwright, 2021; Ford, 2020; Pearson, 2004, 2021).

Transnational Communities: West Indian Cricket Players and Teams

The Caribbean region provides a useful context to examine the interplay between cultural hybridity and resistance efforts by virtue of the geographical and spatial composition of the landmasses. This region was subjected to European colonial rule, particularly from the British, Spaniards, and French from the fifteenth to the twenty-first centuries, albeit to varying extents over time (Horne, 2014a; James, 1963, 2012). A unique aspect of this region that proved to be favorable for revolt efforts in the colonial era was the presence of a numerical majority of Africans compared to Europeans (Horne, 2014a; James, 2012). In addition, the proximity of the landmasses facilitated cultural and political exchanges in more efficient ways compared to other areas of the Americas. More specifically, the Caribbean region was a central location for what Dahinden (2010) described as localized mobile transnational formations. These formations involved high levels of mobility and locality whereby migrants routinely traveled between their native country and other countries. The creation of the West Indian Cricket teams constituted a sport example of a localized mobile transnational formation where ethnic solidarity and reciprocity were exhibited (Dahinden, 2010; James, 1963).

The popularity of cricket in the West Indies dates back to the mid-nineteenth century (James, 1963; Marqusee, 1994/2016). As a European game, cricket in the West Indies was inextricably linked to European colonialism, class stratification, exploitation, and neoliberalism as well as with anti-colonial movements that emerged during the late nineteenth century. Marqusee (1994/2016) highlights the connection between cricket and broader sociopolitical forces during the late nineteenth century: "Cricket becomes the first modern sport at the dawn of the industrial revolution . . . the same forces that changed a folk-game into modern cricket unleashed that revolution: the spread of the market economy, the domination of the state by landowning bourgeoisie, the triumph of private property and law, the revenues from overseas trade and colonial conquest, the movement into cities.... Cricket was not a product of that revolution but a by-product of the conjuncture of social and economic forces which set it in motion" (pp. 59–60).

The attraction of cricket across all social classes in this region reflected what Marqusee (1994/2016) described as the "superimposed English colonial culture" that pervaded every aspect of West Indian society.[3] As a social institution and a cultural practice, cricket served as an extension of the ideological hegemonic apparatus. More specifically, cricket along with other European-influenced sports was increasing in popularity alongside the emergence of racial capitalism (Cooper, 2021; Robinson, 1983/2000). West Indian cricket success during the twentieth century also coincided with Caribbean political independence movements and the bourgeoning Civil Rights and Black Power movements in the United States (Cooper, 2021). More poetically stated, Davis (2009) described the unique role of cricket for the Caribbean masses: "Cricket provided an arena for expressing anticolonial resistance feelings in a socially acceptable manner" (p. 129).

The underlying hypocrisy of English cricket lay in the fact that officials, players, and spectators professed purity, fair play, and gentleman-like conduct while ignoring the racist, sexist, and other discriminatory foundations and norms of the sport (Marqusee, 1994/2016). For example, cricket was synonymous with colonial domination and a mythical English superiority, and thus anyone who challenged this belief was deemed unfit to participate in the sport (James, 1963; Marqusee, 1994/2016). As such, West Indians and other non-Europeans were indoctrinated into a process of assimilation through cricket participation. Contrary to Eurocentric propositions, I argue that cultural assimilation is a form of violence via dehumanization because it presupposes the erasure and minimization of non-European cultures while suggesting human existence and progress is solely associated with Europeans.[4]

In contrast to positive attributions for European culture, in cricket ubiquitous West Indian stereotypes included perceptions of natural ability, violent dispositions, spontaneous behavior, and unsportsmanlike/non-gentleman-like demeanors. From an ontological standpoint, cricket and cricketers represent humanity at its finest, and thus when oppressed groups excelled against their former colonizers these performances and victories constituted an embodiment of resistance and reclamation of their humanity. I refer to this phenomenon as *agentic participatory sporting resistance* whereby a dialectical relationship exists that involves contradictions and tensions between social myths and observed realities, which result in the formation of new schemas, arrangements, and conditions. It is these new formations that carry significant implications for sporting spaces and society more broadly. Thus, as James (1963) professed, cricket was and remains as political as elections, war, and economic trade.

Although cricket began in Europe in the sixteenth century, it was not introduced to the West Indies until the mid-nineteenth century after these lands—and their African-descendant and Indigenous people—were colonized (James, 1963; Marqusee, 1994/2016). Because the Africans who were enslaved on these lands were deemed to be property, everything associated with European culture, including cricket, was viewed as aspirational. James (1963) explained how during his youth in Trinidad his love for cricket and European literature was due to his British-centric socialization. Everything from the naming of buildings, the educational curriculum, social etiquette of elitism and acceptability, standards of beauty, religious beliefs, and even sport were grounded in British cultural standards. Within this context, Trinidadians and other West Indians were treated as inferior and only partially accepted when they assimilated into British ways of doing, being, and thinking. Stated differently, West Indians experienced what Gilroy (1993) described as the state of being *infrahuman*. As such, the cricket space served as a contested battleground for West Indian human dignity and cultural empowerment whereby their presence and success amplified the contradictions of European myths and the colonial project therein. James (1963) succinctly explicated the ontological importance of cricket for West Indians when he said "Cricketers are human" (p. 112). This statement underscores how West Indians in general were not viewed as human, but rather as subhumans or at best infrahumans (Carrington, 2010; Cooper, 2019; Gilroy, 1993). Thus, sport participation carries a different ontological significance for Black people compared to their White counterparts. Human dignity was sought through participation in the European sport of cricket, and Black pride and West Indian independence and self-determination were particularly exhibited through the latter's success, creative expression, and dominance in the sport.

One example of ontological marginalization in cricket during the early and mid-twentieth century was the routine omission of talented Black players from the traveling West Indies team that competed in England and Australia (James, 1963; Marqusee 1994/2016). Those regions' anti-Black racism led to the exclusion of Black West Indians from the West Indies team during the middle of the century, and their absence from the role of captaincy was emblematic of British colonial domination. In other words, the conditions and outcomes of cricket mirrored the status of political relations between West Indian people and their self-government efforts and the British colonial agenda. White fear of Black prominence was a driving force for European colonial practices from the mid-fifteenth century through the mid-twentieth century.[5] Pioneering resistance was one way in which Black West Indian cricketers weakened the chains of European colonialism because it undermined the fallaciousness of innate racial inferiority in a highly public manner. Leadership via captaincy was also a means to reinforce classist assumptions about which gentlemen were best suited to lead versus those who were ill-equipped for these roles; hence, European cricket reproduced intersectional oppressive beliefs and conditions. In an example of pioneering activism, Frank Worrell became the first Black captain of the West Indian team in 1960 and led the squad to a historic victory in England in 1963 (James, 1963). Worrell's securing of the captaincy on a West Indian team and leading this team to victory in England signified how Black sporting resistance can manifest via a transnational formation (Dahinden, 2010; Faist, 2010).

Moreover, Wilton St. Hill, Learie Nicholas Constantine, and George John of Trinidad, George "Atlas" Headley and Frank Worrell of Jamaica, George Challenor and Percy "Tim" Tarilton of Barbados, Sir Clive Lloyd of Guyana, and Sir Isaac Vivian Richards of Antigua are among the prominent Black cricketers of the twentieth century who experienced success on both sides of the Atlantic despite facing anti-Black racism via exclusion,[6] and at times, having their accomplishments minimized by the broader cricket community (Davis, 2009; James, 1963; Marqusee, 1994/2016). When providing an explanation for the omission of legendary West Indian cricketer Learie Constantine from the traveling West Indies team, James (1963) surmised the following conclusion: "[Constantine] would infallibly put all white rivals in the shade. And they [Europeans] were too afraid of precisely the same thing, and therefore were glad to keep him out" (p. 100). In 1928, Constantine put on a legendary performance in England. James (1963) explained its significance within the broader West Indian sociopolitical movement: "Constantine . . . prize pupil of the captain of the West Indies, had revolted against the revolting contrast between his first-class status as a cricketer and his third-class status as a man. . . . The restraints imposed upon him by social conditions in the West Indies had become intolerable and he decided to stand them no longer" (p. 110).

This analysis highlights how West Indians, as well as Black people globally, live multidimensional lives whereby their humanity is always contingent, and they are forced to traverse environments that signal to them respect, dignity, and fairness are transient at best and elusive at worst. Similar to several talented West Indian cricketers of these eras, Constantine migrated from the West Indies to Europe in pursuit of achieving social mobility and reduced racism by virtue of his cricket talent. Hence, these cricketers were not migrating to escape their identities and heritages as West Indians, but rather to elevate their homelands and race via their performances, thus exhibiting a form of stealth migrant sporting resistance.

The stealth migrant sporting resistance referenced here focuses on the relationship between African (Black) sportspersons and the diasporic groups they represent via collective identity. However, I would be remiss if I did not acknowledge how the migration and exploitation of talented Black West Indian cricketers in Europe served as a means to strengthen what Robinson (1983/2000) described as racial capitalism. Because cricket was and remains a European-controlled sport, across the twentieth century it garnered significant attention and investments from corporate and colonial government entities (Marqusee, 1994/2016). Consequently, there was an increased demand for securing talented cricketers, regardless of race, who could enhance the marketability and financial viability of the sport. I posit that cricket organizers, in concert with other neocolonial capitalists, were primarily concerned with attracting more consumers and sponsors to enhance profit margins while simultaneously using the sport to create an illusion of a harmonious multicultural society. In other words, if talented cricketers from diverse backgrounds, such as those from the West Indies, Pakistan, and India, were able to serve as cultural icons for the sport, then criticisms of the racial capitalist social order could be evaded. In neoliberal societies, all commercialized sports are designed to foster neocolonial nationalistic allegiances and quell any forms of radical political socialization and revolutionary activity, particularly anti-capitalist fervor (Cooper, 2019, 2021). Scholars such as Sage (1998) referred to this hegemonic usage of sport as constituting an opiate for the masses whereby spectators' attention is focused on entertainment and distracted from igniting structural transformation. Under these conditions, commercialized sports are weaponized as a powerful form of transnational capitalistic propaganda. Moreover, dating to times of the *maafa*, a primary means by which colonizers maintained their hegemony was by selecting Black exceptions to the rule to serve as buffers against potential revolutionary catalysts (Horne, 2020b). As such, talented athletes, entertainers, and other individuals who were willing to be used to benefit the neoliberal capitalist status quo—without disrupting the foundational structure of the system—were and continue to be identified as prized targets for exploitation.[7]

In the previous chapter, I explained how African (Black) diasporic sporting resistance can be susceptible to hegemonic co-optation when the sportspersons are not explicit about anti-colonial, anti-imperial, anti–White supremacy, and/or anti-capitalist political stances. Similarly, Black transnational sporting resistors such as West Indian cricket players and teams are also vulnerable to being used as pawns for racial capitalists' aims with or without their consent; emphasizing the difference in intentionality aims associated with borderline activist actions versus activism (Cooper 2021; Cooper et al., 2019). As the talent and popularity of Black athletes became more undeniable in the mid-twentieth century, in true capitalist fashion European sport officials sought to exploit the players by separating them from their African cultural roots as well as from any anti-colonial movements in exchange for financial rewards and European nationalistic allegiance (Carrington, 2010; Cooper, 2019, 2021; Mwaniki, 2017). In the case of Black transnational resistors, when they migrate from their native countries to European countries, their physical relocation can turn into psychological, cultural, political, and economic dislocation for the benefit of racial capitalism. In the case of cricket, the most popular and economically viable leagues and tournaments were and remain owned by White capitalists (Marqusee, 1994/2016), which means the structure of these activities are designed to serve the desires of this group. While representation and success for oppressed groups serves the purpose of enhancing racial pride and symbolizing self-determination, these same arrangements can be manipulated to benefit hegemonic classes unless these activities are governed by African (Black) people who embody anti-colonial, anti-imperial, anti-capitalist, and anti–White supremacy orientations.

Moreover, consistent with my previous work (Cooper, 2019, 2021), I emphasize and scrutinize the complexity of any intersectional arrangements grounded in interest convergence. Black West Indian cricket success in the twentieth century, similar to the continued African (Black) athletic success in the twenty-first century,[8] has both strengthened and challenged racial capitalism because of the inextricable connection between the broader ideologies informing the political economies where sport exists and the concurrent and ever-present resistance against these hegemonic conditions.[9] Hence, all racialized sporting spaces constitute dialectical relationships. This analytical point illuminates how the intentions *and* impacts of African (Black) sportspersons are not mutually exclusive, but rather connected in complex ways. As noted in chapter 1, I argue that in order for systems of oppression to be dismantled and for sustained cultural empowerment to be achieved for African people, resistance efforts must move beyond borderline activist actions as the primary form of resistance and involve the activation of multiple forms of activisms that are aligned with social movements and revolutions. These more radically disruptive actions can only be successful if new systems of empowerment are created, protected, and sustained. This is the benefit of aligning specific forms of Black sporting resistance with the Black radical tradition (Robinson, 1983/2000) and with aspects of revolutionary Black ideologies and social movements such as the *Black Liberation Struggle, Black Nationalism, Pan-Africanism*, and *Black Radicalism*. The extent and intensity by which Black sporting resistance aligns with these broader Black struggles will determine the magnitude and temporality or permanency of racial justice efforts locally and internationally.

Notwithstanding the limitations associated with stealth migrant sporting resistance, Black West Indians' disruption of cricket spaces is still noteworthy and emblematic of West Indian independence efforts (James, 1963). Historic West Indian team victories such as the first test win in England in 1950, the 1975 International Cricket Cup (ICC) win in England against Australia by 17 runs, the dominant tour match victories against England in 1976 (3–0), and the West Indies' win over the English in Trinidad in 1994 did more than simply provide evidence of these cricketers' athletic prowess; these feats also symbolized West Indian triumph over centuries of European colonialism (James,

1963; Wilde, 1994). Between the 1980s and the mid-1990s, the West Indian teams compiled a winning percentage greater than 70 percent (Wilde, 1994), which further illustrated their intergenerational self-determination efforts. In a description of diasporic transnational power of Black West Indian cricketers, James (1963) offered the following analysis: "The batsman facing the ball does not merely represent his side. For that moment, to all intents and purposes, he is his side. This fundamental relation of the One and the Many, Individual and Social, Individual and Universal, leader and followers, representative and ranks, the part and the whole, is structurally imposed on the players of cricket" (p. 193).

The connection between player, community, nation, and race is inextricable, and as noted in chapter 2 the vicarious achievement felt by Black West Indians broadly reflected the diasporic resonance of cricket across the West Indies and globally across the Black world. More specific to transnationalism, the essential nature of migration and subsequent victories on European soil amplified the notion that racist myths about Black subjugation were not grounded in biological truths, but rather rooted in pseudoscientific claims and colonial political aims. Akin to the importance of Joe Louis's African diasporic sporting resistance in the boxing ring during the early twentieth century, West Indian cricket success on an international stage during the mid- to late twentieth century was essential to affirm the underlying ethos of the West Indian anti-colonial social movement. The unique appeal of sport as a proverbial site for meritocratic achievement, particularly in transnational spaces, creates a ripple effect between public displays of excellence and reorientations of psychological mental models for both individuals and groups.[10] For West Indians, success on the cricket pitch reinforced confirmation bias about their humanity, pride, and resolve as a people whereas for Europeans these instances of defeat generated cognitive dissonance and a questioning of previous taken-for-granted assumptions about "the Other,"[11] hence the power of *agentic participatory* and *stealth migrant sporting resistance*. In these instances, cricket constituted a vital counter-hegemonic political tool that was complementary to concurrent military, intellectual, economic, and cultural forms of resistance occurring beyond the pitch. In fact, I argue the synchronous impact of collective resistance across distinct milieus is what enables social movements to transform into effective revolutions and later into sustained cultural empowerment.

In concert with transnational activities, West Indian cricketers also exhibited Black sporting resistance by refusing to compete in international spaces. An example of the power of threatening symbolic activism occurred during the 1947–1948 season when the Jamaican cricket team refused to play against England if George Headley was not granted the captain designation (James, 1963). As a result of this concerted disruptive action, Headley ended up playing in one game, which reflected the power of activating sports-based activism.

In another example of symbolic activism, in 1978 Sir Clive Lloyd led a boycott of the Guyana Test Cricket because some of his players were being mistreated (Marqusee, 1994/2016). Although this symbolic activism did not totally upend racism in Guyana Test Cricket, it did garner national and international attention and temporarily ruptured the norms of these sporting spaces. Furthermore, the activation of symbolic activism provided a blueprint for subsequent West Indian resistance efforts within and beyond sporting spaces. West Indian cricket teams also boycotted matches in South Africa to express their support for the anti-apartheid movement of the 1970s (Davis, 2009). This latter instance of symbolic activism reflects the internationalization of Black sporting resistance whereby multiple manifestations of racial oppression were challenged simultaneously. Furthermore, these instances of activism demonstrate how both engagement and disengagement in transnational sport participation can reflect political resistance depending on time, space, and context.

Anti–West Indian racism was also evident in the classification of cricketers as either amateurs or professionals. In the late 1800s, *gentlemen* were considered amateurs and *players* were viewed as professionals. The distinction was made primarily based on race and/or social class. The following description reveals the embedded classism associated with the amateur label: "Being an amateur implied having 'private means', that is, access to capital without recourse to labour. The model for all affluence was landed leisure" (Marqusee, 1994/2016, p. 85). Stated differently, being a professional cricketer was deemed as a lowly profession because those with wealth did not have to earn money through athletic labor. Professionals referred to amateurs as *Sir* or *Mister*. Similarly, cricket clubs were discriminatory and only accessible through membership. Typical members of amateur cricket clubs were landowners and other upper-class professionals (Marqusee, 1994/2016). The professionalization of West Indian players only became a problem when they began defeating British teams. Thus, West Indian players' *agentic participatory sporting resistance* as professionals disrupted the myth of British amateur supremacy.

In concert with these social stratification distinctions, competitions between the West Indies, England, South Africa, and Australia were also initially grounded in imperial relations, as with the case with the establishment of the Imperial Cricket Conference in 1909 led by Lord Harris (Marqusee, 1994/2016). However, *agentic participatory sporting resistance* occurred in 1974 when Sir Clive Lloyd was selected as captain of the West Indies team (Marqusee, 1994/2016). Lloyd's teams exuded a sense of independence and unity. The parallel progress of West Indian independence efforts and the rise of Black West Indian cricket success illustrated the symbiotic relationship between resistance across political and sociocultural contexts. Building on the legacy of West Indian cricketers of the early twentieth century, the success of Garfield "Gary" Sobers, Desmond Haynes, Gordon Greenidge, Keith Boyce,

Vanburn Holder, Joel Garner, and Malcolm Marshall of Barbados, Sir Isaac Vivian "Viv" Richards, Andy Roberts, and Curtly Ambrose of Antigua, Michael Holding and Courtney Walsh of Jamaica, Roy Fredericks and Sir Clive Lloyd of Guyana, Bernard Julien and Deryck Murray of Trinidad and Tobago, and Colin Croft of British Guiana during the mid- to late twentieth century reflected the persistence of Black transnationalism sporting resistance (Joseph, 2017; Riley, 2011; Wilde, 1994).

Another form of resistance exhibited in cricket beyond the victories was the distinctive and stylistic performances. The origins of cricket bowling and batting styles, such as the off-side drive, were grounded in aesthetic standards associated with English elitists (James, 1963). Any excessive use of power and personal expression was viewed as classless and antithetical to the essence of the game. The English style of play was described as pure and traditional, whereas the West Indian style was deemed primitive and unruly (Marqusee, 1994/2016). This dichotomous racist framing is akin to the Apollonian European and Dionysian Brazilian fútbol contrast (Foster, 2003) outlined in chapter 2, which illustrates the pervasiveness of anti-Black racism across multiple sports and geopolitical contexts. These distinctive styles of play reflect Black sporting resistance epistemologically, ontologically, and axiologically because these players demonstrate their kinesthetic intelligence, a different embodiment of an exemplar athlete, and a contrasting values system that communicates that rhythm and style are equally as important as utility when it comes to sport participation.

Moreover, West Indian players' combination of physical and intellectual mastery of the sport was undeniable and personified the power of sport as a counter-hegemonic tool for African diasporic and transnational empowerment. Beyond mere physical achievements, Marqusee (1994/2016) explained the intellectual breakthroughs exhibited with West Indian cricket success in England during the 1980s: "The West Indian fast bowlers in the eighties relentlessly *out-thought the England batsmen*.... Each of the great West Indian quicks—Roberts, Holding, Garner, Croft, Marshall, Ambrose, Walsh—worked to create his own style, experimentally varying height and angle of delivery, line and length. They enjoyed success everywhere, proving themselves in the process among the most adaptable cricketers the world has ever seen" (p. 158).

In response to these distinctive styles of play, British cricket officials created rules to penalize West Indian players. Rule modifications such as neutralizing fast bowling and the disqualification of professional players are two examples of British backlash against West Indian success (Marqusee, 1994/2016). These instances of European backlash via rule changes typify the disruptive effectiveness of Black sporting resistance by West Indian cricketers. Additional British rule changes in the 1970s and 1980s included the increase in the minimum number of overs per day, a counter to the West Indian modifications of the game that included a shorter and faster version known variously as T20, 20/20, or a one-day game (Marqusee, 1994/2016). The West Indian modification of the British pastime was an example of the cricketers' self-determination efforts to define the rules of play by their own terms, which aligned with the anti-colonial tenor of the day. In 1987, English cricket authorities banned flags, banners, and excessive alcohol at cricket tests (Marqusee, 1994/2016). Later drums, whistles, and klaxons were also viewed as deviant by European cricket officials and spectators. In essence, all resemblance of West Indian carnival were deemed unruly.

Instead of assimilating to European cultural norms, West Indian cricketers challenged the epistemological, ontological, and axiological foundations that undergirded the sport. By not being afraid to exhibit their own freedom of movement and change the rules of participation, they communicated to not only their former colonizers, but also to their fellow West Indian and African diasporic community members, that *collective cultural resistance* is essential for full decolonization. No longer would they adhere to imposed ways of doing, being, and thinking. *They would participate on their own terms and elevate their own ingenuity and cultural foundations.* The psychological fracturing of European myths cannot be overstated. Prior to militaristic, economic, and political domination via imperialism and colonialism, Europeans psychologically conditioned non-Europeans to believe the former's views were divine and correct (Carruthers, 1999; Fanon, 1952/2008). Thus, when African (Black) people reclaim and enact their truths, they contribute to a ripple effect of anti-colonial processes. These ideological and behavior constructions constitute what Robinson (1983/2000) described as part and parcel of the Black radical tradition. The ever-present desire and effort to a live free and authentic African existence in a safe and culturally and spiritually affirming space is the foundation of the Black radical tradition. The metaphysical, spiritual, and psychological enactment of this vision precedes physical and material realities—hence, the manifestation of historical consciousness (Robinson, 1983/2000). The *collective cultural resistance* among West Indian cricket teams during the twentieth century reveals the significance of sport as a public platform in terms of shifting attitudes about what is and should be normalized and possible. Thus, West Indian cricketers embodied a *radical imagination of Black sporting resistance.*

More specific to the concept of transnationalism, West Indian cricket teams constituted transnational communities (Faist, 2010) by virtue of including members from anti-colonial nations such as Jamaica, British Guiana, Barbados, Antigua, and Trinidad.[12] West Indian cricketers also personified localized mobile transnational formations whereby they were highly mobile and highly local (Dahinden, 2010). It has been documented that many of these cricketers would return to their native homelands when they were not competing and continued to work in the community to improve the plight of their people (James, 1963). Members of the successful Shannon Club of Trinidad are a primary example of this stealth migrant sporting resistance. Therefore, their transnational performances in cricket *and* their domestic work at home served important political, economic, and cultural purposes. Even though cricket and all sports during that period were designed to reinforce the racial status quo, Black West Indians transformed these spaces into sites of racial contestation and redemption by their presence, performances, and culturally grounded knowledge and values.

Although many of the West Indian transnational migrants traveled to and from England, several others permanently relocated to lands away from their homelands and established their own leagues (James, 1963; Marqusee, 1994/2016). In contrast to localized mobile transnational formations, these West Indian cricketers were transnational outsiders whereby they displayed low mobility and low local anchorage (Dahinden, 2010). According to Dahinden (2010), locality refers to "being rooted or anchored—socially, economically, or politically—in the country of immigration and/or in the sending country; it means developing/having a set of social relations at specific places" (p. 51). These migrants retained their West Indian cultures through music, food, customs, and cricket, but they seldom returned to their homelands after migration. Concomitantly, although they received British citizenship, they were still viewed and treated as outsiders in comparison to native British citizens (Gilroy, 1993). The creation of Black leagues in the face of racial segregation in Europe reflected grassroots activism. This type of activism focuses on fostering racial equity at the local level. In the case of sports, Black leagues not only afforded players an opportunity to display their skill sets, but they also provided a culturally affirming and safe social space for community gatherings. In 1980, the Quaid-e-Azam League was established as an all-Black league (Marqusee, 1994/2016). Along the same lines, legendary West Indian cricketer Sir Clive Lloyd had an event, the Clive Lloyd Cup, named after him. These Black leagues and events were covered by the local Black press, which sought to legitimize the merits of these cricketers and their cultures (Marqusee, 1994/2016). The combination of grassroots and media activism enhanced the respect and visibility of West Indian cricketers and West Indian culture throughout Europe and the world.

Beyond professional leagues, West Indian transnational migrants also created recreational diasporic communities (Bruneau, 2010; Dahinden, 2010; Faist, 2010). In an ethnographic study of an Afro-Caribbean-Canadian adult recreational team called the Mavericks Cricket and Social Club (MCSC) in Toronto, Canada, Joseph (2017) described how the players established diasporic connections through cricket in Canada, the United States, the United Kingdom, and the Caribbeans:

> For the Mavericks [local Afro-Caribbean cricket team], this required neither a trip to Africa nor a flight to the Caribbean. They only need to travel across the

Peace Bridge for a 10-hour drive to New York City, or merely to Ross Lord Park, 30 minutes north of the city of Toronto, in order to forge close bonds with other black people, enjoy Caribbean sport, food, drink and music, and share nostalgic stories in their native languages. Afro-Caribbean migrants used sport and travel within the Black Atlantic as vehicles to create their homeland cultures, resist and promote integration in Canada, overcome racism, and therefore to *be black and Caribbean and Canadian men*. (p. 3)

Transnational familial and kinship networks, emotional connections to a homeland, and cultural formations transcend borders (Faist, 2000). As noted earlier, freedom of movement across borders was a coveted right of formerly enslaved Africans and their ancestors who had these types of opportunities stripped from them during enslavement and subsequent colonial conditions (Franklin, 1947/1974; Gilroy, 1993). During the mid-twentieth century, a wave of Caribbean people migrated to various parts of North America, namely the northeastern United States and Canada. The MCSC comprised Antiguan, Barbadian, Grenadian, Guyanese, Jamaican, and Trinidadian Canadians (Joseph, 2011, 2012a, 2014, 2017). Toronto was a primary destination due to kinship networks, economic opportunities in the metropolitan area, and an openness to international cultures and immigration, albeit one that was also contested at times (Joseph, 2017). As noted by transnational scholars, transnational communities are conducive when ethnic stratification exists in a permanent migration destination (Dahinden, 2010; Faist, 2010). Although cities like Toronto were welcoming to immigrants, ethnic stratification still existed whereby neighborhoods were largely structured along ethnic and class lines. As such, Afro-Caribbean transnational diasporic communities or enclaves were created in Toronto, and Black identity was borderless and de-territorialized through cultural productions such as music, food, and cricket (Joseph, 2017). These local transnational formations constituted grassroots activism by demanding equal opportunities for employment and enjoyment compared to their fellow non-Black Canadian citizens.

In an effort to avoid full assimilation into Canadian culture and retain their Caribbean customs, these transnational migrants continued their homeland practices such as playing cricket and creating a celebratory atmosphere around these matches. This *collective cultural resistance* via the reproduction of familiar activities that have cultural meanings and significance enabled Afro-Caribbean-Canadians to minimize the strain of discontinuity that accompanies migration (Gilroy, 1993; Hall, 2003; Joseph, 2017). More specifically, Joseph (2017) summarized the political significance of West Indian cricket: "Cricket had come to represent a challenge to British hegemony; a black masculine identity associated with strength, speed and dominance; and a space for breaking colonial rules" (p. 162). Hence, Afro-Caribbean blackness was re-created through cricket

(Abrahams, 1983; Joseph, 2017; Wilson, 1973). The re-creation of these memories in Canada as well as during the team's travels to the Caribbeans and Europe reflect what Joseph (2017) called "black plurilocal homespaces" (p. 3). As a form of collective cultural resistance, Afro-Caribbean-Canadians resisted the erasure of their homeland cultures and embodied transnational syncretism whereby they blended African and Western cultural influences (Faist, 2000; Joseph, 2017).

A primary aim of colonialism was to destroy African civilization in totality (Fanon, 1952/2008, 1961/2004; Gordon, 1996; Rodney, 1972; Swan, 2020, 2022; Williams, 1974/1987). For this reason, when African people practice self-definition and self-determination, they resist anti-Black racist oppression. More specifically, there is power in language, music, food, religion, and sport, which embody community cultural wealth (Yosso, 2005) and hybrid resistance (Cooper, 2021). Six forms of community cultural wealth that groups subjected to oppression utilize to resist their marginalization include linguistic capital, resistant capital, navigational capital, familial capital, social capital, and aspirational capital (Yosso, 2005). Collectively and separately, these forms of capital generate a sense of collectivism that combats the divide-and-conquer strategy utilized by colonizers.

With cricket, traditional European norms include limited celebration during matches, longer matches, strict uniform codes, and conservative and Eurocentric expectations for match decorum for players and spectators. In contrast, when Afro-Caribbeans participate in cricket, they promote individual and culturally empowering celebrations during matches, shorter and more fast-paced matches, colorful and less strict uniform codes, and liberal and Afrocentric decorum for players and spectators (James, 1963; Joseph, 2017; Marqusee, 1994/2016; Wilde, 1994). In reference to this distinct atmosphere, Joseph (2011, 2012a, 2014, 2017) described how *liming* at cricket matches for the MCSC included alcohol consumption by players and spectators, loud calypso music, playing of dominoes, city tours, trash talking, gossiping, storytelling, purchasing and selling of symbolic souvenirs, and more emphasis on social engagement and entertainment than winning and compliance to rules. These memories embodied the humanization and healing efforts of a group of African-descendant people who had experienced centuries of displacement and mistreatment (Joseph, 2017). In addition, the hybrid resistance embodied through these transnational formations not only disrupted the vicissitudes of European colonialism in concert with the broader anti-colonial movement in the West Indies, but also sustained a sense of collective identity and ontological security for African migrants across different geopolitical contexts.

Relatedly, Faist (2000) explained how transnationalization occurs in the economic, political, and cultural realms. Economically, transnationalization occurs through the monetary exchanges between communities in a settled land and the homeland. During their travels, the MCSC would not only financially contribute to the businesses and communities of the transnational Caribbean spaces they visited, but they would also send money back to their Caribbean homelands from their earnings (Joseph, 2017). These concerted efforts illustrated a lower level of economic activism whereby small groups exercised their agency, mobility, and resources to financially benefit their native homelands as opposed to solely investing in hegemonic migrant lands or entities. Politically, transnationalization manifests through national, multicultural, and transnational citizenship. Blackness was exuded through Caribbeanness; although Afro-Caribbeans adopted a Canadian national citizenship they also embraced their multicultural and transnational citizenship by identifying with their Caribbean homelands (Joseph, 2017). Culturally, transnationalization involves acculturation, cultural retention, and transnational syncretism via the creation of safe spaces, reciprocal relationships, and cultural distinctiveness (Faist, 2000). The *liming* atmosphere at these cricket matches, the donning of African and Caribbean apparel, and the use of Caribbean team names illustrates cultural transnationalization (Joseph, 2017).

The flows and hybridity of Afro-Caribbean migrants mirrored cultural and political formations associated with the Black Atlantic (Gilroy, 1993; Hall, 2003; Joseph, 2017). Tournaments in places such as Saint Lucia, contested between Afro-Caribbean Canadian, Trinidadian, and Jamaican teams, reflected the creation of a transnational community and mass mobilization activism. At these events, Caribbeans across the diaspora would forge and strengthen relationships, support each other economically, share political information, and foster a deep sense of community. The creation of these conditions amid life in a neocolonial world is invaluable to the intergenerational survival of African diasporic groups. Stated differently, these actions serve as the enactment of the Black radical tradition (Robinson, 1983/2000) in and through sport. The protection and reenactment of empowering cultural practices as a core source of spiritual renewal for African people from antiquity through the transatlantic atrocity and continues in the twenty-first century is reflective of the ontological totality being sustained via Black transnationalism sporting resistance (Cooper, 2019, 2021; Franklin, 1947/1974; Joseph, 2017). Hence, the re-creation of Afro-Caribbean cricket spaces in neocolonial geographies reflects *collective cultural resistance* via agentic resistance, grassroots activism, economic activism, and mass mobilization activism.

Beyond the boundary of the pitch, Black sporting resistance through West Indian cricket has also been exhibited through scholarly and media activism. Such was the case with the consummate West Indian cricket scholar and media activist C.L.R. James. It is worth noting that James's revolutionary fervor and consciousness manifested from his own transnational experiences.[13] He traveled to England in 1932 to support Learie Constantine (James, 1963). During this time, he was exposed to a range of political ideas including the Marxist and Trotskyist philosophies on political economies. This political education facilitated his reexamination of his childhood experiences in colonial Trinidad as well as his previous understandings and valuing of European culture including cricket. Subsequently, James's work more explicitly connected the efforts of Black West Indian cricketers to West Indian nationalist, Labour Party, and socialist efforts. During this same period, there were a number of Black Power organizations emerging in the West Indies including the Afro-Caribbean Movement (Antigua), People's Progressive Movement (Barbados), Black Beret Cadre (Bermuda), Black Socialist Party (Dominica), African Society for Cultural Relations with Independent Africa (Guyana), The Forum (Grenada and Saint Lucia), Black Power Party (Montserrat), Black Power Group (Saint Kitts), Educational Forum of the People and Black Panther Party (Saint Vincent), and National Joint Action Committee (Trinidad and Tobago) (Swan, 2009).[14] The emergence of these groups reflected the growing political consciousness of African people in the Caribbeans regarding Black Power, Black Nationalism, Pan-Africanism, and Black Radicalism.

Moreover, James (1963) was a part of a revolutionary West Indian literary movement that highlighted military, political, economic, and cultural forms of resistance. Along with *Beyond a Boundary*, James authored works such as a biography of Toussaint Louverture of Santo Domingo titled *Minty Alley*; *Cricket and I*;[15] *The Life of Captain Cipriani: An Account of British Government in the West Indies*; *The Black Jacobins: Toussaint L'Ouverture and the San Domingo Revolution*; *Modern Politics*;[16] *Party Politics in the West Indies*; and *Nkrumah and the Ghana Revolution* (James, 1936, 1937, 1963/1989, 1984, 2013, 2014, 2022). James's scholarly activism influenced scores of Afro-Caribbean sport scholars in the twentieth and twenty-first centuries such as Ben Carrington and Janelle Joseph. James was also editor of the politically acclaimed publication *The Nation*, which reflected his activation of media activism. This publication was lauded as the primary source of political information for the People's National Movement of Trinidad. The spirit of the labor and national movement was anti-colonial in nature and centered on West Indian self-governance. As former avid cricketer and later political activist, James (1963) explained his counterargument to those who felt sports, specifically cricket, were beyond the bounds of serious political discussion: "The *Nation* was an official organ and highly political paper. (Some even queried whether such a paper should express an opinion on cricket captaincy at all). They were wrong. This was politics and very serious politics" (p. 231). Specifically, his media activism in *The Nation* was epitomized in his article "Alexander Must Go," which criticized the selection of a White cricketer for the West Indies team over Frank Worrell, who at that time was considered the best cricketer in the region (James, 1963). This media activism contributed to the selection of Worrell as captain of West Indies team in 1960 when they competed in Australia. The performances of the Worrell-led West Indian teams were emblematic of the independence triumphs across the region (James, 1963). The reality of West Indians being able to author their own texts and have this content disseminated across the world signified a shift in the European colonial–dominant narrative that at best misrepresented the experiences and voices of West Indians and at worst ignored them altogether. The vigor, creativity, and passion that West Indian cricketers exhibited on the pitch mirrored the resistance efforts during West Indian independence efforts (James, 1963). The intersection of sport, politics, literature, and media reflects the power of hybrid resistance across geopolitical and sociocultural contexts.

In summary, West Indian cricket emerged concomitantly with West Indian independence efforts and thus sport was an extension of the broader anticolonial political project in the region. Joseph (2017) describes the connection between West Indian cricket and the broader political movement of the 1970s and 1980s: "[B]lack power was symbolised by a man in cricket pads wielding either a bat or a ball as his weapon of choice" (p. 95). Black hybrid sporting resistance was personified in myriad ways, including through agency, pioneering, symbolic, grassroots, mass mobilization, and economic activism. Agentic participatory sporting resistance and stealth migrant sporting resistance were exhibited through victories as well as through fast and distinct forms of batting, catching, throwing, and running (James, 1963; Joseph, 2012a, 2017). Collective cultural resistance was performed through the *liming* atmosphere, Caribbean team names, and culturally empowering uniforms and connections to anti-colonial efforts (James, 1963; James, 2012, 2017). Pioneering resistance was reflected in signature victories and securing captaincy designations (James, 1963; Marqusee, 1994/2016). Symbolic activism and agentic refraining resistance were reflected in boycotts of cricket matches to express the cricketers' demand for racial justice in terms of participation and captaincy opportunities (Davis, 2009; James, 1963; Marqusee, 1994/2016). Grassroots activism was embodied in the formation of local and national teams such as the Shannon Club of Trinidad and the generation of cultural pride across communities in the region. Mass mobilization activism was demonstrated through the transnational formation of the West Indian cricket teams and their demand for inclusion into the ICC (James, 1963; Marqusee, 1994/2016). Economic activism was exhibited when West Indian teams such as the MCSC would intentionally support Black-owned businesses during their international travels as well as when they would send money to their native Caribbean homelands (Joseph, 2012a, 2017). In each instance of resistance, the goal was to amplify West Indian liberation, self-determination, and cultural pride.

Transnational Circuits: Negro and Afro-Latino Baseball Players, Teams, and Leagues

Transnational circuits comprise the cross-border exchange of goods, people, and information that results in symbiotic political, social, cultural, and economic outcomes (Faist, 2000). A primary example of a transnational circuit is the formation of the Negro baseball leagues in the United States during the early twentieth century. In the late nineteenth century, the White mainstream baseball league, the National Association of Professional Base Ball Leagues (NAPBL), instituted a gentlemen's agreement that excluded colored [sic] players (Lomax, 2003). Despite the significant downsides to this racially discriminatory practice, it inadvertently led to the formation of Negro (also known now as African American) and Caribbean baseball teams and circuits that would reach unforeseen heights of popularity in the mid-twentieth century (Bruce, 1985; Burgos, 2007, 2011; Holway, 1988, 1989; Lanctot, 1994, 2004; Lomax, 2003, 2014; Peterson, 1970; Rogosin, 1985; White, 1995). A widely accepted belief holds that these Negro Leagues were solely composed of African Americans (Burgos, 2007, 2011). Even though a majority of the players in these leagues were African Americans, from their inception Black baseball teams in the United States had symbolic and literal ties to their kinship networks in the Caribbean region and Mexico. For example, the cross-border relationships between African Americans and Mexicans dates back to before the U.S. Civil War, when Mexico abolished slavery thirty-six years prior to when its northern neighbor implemented the same measure (Horne, 2005). Throughout the latter half of the nineteenth century, African Americans in the southwestern United States sought to migrate to Mexico as a safe haven from White American terrorism (Horne, 2005). Both African Americans and Afro-Latinos shared a common adversary in White European colonizers and their descendants, and so these groups created symbiotic relationships across borders to enhance their respective livelihoods.

In his book *Playing America's Game: Baseball, Latinos, and the Color Line*, Burgos (2007) explained the significance of this cross-cultural collaboration through sport: "African Americans and Latinos joined forces to create a transnational circuit that operated outside of organized baseball. Understanding this circuit, the actors who created and participated in it, the institutions of which it was made, and the communities that sustained it required an approach that stressed the connections, not the differences, between the English- and Spanish-speaking baseball worlds" (p. xiv).

From the late 1880s until the late 1940s in the United States, nearly all Latinos played in the Negro Leagues, which underscored the fact that the color line largely restricted their participation in White-controlled mainstream baseball as well (Burgos, 2007). The longevity and success of these leagues was directly related to their transnational networks. Given the reality that Black ownership of baseball venues was limited, Black entrepreneurs and players had to rely on networks across state and national lines to establish barnstorming tours for their economic livelihood (Lomax, 2003, 2014), which exemplified their utility of mass mobilization activism.

In addition to Mexico, the transnational networks between the Negro American baseball teams and players also extended to the Caribbean region in countries such as Cuba. The Afro-Cuban and Negro American connections in the Negro Leagues date back to the late nineteenth century. In 1885, the first Black professional baseball team, the Cuban Giants, was established at the Argyle Hotel on Long Island in New York (Lomax, 2003). The team was established under the leadership of Frank Thompson, Stanislaus Kostka (S. K.) Govern, and C. S. Massey (Burgos, 2007). Although none of the players were of Cuban descent, the team's name demonstrated African Americans' affinity for the country just 90 miles south of Florida and particularly its anti-colonial and anti-imperial revolutionary efforts, which aligned with anti–Jim Crow efforts in the United States during the late nineteenth and early twentieth centuries. For example, during the late 1800s, numerous Black newspapers expressed support for the end of slavery in Cuba because African Americans could empathize with being treated as less than citizens in their displaced homeland (Burgos, 2007).[17] As Horne (2018a, 2020a, 2020b) noted, because African Americans were often at a numerical disadvantage in the United States compared to their racist oppressors, they strategically forged alliances transnationally with groups who shared common adversaries. In the case of the Cubans, they also suffered from European imperialism and conquest from the Spaniards, and the U.S. government viewed them as antagonists due to their anti-capitalist, pro-socialist, and pro-communist political leanings (Horne, 2014b).

Beyond the original Cuban Giants, numerous Black baseball teams would adopt similar names, including the Cuban X Giants (Lomax, 2003). Some suggest the choice of the team's name was intended to create the perception among White teams that the players were of Cuban descent, because discrimination against Black people from outside the United States was not as intense as it was toward descendants of those who were enslaved in the United States (Burgos, 2007; Lomax, 2003).[18] In an analysis of Afro-Latino and Negro American relations in baseball during the mid-twentieth century, Burgos (2007) offered the following explanation for the trend among team name selections: "The decision to name themselves the Cuban Giants drew on the ambiguous racial position Cubans occupied in U.S. professional baseball and within U.S. racial understanding" (p. 48). Particularly when teams of the Negro Leagues traveled, if they acted as if they only spoke Spanish they were at times treated more favorably than if they indicated they were Negro Americans who spoke English (Burgos, 2007). Deeply rooted anti–African American sentiment in the United States dates back to the founding of the country in 1776, when a majority of Africans who were enslaved fought alongside the British in hopes of securing their freedom (Horne, 2014a, 2014b, 2018a, 2020a). Because Great Britain was moving toward abolishing slavery—which it did in 1833, more than thirty years before the United States ended slavery after the Civil War in 1865—Africans in the United States did not align with the White Americans who enslaved them (Horne, 2014a). Even following abolition, in the late nineteenth and early twentieth centuries many descendants of White former enslavers retained strong disdain for the African American descendants of their former property. Because of this animus, there was a more lenient color line policy in mainstream semiprofessional and professional baseball for Afro-Latinos, particularly lighter-skinned non-English-speaking persons, compared to that for Negro Americans. The policy thus had its roots in the sociopolitical and economic tensions connected to the counterrevolutionary war of 1776 and the Civil War of 1861–1865 (Burgos, 2007; Horne, 2014a, 2014b, 2018a, 2020a).

Similar to cross-border relationships that led to the successful Haitian revolution (Horne, 2015), connections with Cuban baseball teams reflected the reciprocal relationship between Negro baseball teams of the early twentieth century and their counterparts on the island (Lomax, 2003). After the end of Spanish rule in Cuba in 1898, the country became a popular location for barnstorming tours for American amateur, semiprofessional, and professional teams (Burgos, 2007). In 1899 the Cuban Giants traveled to Saint Augustine, Florida, and Cuba during their inaugural barnstorming tour (Lomax, 2003). The players worked as hotel employees at the Hotel Ponce de Leon. Working at hotels during select barnstorming tours allowed the team managers and players to acquire vital knowledge about Afro-Latinos and other Caribbean cultures (Burgos, 2007). The Cuban Giants' managers, Edward B. (E. B.) Lamar and Clarence Williams, fostered a relationship with the Almendares Blues team manager, Abel Linaries, to create a multiyear barnstorming tour (Lomax, 2003). Abel Linaries's All Cubans team, which became the Cuban Stars in 1905, became the first Cuban team to tour the United States in 1899 (Lomax, 2003). The national and international travel schedule fostered cooperative economics and cultural ties between the teams and their respective communities. Barnstorming tours to Cuba continued through the 1915–1916 season when Andrew "Rube" Foster, known as the founder of Black baseball, took his Chicago American Giants team to Cuba for winter competition and to secure economic benefits (Lomax, 2003). The sports-based hybrid resistance exhibited by the Negro American and Afro-Latino baseball teams included grassroots, mass mobilization, and economic activism amid racially discriminatory social conditions (Cooper, 2021). In contrast to prevailing notions that suggest Africans were complicit in their oppression, the transnational formation of these Negro

American and Afro-Latino alliances underscores how Africans have perpetually been innovative, adaptive, and collaborative with their resistance efforts.

In 1906, three Negro teams (Brooklyn Royal Giants, Cuban X Giants, and Philadelphia Giants) and two Cuban teams (Cuban Giants and Cuban Stars) coalesced to form the National Association of Colored Baseball Clubs of the United States and Cuba (NACBC) (Lomax, 2003). A similar league called the International League of Colored Baseball Clubs in America and Cuba (ILBCAC) was also established in the same year. The ILBCAC was composed of two Negro American teams (Cuban X Giants and Philadelphia Giants), two Cuban teams (Cuban Stars and Havana Stars), and two White American teams (Philadelphia Professionals and Philadelphia Quaker Giants) (Lomax, 2003). This league was born out of the racial realities of the day that prevented Black ownership of facilities and team access to more mainstream economic opportunities. Thus, in true Black transnationalism sporting resistance form, these team managers and players maximized their resourcefulness. I argue that Black sport organizations during the Jim Crow era signified an alignment with the Black radical tradition (Robinson, 1983/2000), which upholds the importance of culturally grounded social structures and organizations created, managed, and owned by and for Black people. Although the NACBC folded within four years and the ILBCAC disbanded after one season, the precedent these leagues set for future Black sport empowerment through transnational ties was invaluable. As examples of mass mobilization and economic activism, these leagues reflected the purpose of what Edwards (2016a) described as the first wave of Black athlete activism between 1900 and 1945, which focused on gaining legitimacy in and through sport. When describing Afro-Latinos' motivation for excelling in baseball during this era, Burgos (2007) offered the following sentiments: "Those who suffered racial exclusion endeavored to challenge claims that they lacked playing skill and 'gentlemanly' comportment. Through their performance on the professional ball fields and their conduct before the sporting public, these men attempted to change perceptions of who could be viewed as a professional ballplayer and as a man" (p. 2).

Both Negro Americans and Afro-Latinos adopted the muscular assimilationism philosophy whereby they believed achievement in baseball would contribute to better treatment for their race in society more broadly (Burgos, 2007; Cooper, 2021; Henderson, 1939).[19] In other words, baseball symbolized more than a leisure activity for entertainment, but rather served as an integral part of the broader political struggle for African diasporic people.

The muscular assimilation philosophy among many African Americans and Afro-Latinos during the twentieth century is not without critique. The integrationist tenor undergirding this belief communicated that merging into White spaces to prove Black worth and equality was the aim. Yet there are a few problematic aspects of this approach. One, it fundamentally ignores the ills associated with racial capitalism (Robinson, 1983/2000). Joining mainstream White baseball leagues or outdueling White players on the field does not challenge the broader economic system that oppresses racialized groups and economically disadvantaged populations. Instead, this approach suggests increased representation and a more favorable position within this system are the primary goals of African Americans and Afro-Latinos. Although nominal gains can be accrued by pursuing increased access to resources for a select minority, the structure remains intact for the majority of racially oppressed people. In other words, true liberation and freedom cannot be experienced in a system of racial capitalism. Hence, I contend the ultimate aim of Black people must be to end all vicissitudes of colonialism, including modern racial capitalism, and replace them with a more egalitarian mode of existence such as African communalism and scientific socialism (Carmichael, 1971; Nkrumah, 1973).

Another issue with the muscular assimilationism approach is the inherent posture that proving Whites wrong about Black inferiority is more important than existing in a space free from racist oppression. For example, it has been noted how leaders of the Negro Leagues such as Rube Foster sought to model these leagues after the White mainstream Major League Baseball (MLB) in an effort to eventually desegregate the latter (Lomax, 2014).[20] By design, racial capitalism creates legal monopolies controlled by Whites and incentivizes assimilation from racialized groups. In the context of the United States, nationalism is synonymous with unwavering adherence to neoliberalism and the presumed White superiority myth. The rejection of these beliefs was endorsed by the Black Nationalism, Pan-Africanism, and Black Radicalism movements, each of whom called for a radical transformation of the United States and internationally (Ogbar, 2020). In contrast, the more popular Civil Rights movement in the United States promoted the idea that equality within the existing system was the benchmark of racial progress (Hine et al., 2006). It is the latter movement that was more closely associated with the political orientations of the Negro Leagues and its supporters. For example, Black media outlets such as *The Pittsburgh Courier* promoted messages calling for the desegregation of MLB and support for the U.S. military effort during World War II (Cooper, 2021).[21]

Given the vulnerable position of African Americans in the United States—as a numerical minority situated in a neocolonial context and geographically separated by water from majority African nation-states—acquiescing to nationalist agendas is more often a strategy of survival rather than an ideal preference. In fact, proponents of Black Nationalism, Pan-Africanism, and Black Radicalism have been targeted by the U.S. government and subjected to imprisonment, exile, and/or death (Ali & Durham, 1975; Robeson, 1958/1998; Ogbar, 2020). I argue that the system of racial capitalism strategically exploited Negro American and Afro-Latino baseball players' affinity for muscular assimilationism to ensure any revolutionary potential for anti-capitalist and anti-U.S.

nationalist efforts could not be exercised through sporting networks. Because sport has served as ideological outpost for nation-states (Sage, 1998), neocolonial capitalist countries use these spaces to advance their political agendas; hence, the weakness of assimilationist efforts, including the actions of Negro American and Afro-Latino baseball players and team managers during the early and mid-twentieth century, further illuminates the need for adopting Black internationalist approaches to achieve universal justice in perpetuity.[22]

Hegemonic groups are not the only ones who use sport to advance their political aims. In both the United States and Cuba, political, labor, and activist groups strategically partnered with baseball promoters, teams, and leagues to promote their messages (Burgos, 2007, 2011; Lomax, 2003, 2014; Peterson, 1970). These efforts reveal how sport as a source of resistance has historically served as a complementary and amplifying tool to mainstream activist efforts beyond sport. In addition to activist groups associated with these baseball teams and leagues, it was not uncommon for select games to be dedicated as fundraisers for charitable causes such as providing money for underprivileged families or community organizations, which reflects advocacy through sport (Burgos, 2007; Cooper, 2021; Lomax, 2014). Along the same lines, grassroots activism was reflected in local-level league formation in urban environments such as Harlem, New York, and Pittsburgh, Pennsylvania (Lomax, 2003, 2014). Mass mobilization activism was exhibited through interstate and international league formations and games, and economic activism was enacted through the creation of business partnerships within and beyond sport (Lomax, 2003, 2014). Political/civic activism was present through the promotion of Black civic engagement and political representation at the local, state, and national levels (Lomax, 2014). Media activism was reflected in the use of newspapers and radio to promote teams and other pro-Black causes, including through outlets such as the *Chicago Defender*, *New York Amsterdam News*, *Pittsburgh Courier*, *Baltimore Afro-American*, *Detroit Tribune*, and *Cleveland Call* (Cooper, 2021; Corbett & Stills, 2007). Pioneering resistance was embodied through Negro American and Afro-Latino ownership, coaching, and legendary players (Burgos, 2007; Cooper, 2021; Lomax, 2003, 2014). Black transnational sporting communities of Negro American and Afro-Latino baseball teams and leagues personified what Edwards (2016b) described as leveraging the power of sport for social change.

Transnational communities are largely sustained by individuals who have acquired migration expertise over time (Bruneau, 2010). One key figure in the facilitation of these relationships was an Afro-Cuban named Alex Pompez (Burgos, 2011). Pompez was a Cuban American who grew up in Key West, Florida, and later moved to Harlem, New York. The following description of Pompez underscores his unique upbringing as a migrant or rather, as a Cuban émigré: "The communities Pompez grew up in featured a mixture of anti-colonial politics, cigar-making, baseball, literature, and music that exposed him to evolving sensibilities about what it meant to be Cuban, a African American, and a first-generation U.S.-born Latino" (Burgos, 2011, p. 5). Pompez's early exposure to the importance of migration between Cuba and Florida for economic, political, and social necessities influenced his professional skill set later in his life as a talented and well-respected transnational scout of baseball players (Burgos, 2011). In 1916, Pompez purchased the Cuban Stars, later known as the New York Cubans, and served as owner of the team until 1950. A few of the notable Afro-Latino players and managers who participated in the Negro Leagues were José "The Black Diamond" Méndez, Orestes "Minnie" Miñoso, Orlando Cepeda, Martín Dihigo, Juan Marichal, Alejandro Oms, Alejandro Pompez, Cristóbal Torriente, Adolfo Luque, Rodolfo Fernández, Rafael Noble, Charlie Rivera, and Armando Vásquez (Burgos, 2007, 2011). Pompez recruited players from Havana, Cuba; Santo Domingo, Dominican Republic; San Juan, Puerto Rico; Harlem, New York; Chicago, Illinois; and Cincinnati, Ohio (Burgos, 2007). Suffice to say, modern-day MLB and its plethora of stars from Cuba, Puerto Rico, and the Dominican Republic owe a debt of gratitude to the pioneering resistance of Alex Pompez.

In the face of racial segregation, Pompez was a leader in pioneering resistance in a multitude of ways. Pompez's pioneering feats reflect his ingenuity: a) first team leader to recruit players from Mexico and the Caribbean region (e.g., Puerto Rico, Dominican Republic, Panama, Saint Kitts, and Saint Thomas) to participate on U.S. baseball teams, b) first to start winter baseball barnstorming in Mexico, c) first to secure stadium leasing and spring training travel schedules for Negro and Afro-Latino teams, d) first to lead a Negro team (Cuban Stars) on a tour of Puerto Rico and the Dominican Republic, e) first to implement Spanish classes at spring training, mentoring programs for Latino players, and intentional housing selection for young players, and f) first Latino director of international scouting in MLB (Burgos, 2011). Pompez was also instrumental in helping Orestes Miñoso become the first Afro-Cuban to integrate MLB, with Miñoso joining the Cleveland Indians and the Chicago White Sox in 1948 and 1951, respectively (Burgos, 2011). Pompez's career titles included Negro Leagues team owner, league vice president, recruiter/scout, businessman, advocate, and mentor. Pompez's bilingualism, familiarity with migration routes, business acumen, and cultural hybridity led to him becoming the most accomplished recruiter of Latin American baseball talent in the twentieth century (Burgos, 2011).

Furthermore, the increased popularity of the Negro Leagues during the 1920s was largely due to the influx of Afro-Latino talent (Burgos, 2007; Lomax, 2014). The emergence of the Negro Leagues in the United States and Afro-Cuban baseball leagues in Cuba coincided with the bourgeoning Universal Negro Improvement Association (UNIA) Black nationalist movement led by

Marcus Garvey. Harlem was the epicenter of the Black nationalist movement, while Cuba claimed the largest number of UNIA chapters outside the United States during the mid-1920s, which underscores the sprawling nature of the African diasporic and transnational collectivism embodied during this era (Guridy, 2013). Not only did African diasporic groups recognize their common identities and struggles, but they understood the power of their unification in all facets of society, including in sport. Thus, Black transnationalism sporting resistance reflected an extension of both the Black radical tradition (Robinson, 1983/2000) and the bourgeoning Black Nationalism movement during the early twentieth century. Relatedly, Burgos (2011) explained the historical connection between what I describe as Black sporting resistance in the early 1900s and the transnational significance of the Negro Leagues: "Through the annals of American sports history, black Americans openly celebrated when Jack Johnson beat Jim Jeffries and listed raptly to Joe Louis's titanic fights with white adversaries. So, too, did they cheer when Negro Leagues all-stars defeated white stars on and off U.S. playing fields. These events not only formed a 'structure of feelings,' they produced a tapestry of understanding that wove a sense of collectivity, pride, and affirmation into the accomplishment of black athleticism" (p. 150).

In 1924, the Negro National League (NNL) and Eastern Colored League (ECL) agreed to participate in a Colored World Series (Lomax, 2014). Key players in the matchup included pitcher José "The Black Diamond" Méndez (a Cuban and Afro-Latino) of the Kansas City Monarchs and third baseman and shortstop William Julius "Judy" Johnson (a Negro American) of Hilldale Athletic Club (Bruce, 1985; Lomax, 2014). The Monarchs emerged victorious, winning five games, and the series recorded over 45,000 spectators and resulted in over $50,000 in revenue (Lomax, 2014). Méndez is considered the first Cuban-born baseball star prior the establishment of the Negro Leagues (NBHF, 2022).[23] He was a valuable contributor to the three consecutive NNL Kansas City Monarch pennant teams between 1923 and 1925. Similar to several Negro American players, Cuban players like Méndez developed their skills under racist conditions. For example, Méndez's experiences working in sugarcane fields conditioned his arm for the pitching he would do as a professional baseball player (NBHF, 2022). Negro American players who grew up in rural areas throughout the United States similarly acquired skills through arduous agricultural and industrial labor (Holway, 1989). As opposed to letting these unjust labor conditions deflate their spirits and restrict their utility, these Black sporting resistors defied the odds placed upon them by excelling in baseball and, more importantly, through their hybrid resistance they advanced the political and racial justice struggles of their day. Stated differently, despite facing the harsh realities of postbellum racism, both Negro American and Afro-Cuban baseball players exhibited *sports-based agentic resistance* by using their talents on the baseball field to express their humanity, cultures, skills, passions, and persistence.

Another key facilitator for the creation and vitality of transnational communities is ethnic stratification (Dahinden, 2010). When African, Latino, and Caribbean migrants relocated to different regions of the United States during the early and mid-twentieth century, there were several central locations where they settled, including places such as Harlem, New York, and Miami, Florida. These urban enclaves were fertile grounds for intercultural mixtures and hybridity (Gilroy, 1993). Because the White racist norms of the era enforced strict color lines, many Latinos (including Afro-Latinos) were deemed as Other and grouped with African Americans. From a survival standpoint, being in proximity to one another created contexts where frequent interactions and relationship building emerged. As Faist (2010) states, transnationalism manifests through informal and formal relationships. In the case of the Negro Leagues, informal social relationships evolved into the creation of formal institutions such as baseball leagues and related businesses (Burgos, 2007, 2011; Lomax, 2003, 2014). For example, one of the hallmark events of the NNL was the annual championship series. The 1935 NNL championship series, considered the greatest in Black baseball history, was played between the Pittsburgh Crawfords and the Cubans and featured some of the best Negro American players, such as Josh Gibson, James "Cool Papa" Bell, Oscar Charleston, Sam Bankhead, Jimmy Crutchfield, and Leroy Matlock, and the best Cuban players, such as Martín Dihigo, Ramón Bragaña, Horacio "Rabbit" Martínez, Alejandro Oms, Lázaro Salazar, and Lefty Tiant (Burgos, 2011). The East-West Classic in New York City attracted over 42,000 spectators, which was an impressive turnout for any major entertainment event during the mid-1930s (Burgos, 2011; Lomax, 2014). The symbiotic relationship between the Negro Leagues and local Black businesses not only led to legendary contests, but also successful community building via economic and sociocultural empowerment (Bruce, 1985; Burgos, 2007, 2011; Holway, 1988, 1989; Lomax, 2003, 2011; Peterson, 1970). Hence, these transnational circuits manifested into sports-based mass mobilization and economic activism.

Moreover, the innovative and barrier-breaking strategies exercised by baseball influencers such as Alex Pompez mirrored the energy and contributions of the Harlem Renaissance movement in the 1920s and 1930s (Cooper et al., 2020). A prime example of this interplay was reflected in the popularity of the Dyckman Oval park in New York City. Burgos (2011) highlighted the significance of this facility and its location: "Dyckman Oval soon emerged as Harlem's sporting playground, hosting Negro Leagues baseball contests, black professional and college football games, [and] boxing and wrestling cards that featured African American and Latino athletes.... The Dyckman scene was hopping, providing Harlem residents a haven at a time when they could not attend Harlem entertainment venues that were segregated, such as the Cotton Club. Jazz musicians, entertainers, local politicians, race leaders, and sporting figures such as Joe Louis and Jesse Owens in addition to the everyday fan visited the Oval" (p. 86).

During Pompez's growth in Harlem in the early to mid-1900s, the Harlem Renaissance was celebrating the intellectual, artistic, and political contributions of renowned African Americans and Caribbean migrants such as W.E.B. Du Bois, James Weldon Johnson, Madame C. J. Walker, Claude McKay, Marcus Garvey, James Baldwin, Zora Neal Hurston, Harry Belafonte, Augusta Savage, John Henrik Clarke, Paul Robeson, Charlie Parker, Father Divine, and Arturo "Arthur" Schomberg (Burgos, 2011; Cooper, 2021; Cooper et al., 2020; Hine et al., 2006). The cultural amalgamation in Harlem during this period contributed to this location being a prime destination for African diasporic expression and existence. The bourgeoning success of the Negro Leagues as a transnational circuit reflected the broader social and political advancements by Black people in the United States during the New Negro era between the late 1890s and the early 1950s (Cooper, 2021; Early, 2008). Since African Americans were largely marginalized from the mainstream political economy, the Negro Leagues relied on underground economies to fund their enterprises (Burgos, 2011; Lomax, 2003, 2014).[24] Although these practices were frowned upon by some contemporary onlookers, they reflect the adaptive tactics African Americans, Afro-Latinos, and Afro-Caribbeans employed to create and sustain their businesses in a society that sought to strip them of any form of ownership and economic vitality. The shared experiences with being oppressed and a mutual desire to embody a sense of humanity and community strengthened these groups' African diasporic interdependence.[25] The symbiotic relationships fueled the success of transnational formations such as the Negro Leagues, Afro-Latino baseball leagues, Black media outlets, and Black-owned entertainment venues.

In addition, enslavement and post-slavery oppression conditions unintentionally fostered a keen sense of resourcefulness and use of migration routes and exchanges among African people. Knowledge of borders, neighborhoods, and cultures served as a vital asset not only for migration experts such as Alex Pompez and Rube Foster, but also for Negro American and Afro-Latino players as well (Bruce, 1985; Burgos, 2007, 2011; Holway, 1988, 1989; Lanctot, 1994, 2004; Lomax, 2003, 2014; Peterson, 1970; Rogosin, 1985; White, 1995). However, the transnational circuit was not unidirectional. In fact, several Negro American players such as Satchel Paige, James "Cool Papa" Bell, and Josh Gibson migrated to Mexico, Cuba, Puerto Rico, and the Dominican Republic to participate in leagues during their domestic off-season as well as later in their careers when there were better economic opportunities outside of the United States (Lomax, 2014). Similarly, several Afro-Latinos would migrate and play in the Caribbean region as well as the United States. For example, Martín Dihigo played in Venezuela, Cuba, Mexico, the Dominican Republic, and the United States (Burgos, 2011). As a transnational circuit, these leagues and the cross-border entrepreneurial partnerships they enabled created economic opportunities, a sense of community, and meaning for Negro American and Afro-Latino managers, players, umpires, media, and spectators (Burgos, 2007, 2011; Lomax, 2014; Peterson, 1970).

The African diasporic influence on the internationalization of baseball extended beyond Latin America and into areas such as Asia. For example, in 1927 the Philadelphia Royal Giants of the NNL traveled to Japan to participate in a series of games with local teams (Koshiro, 2003). This occurred four years prior to an all-White MLB all-star team visiting Japan, a fact that did not go unnoticed by the Japanese (Koshiro, 2003) and one that underscores how Black transnational sporting resistance fosters *inter-diasporic alliances*. Horne (2018b) highlighted how the mutual respect and support between African Americans and Japanese, which dates back to the late nineteenth century, continued through the post–World War II years when Afro-Asian solidarity emerged alongside the bourgeoning internationalist political movements. In addition, Koshiro (2003) noted how African American freedom struggles inspired scores of Japanese who were not only seeking to improve human rights conditions within their own country, but also working to strengthen trans-Pacific Afro-Asian relationships. Collectively, the hybrid resistance of African Black diasporic baseball players, managers, owners, business leaders, and media throughout the late nineteenth and early twentieth centuries exemplified how transnational connections have been a central source for intergenerational liberation and empowerment efforts within and beyond sporting spaces.[26]

Transnational Kinship Groups: Colored Hockey League of the Maritimes

Following the Emancipation Proclamation of 1863 and the ratification of the Reconstruction Amendments in 1865, thousands of Africans who were enslaved in the United States sought to migrate northward away from former Confederate states to seek refuge from White racial oppression (Franklin, 1947/1974; Hine et al., 2006). Concurrently, at the turn of the twentieth century, several Caribbeans including Jamaicans and Trinidadians were also migrating north for similar reasons (Fosty & Fosty, 2008). One common destination where these groups arrived to form transnational kinship groups (Bruneau, 2010) was Halifax, Nova Scotia (Fosty & Fosty, 2008). The mass migration of Africans who were formerly enslaved in the United States and Jamaica to Canada dates back to the late eighteenth century. In 1796, the British agreed with the Canadians to relocate the Maroons from Jamaica to Nova Scotia to have their own territory (Fosty & Fosty, 2008). The Maroons are widely celebrated as one of the most effective anti-colonial groups of Africans in world history, particularly within the Western Hemisphere (Horne, 2014a; Ogbar, 2020; Robinson, 1983/2000).

Along with the Maroons from Jamaica, Africans who were enslaved in the United States migrated to Nova Scotia to form the territory that would become known as Africville (Fosty & Fosty, 2008; Lawson, 1972). Per the agreement between the British, Canadian, and Jamaican governments, Africville was on land that was owned by Jamaica (Lawson, 1972). Both groups' lineages and their respective efforts to upend European colonizers in the United States and Caribbeans are noteworthy and illustrate how *societal-centric resistance* informs and strengthens subsequent *sport-based resistance*.[27] In other words, the formation of the Colored Hockey League of the Maritimes in Africville was birthed out of the spirit of resistance from the transnational migrant Maroons of Jamaica and Africans who were formerly enslaved in the United States who fought for their freedom, sovereignty, and humanity. The founders and supporters of this league understood what Robinson (1983/2000) described as a part of the Black radical tradition whereby understanding the significance of self-controlled social structures and organizations is foundational to Black liberation and empowerment efforts. The creation of this separate territory also reflected the Black nationalist tenor of the era, which championed racial separation so Black people could build their own communities with minimal interference from Whites (Ogbar, 2020).

Based on their historical research, Fosty and Fosty (2008) described the significance of Africville: "A community strong in its roots and heritage, where Blacks engaged in farming, logging, local construction, and fishing, a place where families worked to establish businesses, permanent churches, and a better life for all" (p. 31). According to Faist (2010), transnational spaces are "relatively stable, lasting and dense sets of ties reaching beyond and across borders of sovereign states" (p. 13). Thus, Africville constitutes a transnational space. The fact that the residents of Africville were individuals and groups who escaped enslavement and overcame revolutionary war conditions provides a necessary context for understanding their resistance efforts in Canada during the twentieth century (Fosty & Fosty, 2008; Horne, 2020a).[28] The conditions they experienced in the United States and Jamaica in concert with the historical consciousness they possessed by virtue of their connections with their ancestors (Robinson, 1983/2000) equipped them with the resolve and resourcefulness to build a thriving Black community in Nova Scotia.

The origins of hockey in Canada are traced to the early 1800s, but, like many aspects of Canadian society, Africans had been largely excluded from the sport (Fosty & Fosty, 2008). As a result, in 1895, a group of religious African transnational migrants from the United States and Caribbean region including

James A. R. Kinney, James Robinson Johnston, James Borden, and Henry Sylvester Williams (also the founding organizer of the inaugural Pan-African Conference in 1900) established the Colored Hockey League of the Maritimes.[29] Fosty and Fosty (2008) illuminate the important role of Williams's political leadership style and cultural orientation: "Williams' genius was a key element in the efforts to create Black awareness and to promote Black pride. In doing so, he would work to preserve and promote Black consciousness, Black respect for the past, and a burning memory of the struggle that was the language and experience of the Black race on North American shores. *The Code of the Underground Railroad* would become the language of the Colored Hockey League" (p. 55).

Consistent with the core purpose of Black sporting resistance, the Colored Hockey League of the Maritimes was an extension of the concurrent Black political struggles within Nova Scotia and throughout the Black world. As such, the ethos and spirit of the intergenerational Black Liberation Struggle, Black Nationalism, and Pan-Africanism social movements was manifested through the transnationalism sporting resistance of the Colored Hockey League with the establishment of social formations, entrepreneurship, and reciprocity and solidarity with kinship networks. The purpose and structure of the league, the league officials, the players, the spectators, and the league partners such as local Black churches, collectively embodied the message of Black self-determination and collectivism. Moreover, Williams's strategic use of the media and oratory to convey Black pride was not only intended for Africville community members, but also for White Canadians in local areas who harbored racist beliefs about the civility, business acumen, and hockey prowess of Black people. Irrespective of their pre-migration homesites, the members of the Colored Hockey League galvanized around their racial, Pan-Africanist, and religious identities.[30]

The central location for the town and the league organizational activities was a church originally named Campbell Baptist Church and which was later known as African Baptist Church (Fosty & Fosty, 2008). The African Baptist Church was a part of the African Baptist Association (ABA), which was formed in 1854 and included Cornwallis Street Baptist Church, Preston Baptist Church, Beech Hill Baptist Church, Hammond Plains Baptist Church, Bear River Baptist Church, Digby Joggins Baptist Church, Moose River Baptist Church, Granville Mountain Baptist Church, Weymouth Falls Baptist Church, and Yarmouth Baptist Church. Two of the league's founders, James Robinson Johnston and James A. R. Kinney, were preachers at Cornwallis Baptist Church. Within this context, sport participation was closely aligned with religious practice as well as with African self-determination values as promulgated by prominent African American intellectual Booker Taliaferro Washington (Fosty & Fosty, 2008). Along the same lines, the virtue of muscular assimilationism was championed by the league whereby Black excellence in sport was pursued with dignity and grace to break down racial barriers in other aspects of society (Cooper, 2021; Henderson, 1939). In other words, sport was viewed as a vital space where Black people could demonstrate they were not inferior to their White counterparts and thus deserving of equal and fair treatment irrespective of the context.

The four disciplines or core values of the league included "self-discipline, professionalism, skill and teamwork" (Fosty & Fosty, 2008, p. 77). The teams in the league played an average of six to eight games per season and attracted over double the attendance to their games compared to other Canadian leagues in Nova Scotia. For example, the Colored Championship in 1898 between the Halifax Eurekas and the Dartmouth Jubilees was considered a success in terms of organization and execution; the Eurekas emerged victorious 6–3. Later in 1901, over 1,200 attendees watched the African Sea-Sides defeat the West End Rangers 3–2 in the Inter-Provincial Maritime Championship. Related to their resourcefulness, the league played games on frozen ponds between 1906 and 1911 after being denied access to arena ownership. A common theme of African diasporic and Black transnational groups is the keen ability to adapt to unfavorable circumstances and create positive communal experiences through distinct cultural practices and ingenuity. The establishment of this league influenced the creation of Black baseball teams in New Brunswick as well, which reflects the ripple effect of pioneering resistance (Fosty & Fosty, 2008). Thus, the league and its teams reflected small-scale migrant entrepreneurship (Faist, 2010) and highlight how Africville and the Colored Hockey League embodied transnationalism via grassroots and economic activism as well as through pioneering resistance.

A common feature of Black sporting resistance across the globe is agentic participatory and pioneering resistance through distinctive styles of play. Scholars have described this type of resistance as the Black aesthetic (George, 1992) and performative Black masculinities (Cooper, 2019). One example of this type of expression is the cakewalk dance done on skates by Black hockey players in the league, which was an ode to the chalk line walk-dance that was popular on plantations in the southern United States (Fosty & Fosty, 2008). Similar to the vaudevillian performances of the Negro Leagues players in the United States (Lomax, 2014) and the juba dance among Africans who were enslaved in the United States during the antebellum era (Wiggins, 2018), the cakewalk dance was used to mock upper-class Whites' preference for Victorian norms of respectability. The use of sarcastic humor, only fully understood by those who share a common experience of racial oppression, was an example of agentic resistance. This dance communicated the mutual feelings of rejecting European standards and a sense of collective memory (both real and imagined) of a homeland where freedom of movement and expression are normalized.

Similar to other sports, Black hockey players' unique playing style involved speed, athleticism, physicality, and creativity, thus embodying sporting resistance ontologically. In addition, Black pioneers in the Colored Hockey League such as Eddie Martin (who introduced the slap shot) and Henry "Braces" Franklyn (who created the flopping save) innovated moves that became central to twentieth- and twenty-first-century professional hockey across the world (Fosty & Fosty, 2008). Although mainstream hockey spectators misapply the pioneering feat of the flopping save to Jacques Plante, it has been documented that Franklyn introduced this goalkeeping style in the late 1800s (Fosty & Fosty, 2008). The erasure of seminal contributions is emblematic of colonial rule, and thus Fosty and Fosty's (2008) historical archiving and historiography of Black sporting accomplishments such as the Colored Hockey League of the Maritimes and its organizers, coaches, and players serves as a vital form of scholarly allyship.[31]

Because the accepted hockey rules and norms did not permit certain types of play, Black hockey players in this league utilized this space to liberate themselves literally and figuratively. Black people's agentic use of space and their bodies in neocolonial contexts is a battle for selfhood, humanity, and belonging (Carrington, 2010). Freedom was and remains associated with the ability to use your mind and body in ways of your choosing as opposed to being controlled by others. Dance, verve, and performance as valued distinctive cultural practices are prevalent across African societies (Asante, 1990, 2003; Asante & Mazama, 2005). Relatedly, Black *agentic participatory sporting resistance* is exhibited in multiple ways: a) through skill proficiency, which debunks the myth of innate inferiority and perceptions of laziness; b) through performative displays of creativity, which undermine Eurocentric norms of standardization and rigidity; c) through teamwork, which demystifies the stereotype that Black people are inherently selfish and not trustworthy; and d) through team and league organization, which refutes the notion that Blacks are incapable of excelling in leadership roles.[32]

Another aspect of freedom and agentic resistance for Black people, particularly those who were formerly enslaved, is the ability to name oneself. The team names used in the Colored Hockey League of the Maritimes were connected to Black empowerment experiences and memories. One team, the Mossbacks of Hammond Plains, attributed their name to a secret code on the Underground Railroad that referenced moss growing on trees as a guide for the northward direction to Canada (Fosty & Fosty, 2008); Black baseball teams in the same region would also adopt culturally empowering team names. Another hockey club took the name Eurekas, a term originated from Greek that translates to "I have found God," which reflected the spiritual foundation of the African-based league (Fosty & Fosty, 2008). There were also names that highlighted the political landscape at the time. For example, the Independent

Stars' team name symbolized the freedom Black people were seeking through establishing separate territories; the Jubilees' team name was a reference to the British abolition of slavery; and the Victorias' team name represented victory over European oppression, rather than celebrating Queen Victoria (Fosty & Fosty, 2008). Along the same lines, the Sea-Sides (SS) team name carried a dual meaning: on the one hand, it was a geographical reference to the harbor border where Africville was located, and on the other, the "SS" signified *slave stealer* or *slave salvation*, a reference to allies who assisted Africans in America to escape to freedom (Fosty & Fosty, 2008). The intentional and culturally grounded naming of these teams illuminates what Robinson (1983/2000) described as the *historical consciousness* and social experiences that are a part of the Black radical tradition. As noted earlier, agentic resistance refers to individual or group actions that seek to convey a culturally situated form of personal expression or disposition (Cooper, 2021). Thus, the intentional naming of hockey teams after culturally significant meanings underscores how Black people's embodiment of *collective cultural resistance* traverses all aspects of life, from the most subtle form via a team name to the most apparent presentation through a distinctive style of play.

The Colored Hockey League of the Maritimes also illustrated sports-based hybrid resistance. As a transnational kinship community, it reflected networks for social, political, and economic empowerment (Faist, 2010). Economic and grassroots activism were reflected in the small-scale migrant entrepreneurship within the league and its events such as the Colored Championship and Inter-Provincial Championship (Cooper, 2021; Fosty & Fosty, 2008). Fosty and Fosty (2008) detail the influence of the league and its participants as a part of the pantheon of Black sporting resistance: "Thus, by creating teams of Blacks, skilled in hockey, and led by respected Black religious leaders, the Colored League was not only challenging the traditional Canadian hockey status quo, but was also challenging both religious and scientific extremism as well. The league, by its very existence, gave Blacks hope, setting itself up as a symbolic target for anyone who sought its failure or demise. The Colored Hockey League of the Maritimes changed the way hockey was seen and played in early Canada" (pp. 220–221).

The emphasis on the impact of religious activism with other forms of hybrid resistance is particularly important because religious institutions have served as central organizing and redeeming spaces for Black empowerment intra- and internationally for centuries (Franklin, 1947/1974; James, 2012). The pervasiveness of racial capitalism (Robinson, 1983/2000) prevented the league from experiencing more longevity and having a broader impact. Nonetheless, despite encountering numerous pre- and post-migration barriers, the Africville community members' collective resilience and resolve enabled them to build successful businesses and organizations that uplifted their race. Their efforts had a ripple effect on Black communities throughout Nova Scotia as well as on White communities who witnessed the intellectual and physical prowess of people who were fallaciously deemed inferior. The courage and vision of these organizers, coaches, and players paved the way for future desegregation efforts in sport, including that of the National Hockey League (NHL) in 1958 with the drafting of Willie O'Ree (Cooper, 2021; Murray, 2007).

Localized Diasporic Transnational Formation: Black Rens/Harlem Renaissance Basketball Team

Transnational formations can manifest in multiple ways based on the extent and frequency of mobility and locality (Dahinden, 2010). One type of transnational formation that involves low physical mobility and a high degree of local ties is called a localized diasporic transnational formation (Dahinden, 2010). The New York Renaissance/Harlem Rens, also known as the Black Rens, are an example of a localized diasporic transnational formation. In 1922, William Roche, a transnational migrant from Montserrat, created the Sares Realty Company and subsequently bought land where the Harlem Renaissance Casino was developed (George, 1992). In the same year, Robert "Bob" L. Douglas, a native of Saint Kitts who migrated to Harlem during his youth, partnered with the Renaissance Casino to establish a professional basketball team (George, 1992; Rayl, 1996). The Harlem Renaissance team, affectionately known as "the Rens," debuted at the casino on November 30, 1923, in a game against the Chicago Collegians; the home team emerged victorious by a score of 28–22. Leon Monde, Hy Monte, Zack Anderson, Clarence "Fats" Jenkins, and Frank "Strangler" Forbes were the original Rens players (George, 1992). Prior to starting the basketball team, Douglas organized the Caribbean Athletic Club, which included a cricket team and a basketball team (George, 1992). At the time there were a group Black athletic clubs in Harlem that competed against each other, including the Spartans, Saint Philip's Church, the Alphas Club, and Salem Church. The formation of these local athletic clubs in partnership with Black churches and businesses illustrated the spirit of African diasporic cooperative economics. This grassroots and economic activism centered on Black self-determination, economic empowerment, and communalism despite living in a society grounded in anti-Black racism with limited sporting and employment opportunities.

Harlem was a primary destination site for transnational migrants from the West Indies.[33] In the early 1900s, one out of every five thousand Black people in New York City were transnational migrants (Rayl, 2017). The influx of West Indian migrants during the early 1900s, along with the Great Migration of Black Americans from the southern United States, created a distinct cultural milieu for entrepreneurship, political movements, and social exchanges (Hine et al., 2006). The message spread by Black transnational luminaries such as Marcus Garvey was palatable in places like Harlem because there was a confluence of transnational migrants who possessed business acumen, racial pride, and cultural loyalty to their ethnic groups and native homelands. Furthermore, the ethnic stratification in the transnational formation of Harlem was conducive to the cultivation of grassroots activism via the establishment of Black-owned businesses and galvanization of political power as well as for mass mobilization activism in terms of the international reach of the Harlem Renaissance movement (Cooper, 2021; Cooper et al., 2020). Douglas's relationships with numerous luminaries of the Harlem Renaissance era enhanced the popularity of the franchise and the emergence of the Harlem Rens, as the name suggests, coincided with the bourgeoning resonance of the Harlem Renaissance and New Negro movement in the United States.

The New Negro era comprised Black leaders who grew up during the post-emancipation periods in the United States and Caribbean region (Early, 2008). This new group of Black Americans and transnational migrants was emboldened to confront the vicissitudes of White racism in every facet of society, and sport was no different. In an analysis of the role of the Rens within the broader context of the New Negro movement, Rayl (2017) offered the following summary:

> With the Harlem Renaissance and expression of the "New Negro" in full swing, Douglas mirrored Marcus Garvey as an example of black entrepreneurship, negating the stereotype that blacks lacked intelligence or motivation to achieve. Black basketball served as a symbol for Harlem blacks in the 1920s. By defeating white teams, blacks could dispel the notion of their athletic inferiority and attain equality with their white counterparts—at least on the basketball court. Challenging the supremacy of the Original Celtics not only drew respect from fans, players, and coaches but also demonstrated that blacks could compete successfully against the best team whites could offer. (p. 159)

Douglas's team ownership also reflected sports-based economic activism. Since the inception of organized sport in the United States, Blacks have been systematically denied access to ownership of teams and facilities (Cooper, 2021). Team ownership separate from a league provided Douglas and his advisers with full control of the revenue streams and business decisions of the team, which enabled them to sustain a two-decade period of success (Rayl, 1996). The relationship with the Renaissance Casino was also pivotal to the success of the basketball team in terms of attendance and gate receipts. The Renaissance ballroom was the site for numerous Black social and political events, dinners, dances, celebrations, and sport competitions (Rayl, 2017).[34] The basketball games were played on the ballroom dance floor next to a bandstand area where music complemented the entertaining athletic performances (George, 1992). There would often be dances after the game.³⁵ The intentional cultivation of this atmosphere reflected *collective cultural resistance* whereby multiple facets of African cultural expressions are coordinated concomitantly and sequentially with the same core aim of manifesting epistemological, ontological, and axiological freedom. Hence, collective cultural resistance including efforts involving sport underscore how Black sporting resistance is embedded within the Black radical tradition (Robinson, 1983/2000). In concert with the culturally empowering environment at Rens' games, Douglas also leveraged his ownership to engage in pioneering practices such as providing players with monthly contracts and travel with a custom team bus for barnstorming tours (George, 1992). Thus, Black team ownership in conjunction with the utilization of transnational networks in urban enclaves such as Harlem facilitated the creation of vibrant local economies when not disrupted by White oppositionists.

In addition, Black social networks were essential to the success of the Rens. The franchise had a symbiotic relationship with multiple Black institutions in Harlem. For example, the Renaissance ballroom hosted numerous functions for Saint Martin's Episcopal Church and other Baptist, Methodist, and Catholic churches (Rayl, 2017). Similar to the Colored Hockey League of the Maritimes (Fosty & Fosty, 2008) and the Civil Rights movement (Hine et al., 2006), the strong connection with Black churches was instrumental for marketing, promotion, social connectivity, and revenue generation. Baptist and Methodist churches were popular among Black Americans and Episcopal and Catholic churches were more popular among Caribbean immigrants (Burgos, 2007, 2011; Horne, 2014b; Rayl, 2017). Another institution that was integrally connected to the Rens and their success was the local Black media, specifically the *New York Amsterdam News* (Rayl, 2017). Douglas had a close relationship with the owner of the publication, Dr. P.M.H. Savory, and several of the journalists such as Romeo Dougherty, who was a transnational migrant from the West Indies (Rayl, 2017). The *New York Amsterdam News* was among the central sources of Black political, social, cultural, and economic communication during the New Negro era and featured prominent Black leaders such as W.E.B. Du Bois and Reverend Adam Clayton Powell (Early, 2008). Thus, the media coverage of the Rens in this publication outlet aligned with the broader political efforts during the New Negro and Harlem Renaissance eras, which centered on anti–Jim Crowism, Black pride, self-determination, and Pan-African connections. Media coverage was essential for generating mass interest in the team. The activation of these institutional relationships across and within Black communities exemplified hybrid resistance in a Jim Crow society.

In addition to media coverage, participation in the sport of basketball alone was a form of collective cultural resistance. Basketball was established in Springfield, Massachusetts, by a White Canadian educator named James Naismith in 1891 (Henderson, 1939). A few years after its creation, the game was introduced to African Americans by Edwin Bancroft (E. B.) Henderson, and it was intended to promote the philosophy of muscular assimilationism (Henderson, 1939). The game served multiple purposes for the Black community. One, it served as a means to build healthy minds, bodies, and spirits for productive citizenship, community building, and family structures. Two, it helped prove to mainstream Whites that Black people could perform at comparable, if not better, levels of success in athletic spaces when granted a semblance of equitable access to opportunities. These performances were believed to improve access to resources within and beyond sport by indisputably proving Black people's abilities when insurmountable racist barriers were removed (Cooper, 2021; Henderson, 1939). When the American Basketball League (ABL) was established in 1925, Black players, teams, and coaches were excluded (Henderson, 1939). As a result, Black sportspersons were forced to create their own spaces and organizations for sport opportunities.

Similar to the semiprofessional and professional Negro baseball teams of the 1930s, a primary strategy for economic viability pursued by the Rens was barnstorming (George, 1992; Rayl, 1996, 2017). During these tours, the Rens played games against teams at historically Black colleges and universities (HBCUs) and stayed on their campuses for housing (Rayl, 2017). These kinship networks facilitated successful barnstorming tours, and these traveling circuits were similar to the famous Underground Railroad networks whereby Black people relied on interstate relationships, shared values, and coveted agreements to sustain their livelihoods. Hence, the Rens reflected hybrid resistance via entrepreneurial transnational formations during the New Negro era in the United States.[36]

In addition to being Black owned, the Rens' success on the court also reflected pioneering activism. Over a 16-year span (1923–1939), the team boasted a winning percentage of .871 (2,318 wins and 381 losses), including numerous notable victories against all-White teams (George, 1992; Rayl, 1996). For example, in December 1925 the Rens defeated the Original Celtics of New York, 37–30, at the Manhattan Casino in front of three thousand attendees (Rayl, 2017). The Original Celtics, along with the South Philadelphia Hebrew Association, were the Rens' biggest rivals (George, 1992). Although the owners of each team were colleagues, these interracial contests were largely grounded in economic interest convergence.[37] As noted, within a system of racial capitalism (Robinson, 1983/2000), oppressed groups are forced to engage in compromising decisions for survival. Thus the Rens and their Black transnationalism sporting resistor counterparts were only able to achieve marginal progress insofar as it benefited the dominant racial groups. Even though White teams such as the Celtics often profited more from the gate receipts than the Rens due to the exploitative racist norms of the era, these contests still mitigated the separate and unequal practices that were ultimately outlawed by the mid-twentieth century (Cooper, 2021; George, 1992; Rayl, 2017). Therefore, the Black sporting resistance exhibited by teams such as the Rens played a notable role in advancing racial equality in the United States by testing out the breaking of barriers within the coveted space of sports.

The Rens' most successful season, the 1932–1933 campaign, included eighty-eight wins in a row, which broke the previous record held by the all-White Original Celtics (Rayl, 1996).[38] In 1937, the Rens defeated the Original Celtics, 40–31, in Louisville, Kentucky, in what was recognized as the first interracial professional basketball game in the United States (Rayl, 2017). Prior to that, the Rens had been considered an amateur team (Rayl, 1996). The athletic excellence of the Rens advanced the cause for racial equality because they showed on multiple occasions that talent was not restricted to one race, and if opportunities continued to be denied to Black people then it was not because of their genetic composition, as promulgated by the White superiority myth (Sailes, 2010). The team's distinct style of play included consistent ball movement versus excessive dribbling, less emphasis on individual success, intense defensive sets, and quick cuts, passes, and drives to the basket (George, 1992). The Rens were also the first all-Black team to win the renowned World Championship Tournament for Basketball Champions in 1939 and join the National Basketball League (NBL) in 1948 (George, 1992; Rayl, 1996). The admittance into the NBL came after years of requesting membership and being denied access due to racial discrimination. These notable accomplishments underscore how pioneering activism does not only constitute the single act of breaking a barrier, but rather an accumulation of efforts that contribute to those moments. The preceding success, persistence, and resolve of the Rens from prior to 1939 through 1948 created conditions for future Black pioneering achievements in sport throughout the twentieth and twenty-first centuries.

In the late 1920s, the Rens pursued legal activism to challenge the racial discrimination associated with the Original Celtics' roster policy. The Rens won the lawsuit and subsequently Eyre Satch, Clarence "Fats" Jenkins, Charles "Tarzan" Cooper, and Bill Yancey signed contracts to play for the Original Celtics (Cooper, 2021; Cooper et al., 2020; Rayl, 2017). The success of this legal activism served as a major precedent for Black people in the United States. For one, it signified that the fight for racial integration would have to be won in the legal system in concert with broader efforts in society. Two, it provided a blueprint for future sport integration pursuits such as the fight to end the reserve clause in MLB in the 1970s,[39] removal of the age restriction in the National Basketball Association (NBA),[40] and increased players' rights and freedom in salary and contract negotiations in the NBA post-1970 (Cooper, 2021).[41]

Later in 1948, the Rens were admitted into the NBL when they replaced the Detroit Vagabond Kings and the team's name was temporarily changed to the Detroit Rens (Rayl, 2017). In 1963 the Rens became the first all-Black basketball team to be inducted in the Basketball Hall of Fame; in 1972 Bob Douglas became the first Black person to be inducted. The legacy of the Rens' hybrid resistance lies in their blueprint for Black ownership, breaking the color line, and paving the way for Black players' rights in professional sport organizations. The transnational formation of the Rens in Harlem, New York, during the height of the New Negro era and Harlem Renaissance movement facilitated the success and long-term impact of this Black sporting resistance organization.[42]

The Transnationalization of (Ro-day-o) Rodeo: Shadow Riders of the Subterranean Circuit

The transnational nature of rodeo, also referred to as *charrería* or ro-day-o,[43] has origins in Mexico with festival pastimes. Later in the nineteenth century this activity became popular in the United States (Pearson, 2021). Spanish conquistadors who colonized Mexico brought cattle and horses with them during the sixteenth century. Indigenous Mexicans participated in Spanish bullfighting, which was the precursor to modern rodeo (Pearson, 2021).[44] Historians have noted that Black people were present in modern-day Texas, previously Mexican territory, dating back to the fifteenth century and before Anglos arrived on the land (Barr, 1996; Horne, 2005; Katz, 2005; Pearson, 2021). Robinson (1983/2000) also documented how African American and Indigenous Mexican relations dated back to the sixteenth century when those who escaped slavery in America would seek refuge with native settlements; these groups would be described as *cimarrones* by the Spanish and *Maroons* by the English. Due to the cultural fusion in the Texas Gulf Coast region during the fifteenth and sixteenth centuries, Pearson (2021) described this area as a place where "Afro-Spanish-Indian culture" was created (p. xii). The presence of these *inter-diasporic alliances* served as a vital foundation for the subsequent Black sporting resistance embodied in ro-day-o in the nineteenth, twentieth, and twenty-first centuries. It is worth noting that under the leadership of a president of African descent, Vincente Guerrero, Mexico abolished slavery in 1829, more than thirty years before the United States did, and thus Mexican abolitionists and African Americans strengthened their long-standing relationship during this era (Horne, 2005).

Following the Civil War, thousands of African Americans migrated from the southern regions of the United States to the Midwest, Northeast, and West regions to pursue a better quality of life compared to their previous enslavement (Ford, 2020). Several African American migrants found work as "migrant farmers, domestics, livestock caretakers, and cowboys" (Pearson, 2004, p. 192). When the cattle industry expanded in the late nineteenth century, scholars estimate African Americans constituted nearly one-fourth of all working cowboys, including an estimated 9,000 cattle industry workers (Barr, 1996; Cartwright, 2021; Pearson, 2004, 2021). African American cattle drivers of this era would travel throughout the American West as well as to Mexico and Canada (Pearson, 2004). As rodeos expanded in popularity throughout the late nineteenth and early twentieth centuries, these activities were enjoyed by African Americans, Mexicans, Native Americans, and White Americans (Blanchard, 1995; Pearson, 2021).

Similar to their Negro Leagues counterparts, at times Black cowboys would seek to pass as Native American or Mexican or use non-racial aliases such as "The Dusky Demon" or "Gaucho the Corral Dog" in order to receive favorable treatment in terms of admittance to rodeo competitions, which underscores the depth of early twentieth-century anti-Black racism toward Africans who were descendants of those who had been enslaved in the United States (Ford, 2020, p. 119). For example, due to racial discrimination, it was not uncommon for Bill Pickett, a legendary African American cowboy, to dress up as a Mexican toreador to gain access to certain venues because Black cowboys were banned (Pearson, 2004). Given the racist tenor of the day, Black people were not always referred to as cowboys in an endearing manner or even by their names; instead, they were often described by their race, which was meant to dehumanize them (Ford, 2020; Pearson, 2021). Cartwright (2021) explained the unique application of the term *cowboy* when attributed to African Americans during the nineteenth and twentieth centuries:

> The concept of a cowboy as the victor in a battle between humans and beasts carries a special connotation for African Americans that unmoors much of our understanding of who cowboys were and why they are important in the story of American identity. The rodeo itself, as a competitive exhibition of athletic skill, was and is a venue in which Black cowboys could vie for legitimacy not only as exemplars of the American spirit but also as leaders within their industries.... The political connotations of Black athletic excellence and the ways in which Black athletes have historically used their popularity and influence to fight racism are part and parcel of the story of Black cowboys. (p. ii)

This understanding of the role and impact of Black cowboys and cowgirls during the nineteenth and twentieth centuries extends Edwards's (2016a) conception of the first wave of Black athlete activism, which focused on gaining legitimacy. The first wave of Black athlete activism started in 1900 (Edwards, 2016a), but the inclusion of Black cowboys and cowgirls' efforts indicate this wave of sport activism predates 1900. Furthermore, Cartwright's (2021) analysis reiterates the symbolic power of agency as a form of Black sporting resistance whereby athletic participation and performances constitute an overlooked yet significant method of sport activism under certain conditions.

In response to being largely excluded from the mainstream Professional Rodeo Cowboys Association (PRCA) and United States Team Roping Championships via unwritten agreements, the creation of rodeo events and organizations such as the Boley Rodeo (established in 1905), Southwestern Colored Cowboys Association (SCCA; established in the late 1940s), Okmulgee Colored Round-Up Club (first all-Black rodeo; created in 1956 and built an arena for an annual rodeo in 1958), Prairie View Trail Riders Association (established in 1957), Southwestern Colored Rodeo Association (SCRA; established in 1960), Latting Rodeo Company (LRC; established in 1964), Black Rodeo Association (BRA; established in 1969), American Black Cowboy Association (ABCA; established in 1969), Cowboys of Color Rodeo Series (previously known as the Texas Black Rodeo; established in 1974), Black World Championship Rodeo (incorporated in 1985; first event held in 1986), Bill Pickett Invitational (established in 1984), Real Cowboys Association (RCA; founded in 1990), C91 Ranch and Livestock Rodeo Productions (established in 1999), and the National Multicultural Western Heritage Museum and Hall of Fame (NMWHMHF; previously known as the National Cowboys of Color Museum and Hall of Fame and established in 2001) signified the intergenerational presence of Black grassroots, mass mobilization, economic, and scholarly activism (Cartwright, 2021; Ford, 2020; Pearson, 2004, 2021). Similar to the aforementioned social formations, transnationalization (Faist, 2010) in Black sporting resistance is often reflected in the mobilization of resources and activation of cooperative economics across borders and ethnic and cultural groups. These Black rodeo events and organizations were covered by the Black press, and in several instances funds generated from these events would be transferred to philanthropic causes. For example, in 1950 the Texas Championship Colored Rodeo donated the revenue from this event to a local orphanage (Ford, 2020). Albeit not disruptive as activism, this form of advocacy is notable and contributes to positive social change within marginalized communities, and thus serves as a meaningful form of resistance through sport.

Alongside the formation of associations and events, pioneering activism has been reflected in the sporting achievements of Black cowboys and cowgirls:

- *Jesse Stahl*—a pioneer rider of "Glass Eye" in 1912, inventor of the rodeo technique called "hoolihanding,"[45] and considered one of the best bronc riders of all time (Pearson, 2021, p. 36);
- *Sherman Richardson*—Southwestern National Cowboys Association all-around title winner in 1946;
- *Willie Thomas*—participated at the Diamond L Ranch for the first time in 1948;
- *Cleo Hearn*—joined the PRCA in 1959; first African American to win the calf (tie down) roping at a major rodeo in 1970 at the

Denver National Western Stock Show and Rodeo; in 1971 he founded the Texas Black Rodeo (later renamed the Cowboys of Color Rodeo in 1995); in 2022 he was inducted into the National Cowboy Museum and Hall of Fame;

- *Tex Williams*—won the saddle bronc riding event at the age of 14 at the Southwestern National Cowboys Association (SNCA) in 1963 and became the first African American to win a Texas state high school rodeo title as a junior in 1967;
- *Myrtis Dightman*—first Black cowboy to participate at the National Finals Rodeo in 1964,[46] first Black cowboy to qualify for the National Finals Rodeo in 1966, and first African American inducted in the Professional Bull Riders (PBR) Ring of Honor;
- *"Cowtown Gene" Walker*—first Black cowboy to qualify for the College National Finals Rodeo in 1967;
- *Ervin Williams*—first Black cowboy to win Oklahoma state rodeo title in 1983;
- *Clarence LeBlanc* and *Kenneth LeBlanc*—first brothers to qualify for the International Finals Rodeo (IFR) in the same event in 1985;
- *Dwayne Hargo Sr.*—first Black cowboy to win the Wrangler Freestyle Bullfighting Tour at National Finals Rodeo (NFR) in 1989;
- *Fred Whitfield*—won first of eight PRCA world titles in 1991 and was inducted into the National Cowboy Hall of Fame in 2000 and Pro Rodeo Hall of Fame in 2004;
- *Clara Brown*—first African American inducted into the National Cowgirl Hall of Fame in 1997;
- *Willie Thomas*—2008 NMWHMHF inductee; and
- *Ezekiel Mitchell*—first African American to win the PBR Touring Pro Division in 2017 (see Cartwright, 2021, and Pearson, 2021, for an extensive listing and discussion of African American rodeo pioneers).

These feats are particularly noteworthy because in the late nineteenth and early twentieth centuries Black cowboys and cowgirls were largely prohibited from mainstream rodeo events, and when they were included, it was often as exhibition performers rather than as competitors (Ford, 2020). In addition, Pearson (2021) noted how African American pioneers who were early cardholders of the RCA, such as Willie Thomas, were also transnational migrants who would travel outside the United States to participate in events such as the Calgary Stampede in Canada. Highly acclaimed Black rodeo cowboys such as Bill Pickett exemplified localized mobile transnational formations in that they were both highly mobile and highly localized (Dahinden, 2010). In terms of mobility, Pickett performed throughout the United States, Canada, Mexico, South America, and Europe over the course of his career (Cartwright, 2021). Amid these global travels, he also retained his strong familial and social networks in Oklahoma and Texas in the United States (Cartwright, 2021). Hence, competing and winning in rodeo competitions, nationally and internationally, became an aspirational goal of Black cowboys and cowgirls seeking to gain legitimacy in an anti-Black racist society and the sporting space of rodeo.

Along with pioneering accomplishments, Black cowboys and cowgirls were also rodeo innovators. For example, Bill Pickett popularized "bulldogging" or steer wrestling,[47] which involves jumping off a horse to wrestle a steer to the ground; this move became celebrated throughout the United States and Mexico (Ford, 2020). Pickett's popularity increased to the level that some of his events would attract 20,000 attendees (Ford, 2020). During the twentieth century, it was common practice for Black cowboys to only be allowed to compete before or after mainstream rodeo events when crowds were not present, which was referred to as *slack competition* (Pearson, 2021). Despite the racially discriminatory nature of this practice, Black cowboys would make the most of these opportunities and win events such as bull riding, which would open the doors for future racially integrated rodeos (Pearson, 2021). Once again, racial capitalism (Robinson, 1983/2000) creates conditions that perpetually disadvantage Black people and force them to adapt in ways that differ from how they would exist under more favorable conditions. In other words, rather than being relegated to pre- or post-event exhibitions or being forced to travel across borders for participation and economic opportunities, Black people in a world free from anti-Black racism would be able to create their own vibrant sporting spaces and thrive without any marginalization within or across borders.

In 1999, Angel Floyd exhibited economic and mass mobilization activism with the creation of C91 Ranch and Livestock Rodeo Productions (Cartwright, 2021). Black women's entrepreneurship among the Black rodeo circuit signified racial and gender progress. During the early 2010s, Black cowgirls began receiving increased recognition such as being inducted into the National Cowgirl Hall of Fame. For example, Patricia E. Kelly was inducted in 2015 and Mayisha Akbar in 2019 (Cartwright, 2021). These pioneering accomplishments coincided with the broader Black Lives Matter (BLM) movement and reflected a precursor to what Edwards (2020) described as the fifth wave of Black athlete activism, one centered on Black women. The accomplishments of Black cowboys and cowgirls and their hybrid resistance was integrally connected to the Black freedom struggles of the nineteenth and twentieth centuries. These sportspersons demanded legitimacy and respect from the cattle herding and rodeo industries and excelled during eras where intense anti-Black racism was pervasive.[48]

Beyond performances within the rodeo venue, the spectator atmosphere at Black rodeo events was unique and reflected *collective cultural resistance*. The

Mexican concept and atmosphere of *charrería* (rodeo) is akin to West Indian/Caribbean concept of *liming* with cricket (James, 1963; Joseph, 2012a, 2014, 2017) and the HBCU sporting diaspora (Cavil, 2015) whereby sporting activities were enmeshed within broader cultural rituals, traditions, and celebrations. This *collective cultural resistance* at the grassroots level has been a primary source of empowerment for African people since antiquity (Cooper, 2021; Gilroy, 1993). The existence of these types of activities contrasted mainstream European etiquette and embodied sporting resistance epistemologically, ontologically, and axiologically. *Charrería* events include "ranch-related competitions featuring horsemanship, roping skills, acrobatic stunts, and pageantry" (Pearson, 2021, p. 4). Instead of European colonizers, working-class multiracial independent contractors, also known as *vaqueros*, were the creators of modern-day rodeo. Their numbers included *mestizos*, who were people of Native American and Spanish descent; American Indians; African Americans; mulattos, also known as interracial or mixed-race people; and *criollos*, who were Spanish people born in North America (Pearson, 2021). Throughout the American West, African Americans, Mexicans, Chinese, and Native Americans worked in the cattle business (Ford, 2020). Hence, rodeo was a by-product of transnationalization (Faist, 2000). Similar to Gilroy's (1993) conception of the Black Atlantic being a result of cultural hybridity and creolization, rodeo was birthed from cultural exchanges and flows via *inter-diasporic alliances* rather than its emergence being from a single ethnic group.

Moreover, Black rodeo events would often have culturally endearing titles such as the Juneteenth Rodeo Series, which celebrated the symbolic abolition of chattel slavery in the United States in 1865 (Ford, 2020). Most Black rodeos hosted throughout the United States occur on Juneteenth or what is referred to as "'Cowboy Christmas' in black rodeo circles" to celebrate the proverbial end of slavery against African Americans (Pearson, 2004, p. 197).[49] In contrast to White rodeos where country music is played, Black rodeos play rhythm and blues (R&B), hip-hop, and zydeco music,[50] which reflects *collective cultural resistance* to anti-Blackness. Similar to HBCU homecomings, the food, music, specialty events, and pre- and post-event festivities (e.g., the rodeo dance) of Black rodeos embody both the intercultural fusion of the African diaspora as well as the uniqueness of African American culture in the Texas Gulf Coast region (Cavil, 2015; Cooper, 2021; Pearson, 2004, 2021). Thus, the meaning and structure of these activities as well as *who* could participate in them and *how* they could participate in them were rooted in African and Indigenous cultural foundations rather than Eurocentrism. This embodiment is the essence of Black sporting resistance across time, space, and context as well as a reflection of creolization, cultural hybridization, and transnationalization in and through sport.

The racist social order of the nineteenth and early twentieth centuries prevented Black cowboys and cowgirls from participating in mainstream rodeo circuits until 1950 (Pearson, 2021). Similar to other sports such as boxing and baseball, the harsh labor conditions facing African Americans, albeit unjust and immoral, enabled them to develop skills that would be transferable to success in activities such as rodeo. For example, Pearson (2021) highlighted how African Americans' involvement in livestock management cultivated their knowledge and abilities for managing horses. In true sport activist nature, Black cowboys in Texas exhibited mass mobilization (organizational) and economic activism through their establishment of the "Soul Circuit," or what Pearson (2004) termed the "Shadow Riders of the Subterranean Circuit" (Pearson, 2004, p. 190).[51] Pearson (2021) captures the cultural significance of Black rodeos during the early to mid-twentieth century in the Texas Gulf Coast region: "black rodeos like their Negro Leagues counterparts were salient contributors to the black 'eco-system' in their respective communities. For example, at times they were a source of entertainment and pride; a vehicle for seasonal employment; a galvanizing entity for political activism; an economic revenue generator for sport entrepreneurs and small business owners; as well as educational forums" (pp. 39–40).

Collectively, these impacts reflect hybrid resistance via the activation of agency, pioneering, advocacy, grassroots activism, mass mobilization activism, political/civic activism, and economic activism. Key characteristics of the Subterranean Circuit include predominantly African American riders; minimal mainstream media coverage and historical accounts of the events; sites for the events in small, remote, rural locations in the outer regions of Houston, Dallas, and San Antonio, Texas;[52] attendees who were committed supporters; and the presence of African American cultural foods such as fried fish and boudin (Pearson, 2004). In addition, Pearson (2004) highlighted how African American rodeo cowboys often worked full-time jobs and were restricted to rodeo participation on the weekends and at venues that were relatively close to their homes. In other words, the impact of racism on their economic plight limited their mobility as well as the time that they could spend on the sport. Thus, the Shadow Riders of the Subterranean Circuit reflected what Dahinden (2010) defined as localized diasporic transnational formations whereby they exhibited low physical mobility with a high degree of local ties. The lack of high revenue generation, ownership of arenas, and marketing resources resulted in the circuit organizers relying on word of mouth and tight-knit networks to sustain support for these grassroots events (Pearson, 2004).

This Subterranean Circuit provided the foundation for the modern U2 Rodeo Cowboys of Color rodeo series, which was established in 1984 and revised in 2001 (Pearson, 2021). Many of the largest and most popular Black rodeos were established during the latter half of the twentieth century (Ford, 2020). According to Pearson (2021), the Cowboys of Color rodeo series is the largest and most ethnically diverse rodeo in the world. Led by Cleo

Hearn, the U2 Rodeo was established to promote awareness of and access for African American cowboys' and cowgirls' involvement in rodeo. This innovative rodeo company successfully secured multiple sponsorships, which enabled the organization to redirect funds that typically went to White stakeholders and communities to African American benefactors (Pearson, 2004). The U2 Rodeo's hybrid resistance resulted in the creation of one of the most popular rodeo series in the world and heightened the visibility and presentation of Black cowboys within the PRCA (Pearson, 2021). The success of the company involved collaborative efforts with various stakeholders who support racial equality (e.g., select stock contractors, sponsors, veterinarians, and vendors) (Pearson, 2021). The fact that the Cowboys of Color series was among the "only minority oriented rodeos that used contemporary technological advances to advertise" (Pearson, 2004, p. 194) illuminates how this organization embodied Edwards's (2016a) fourth wave of Black athlete activism centered on using technological and economic resources to secure power in sport.

Additionally, the research of scholars such as Demetrius Pearson (2004, 2021) and Mia Mask (2023) reflects scholarly activism to combat the whitewashing of rodeo history that distorts White European involvement in the sport and marginalizes African Americans', Mexicans', and Native Americans'/Indigenous peoples' contributions to the sport. In analysis of the anti-Black racist scholarship on rodeo, Pearson (2021) offered a cogent critique:

> However, as more Anglos acquired land and gravitated toward the cattle industry the tone, tenor, and image changed, as well as certain cultural perceptions. This was due in part to the mythical legend, lore, and fictional accounts of the Anglo cowboy herder propagated by the many dime novels and baseless artistic renderings of the western frontier. Often depicted in Western movies as evil, corrupt bandits are in stark contrast to the created image that underscores the enduring Anglo cowboy of the Old West. In essence, the name and embodiment of the original cattle herder or vaquero/charro was "hijacked" and "whitewashed" since the mid-nineteenth century. (p. 4)

Among the primary tools of racist ideological hegemony is the creation and promulgation of mythical histories that position White Europeans as saviors and Black Africans and Indigenous people as deviants and savages (Carruthers, 1999). These fallacious stories have also been changed in other areas of North America such as in Canada. For example, John Ware, an African who was formerly enslaved in the southern United States and later migrated to Alberta, Canada, became one of the most celebrated cowboys among Canadian cowboy circuits, although his greatness has still been marginalized in scholarly literature (MacEwan, 1960). Akin to his Black transnational sporting resistor peers, Ware developed his knowledge of cattle under racially oppressive conditions in the southern United States in the late 1800s (MacEwan, 1960). During his time in Canada, Ware became known as a bronc buster champion and a legend of steer wrestling, an event that would become a central feature of the Calgary Stampede (Burgess, 1993; MacEwan, 1960). Hence, the debunking of fallacious racist narratives or the whitewashing of cowboy and cowgirl history and the concurrent presentation of factual counternarratives of Black diasporic cowboys and cowgirls serves as a powerful example of scholarly activism and allyship.

Summary

In this chapter, I outlined how select Black sportspersons, teams, and leagues constitute transnational formations. Using strategies that were effective during the precolonial and colonial eras, these Black sportspersons relied on reciprocity, kinship networks, cross-border mobility, and small-scale entrepreneurship (Dahinden, 2010; Faist, 2010) to create culturally empowering and economically viable sport teams and leagues. The creation of these spaces through mobilization efforts reflected the following prophetic phrase expressed by Robinson (1983/2000) when referring to the courageous resistance actions of African freedom fighters: "They lived on their own terms" (p. 170). Key terms presented in this chapter were *stealth migrant sporting resistance, agentic participatory sporting resistance, agentic refraining sporting resistance,* and *radical imagination of Black sporting resistance.* As transnational communities, West Indian cricket players and teams symbolized West Indian self-determination and anti-colonialism across the Atlantic and Pacific (James, 1963; Joseph, 2011, 2012, 2014, 2017; Marqusee, 1994/2016). The collection of players from Caribbean nation-states such as Trinidad, Jamaica, Barbados, Antigua, and British Guiana (now known as Guyana) represented the transnational formation of the West Indian teams during the mid-twentieth century. Negro American and Afro-Latino baseball players, teams, and leagues of the early to mid-twentieth century embodied transnational circuits (Burgos, 2007, 2011; Lomax, 2003, 2014). Cross-border relationships and events fueled the international success of numerous players, managers, owners, scouts, media personnel, and business leaders. In partnership with African Americans, sportspersons from Cuba, Puerto Rico, the Dominican Republic, Panama, Mexico, Saint Kitts, and Saint Thomas formed successful transnational circuits that circumvented anti-Black racism in North and Latin America and the Caribbean region.

The Colored Hockey League of the Maritimes reflected a transnational kinship group (Cooper, 2021; Fosty & Fosty, 2008). The collective efforts of African Americans who had escaped slavery in the United States and the Maroons of Jamaica who had fought against British colonial rule led to the formation of a pioneering hockey league in Africville, Nova Scotia. The connection to the Black churches in the area was an integral part of the teams' formation and successful existence. The Harlem Rens basketball team of the 1920s–1950s was an example of a localized diasporic transnational formation (Cooper, 2021; Henderson, 1939; Rayl, 1996, 2017). Established in the Pan-African epicenter of Harlem during the 1920s, the team personified the ethos of the New Negro era and Harlem Renaissance movement (Cooper, 2021; Cooper et al., 2020). Led by their transnational migrant team owner, Bob Douglas, the team would go on to have a historic run as the first all-Black team to beat all-White teams and achieve a legendary win streak in the early 1930s, which resulted in their Hall of Fame induction in 1963 (Rayl, 2017). The transnationalization that produced the sport of rodeo was exemplified by Black cowboys and cowgirls of the southwestern United States and Mexico and illustrated Black sporting resistance between the late nineteenth and twenty-first centuries (Mask, 2023; Pearson, 2004, 2021). Each of these transnational formations utilized hybrid resistance to challenge the status quo and create new opportunities for Black people locally and internationally.

4

Revolutionary Consciousness

• • • • • • • • • • • • • • • • • • • •

Black Internationalism
Sporting Resistance

> While the breach could never be fully compensated for, at the very least, the efforts to set things right would entail a revolution of the social order—the abolition of slavery, racism, domination, and exploitation, the realization of justice and equality, and the fulfillment of needs. (Hartman, 1997, p. 76)

Black internationalism as a movement and paradigm emerged during the mid-twentieth century during the Cold War (Burden-Stelly & Horne, 2020). While intense military conflict was mounting and nationalistic loyalties were being expressed, there was also a growing contingent of international groups who were championing anti-war positions. Revolutionary consciousness emerged among prominent Black American intellectuals, such as William Edward Burghardt (W.E.B.) Du Bois during the early to mid-twentieth century, who were influenced by various ideologies including Black radicalism and Marxism (Robinson, 1983/2000). In an analysis of this era and the emergent hybrid ideology, Robinson (1983/2000) observed that "Revolutionary consciousness had formed in the process of anti-imperialist and nationalist struggles.... The idiom of revolutionary consciousness had been historical and cultural rather than the 'mirror of production'. The ideology of the Black struggle ... had achieved the force of a historical antilogic to racism, slavery, and capitalism" (p. 240).

Along the same lines, prominent activists such as Paul Robeson voiced scathing critiques of imperialist countries who were violating human rights both domestically and internationally. During this same period, international sporting events took on increased political significance.[1] For example, the 1936 Olympics in Berlin, Germany, was marred by the proliferating fascist movement led by Adolf Hitler. The 1940 and 1944 Olympic Games were canceled due to World War II (Arnaud & Riordan, 1998; Boykoff, 2016).[2] The 1968 Olympics in Mexico City, Mexico, was the site for the most renowned display of athlete activism in sports history, that of Tommie Smith and John Carlos's famous Black Power salutes (Edwards, 1969/2017).[3] In 1976, multiple African countries boycotted the Olympics in Montréal, Canada, to express their discontent with New Zealand being permitted to participate after maintaining relations with South African sport organizations during the apartheid era (Bass, 2002; Donnelly, 2008). Several countries, including the United States, boycotted the 1980 Olympics in Moscow, Russia during the Cold War. Aside from Olympic events, several Pan-Games and world championships were either boycotted or became sites for athlete protests of political and military decisions of certain nation-states (Boykoff, 2016; Cooper, 2021). In an analysis of the politicized nature of sporting events, Arnaud and Riordan (1998) outlined common juxtapositions observed in mainstream media during the mid-twentieth century: "Sporting competition was thus, circumscribed by political considerations that often transformed purely sporting contests into other rivalries: communism v. capitalism, fascism v. liberal democracy, communism v. social democracy" (p. 2).

In contrast to the traditional sport ethic of keeping politics separate from these endeavors, numerous Black sportspersons have refused to ignore social injustices for the sake of preserving social norms and the comfort of elite economic groups. Instead, Black internationalist sportspersons have viewed themselves as global citizens who have a moral obligation to utilize their platforms and resources to advance broader social movements and improve human rights. For example, Thomas (2012) surmised that the historic 1968 protests of Tommie Smith and John Carlos were perceived by the athlete activists as "the equivalent of taking the United States before the United Nations on charges of violation of international law" (p. 134). Albeit hyperbolic, Thomas's point here was to emphasize how Smith and Carlos sought to use their platform through sport to garner international attention and accountability toward the United States for its intergenerational inhumane treatment of Black people without penalty.[4] Black internationalist sportspersons are inherently activists because they possess and express the intention of upending hegemonic status quos by addressing concrete injustices. These individuals and groups join or align their efforts with non-sport activist groups. They understand the leverage power of sport and often sacrifice athletic glory and economic opportunities for the greater good of humanity (Edwards, 2016b); thus, they embody a teleological ethical orientation.

One distinction between *Black internationalist sporting resistance* and diasporic and transnational sporting resistance is the inherent enactment of political activism. My colleagues and I defined political activism as "the direct challenging of oppressive ideologies, structures, and systems connected to controlling governments and related entities" (Cooper et al., 2020, p. 101). Oppositionists for Black internationalists are fascist, imperialist, racist, and capitalist governments and related entities. Although diasporic and transnational resistance can involve political activism, it is not inherent to these types of resistance.[5] In addition, military and legal activism are also more common in Black internationalist resistance when compared to diasporic and transnational resistance. Illuminating the nature, strategies, tactics, and impact of different types of international resistance is a core purpose of this book. One consummate Black internationalist who was a former athlete is Paul Robeson. The legacy of Robeson inspired scores of anti-colonial activists within and beyond sport throughout the twentieth century. A standout football player at Rutgers University who had a short professional football career, Robeson chose to follow his convictions to ignite social change off the field. After retiring from sport, Robeson went on to earn a law degree and later became a world-renowned actor and singer who used his talents, relationships, and platforms to openly challenge imperialist and capitalist nation-states, particularly his own country, the United States of America (Robeson, 1958/1998). In his examination of the Pan-African and internationalist ethos emerging among African Americans like Robeson in the mid-twentieth century, Williams (2012) said, "Whether real, or imagined, in most cases, a little of both, the threats and the promises of a global Black Power movement had influence and power beyond the boundaries of the United States. Its principles were internalized, reimagined, imported, and exported by African Americans, who were respected members of a worldwide freedom struggle" (p. 165).

Robeson was a by-product of Cold War politics and the growing internationalization of the freedom struggle for all oppressed people. The Communist Party of the United States of America (CPUSA) increased in popularity during the 1930s (Horne, 1985; Munro, 2008). Robeson was associated with the CPUSA as well as the Communist Party of Britain; these organizations were among the strongest opponents of fascist regimes across the world, but particularly in Europe and the United States (Horne, 1985, 2016; Munro, 2008).

Robeson's connections to these organizations were dangerous given the Red Scare in the United States throughout the Cold War (Horne, 1985, 2016). In 1942, Robeson would become a cofounder of the Council of African Affairs (CAA). The CAA launched efforts in South Africa, Nigeria, and Kenya (Anderson, 2012). In 1949, Robeson delivered a speech at the Paris World Peace Congress in front of more than eighteen hundred delegates from sixty nations (Robeson, 1958/1998; Thomas, 2012). In his speech, he condemned U.S. capitalism, nationalism, imperialism, and militarism while praising the Soviet Union for its humanitarian efforts for African countries and support for African Americans (Thomas, 2012).

On December 7, 1951, Robeson coauthored a petition to the United Nations titled *We Charge Genocide*, seeking to indict the United States on its anti-Black oppression dating back to the founding of the country (Anderson, 2012; Robeson, 1958/1998). The writing and submission of this UN petition was an example of legal activism, which involves "the use of the judicial and legal systems to challenge unjust laws, policies, and/or practices (i.e., enforcements) in the pursuit of justice and equitable treatment" (Cooper et al., 2020, p. 102). Typically undertaken prior to military and political activism, legal activism has been a central tool for upending oppressive regimes because it changes the contexts of what is considered legal, ethical, and moral in each distinct geopolitical milieu. For example, the abolition of slavery, desegregation efforts, immigration opportunities, and access to material resources have all been pursued and secured to an extent by legal activism at the national level via a supreme court and at the international level via the UN or International Criminal Court (ICC). Even after his athletic career concluded, Robeson remained connected with Black athletes such as Joe Louis and inspired others such as Muhammad Ali and Arthur Ashe. This chapter on *Black internationalist sporting resistance* is dedicated to Paul Robeson for his courage, conviction, and sacrifices made both during and after his athletic career. Within this chapter, I highlight examples where Black internationalist sportspersons championed anti–white supremacy/continental unity, anti-colonialism/self-determination, anti-imperialism/revolutionary transformation, anti-sexism/radical humanism, anti-capitalism/socialism, and anti-war/durable peace (Burden-Stelly & Horne, 2020; Horne, 2014a).

As a self-identified Black person and African American and a scholar on African American athletes, in this chapter I highlight how this diasporic subgroup engaged in international coalition building. I recognize the limitations of this approach, but rather than view it as a shortcoming I interpret it as a unique strength of this research. Moreover, I understand the value of identifying connections between a specific diasporic group, such as African Americans, with their international comrades and allies such as continental Africans, Afro-Caribbeans, Afro-Latinos, Aboriginals, anti-colonialists, anti-imperialists, and anti-fascists. It is also worth noting that in this chapter I incorporate examples of Black internationalist sporting resistors from places such as South Africa, Nigeria, England, Canada, and the First Nations of Australia. Furthermore, I believe the current text not only adds to extant literature on the topic, but also provides pathways for future inquiries to explore similar topics from different positionalities and analytical data points across the globe. In summary, the framing of this chapter aligns with the legacy scholarship of African American exemplar historian and internationalist Gerald Horne, who has grounded his international analyses in the perspectives, experiences, and efforts of African Americans across time, space, and context in connection with their diasporic counterparts and allies abroad (Horne, 1985, 1994/2020, 2013b, 2014a, 2015, 2016, 2018a, 2020b).

The Anti-Apartheid Movement and Mass Mobilization Sport Activism for Human Rights

South Africa began instituting the apartheid regime in 1948. By 1985, an all-sport boycott of South Africa had been enacted (Bass, 2002; Donnelly, 2008; Edwards, 1969/2017). Scholars have noted how although sport was not the primary reason why the apartheid regime ended in South Africa, it did play a meaningful role (Bass, 2002; Blackman, 2012; Donnelly, 2008; Edwards, 1969/2017). Because South Africa and the United States were Cold War allies, the U.S. government and United States Olympic Committee (USOC) were reluctant to support sanctions against the apartheid state (Blackman, 2012; Edwards, 1969/2017). The United States had hoped Black athletes would be grateful for the opportunity to represent "their" country and acquiesce to the adage of keeping sport and politics separate. Yet the emergence and vitality of the Black Power, Civil Rights, and anti-war movements of the 1960s greatly influenced the consciousness, activism, and ontological security for resistance efforts among Black athletes in the United States (Blackman, 2012; Cooper, 2021; Edwards, 1969/2017). When analyzing the Pan-African influence on Black Power and Civil Rights efforts in the United States, Blackman (2012) notes that "The prevalence of African liberation movements, many of which were engaged in armed struggle for the control of land and economies, further legitimized such Black Power arguments. As a result, Pan-Africanism, the belief that the liberation of one people of color further delegitimized the subjugation of other peoples of color, expanded among African Americans. The resulting activity included African American participation in a sports boycott, which was initiated by the international campaign to bar SAOC [South African Olympic Committee] from the 1968 Olympics" (p. 3).

The politically conscious, courageous, and confident collection of African American athletes during this era began to identify parallels between their struggles at home and those abroad (Ashe & Ramperstad, 1993; Bass, 2002;

Blackman, 2012; Edwards, 1969/2017). This heightened awareness was generated by multiple factors: a) converging issues impacting African Americans and continental Africans, b) the expansion of Black nationalist and internationalist movements, and c) the increased tensions and hypocrisies associated with the Cold War. Alliances with anti-apartheid African countries were strategically pursued because African American internationalists understood the inextricable connections between dismantling racism across geopolitical contexts (Blackman, 2012; Robeson, 1958/1998).

International coalition building among Africans and their allies was reaching an apex in the 1950s. For example, in 1955, the Bandung Conference was held in Indonesia with twenty-nine decolonized states in attendance, which reflected the emergence an Afro-Asian bloc (Burden-Stelly & Horne, 2020; Thomas, 2012). This international event focused on the shared liberation struggles in Africa, Asia, and North America (Thomas, 2012). In 1958, Kwame Nkrumah, president of newly independent Ghana, hosted the All African People's Conference in Accra, Ghana (Williams, 2012). In the same year, under the leadership of Dennis Brutus, a member of the African National Congress (ANC) and South African Communist Party (SACP), the South African Sports Association (SASA) was formed to combat apartheid rules that barred Black South African participation on national sport teams (Blackman, 2012). During SASA's first year of existence, they practiced media activism by sending multiple communications to international sport organizations, including the International Olympic Committee (IOC), about the unjust treatment of Black South Africans under apartheid (Blackman, 2012). The efforts of the SASA led to the all-White South Africa soccer team being banned from the 1958 Fédération Internationale de Football Association (FIFA) World Cup. Despite these efforts, international awareness of and support for harsher sanctions on South Africa only gradually gained acceptance.[6] The Soviet Union was among the first supporters of the anti-apartheid effort, and in 1958 it expressed that apartheid laws prohibiting non-whites from participation on South Africa Olympic Committee (SAOC) teams were a violation of Principle I, Clause 25 of the Olympic Charter (Blackman, 2012).

In terms of Black athlete involvement in anti-apartheid efforts, in 1963 Jackie Robinson worked with the American Committee on Africa (ACOA) to pressure the IOC to ban South Africa from the 1964 Olympics until its apartheid practices were eliminated (Blackman, 2012). In 1965, the African Games banned South Africa and Rhodesia from participation (FEI, 2022). However, it was not until the late 1960s that a critical mass of African Americans were more outwardly supportive of anti-apartheid efforts. Williams (2012) captured the emerging international consciousness among scores of African Americans by the late 1960s: "African Americans began seeing the connections between their plight against 'American apartheid' and colonialism in Africa and Third

World countries around the world" (p. 151). On November 22–23, 1967, the National Conference on Black Power was hosted at Second Baptist Church in Los Angeles (Edwards, 1969/2017).[7] The theme of the conference was "Liberation is a Coming from a Black Thing" (Thomas, 2012, p. 138). The chairman of the event was Dr. Harry Edwards of San Jose State University (SJSU). Along with Edwards, local political activists including members of the bourgeoning Student Non-Violent Coordinating Committee (SNCC) assisted in the planning and implementation of this important conference. As the leader of the Olympic Committee for Human Rights (OCHR),[8] Edwards strategically aligned himself with Civil Rights leaders who were internationally connected such as Reverend Dr. Martin Luther King Jr. of the Southern Christian Leadership Conference (SCLC); Dr. Louis E. Lomax, Floyd McKissick, and Ray Ennis of the Congress of Racial Equality (CORE); Kenneth Noel, H. Rap Brown, Stokely Carmichael (later known as Kwame Ture), and James Forman of the SNCC; Huey P. Newton of the Black Panther Party of Self-Defense (BPP); Omar Ahmad of the 1967 Black Power Conference; Samuel J. Skinner Jr. of the *San Francisco Sun Reporter*; and Dick Gregory (Edwards, 1969/2017).[9] The fact that the six OCHR demands were nearly identical to The Black Power Manifesto and Resolutions outlined at the second annual National Conference of Black Power (NCBP) on July 20–23, 1967 in Newark, New Jersey, underscores the significant influence of the Black Power movement on Edwards's leadership and the OCHR (Blackman, 2021).[10] In other words, the OCHR and the subsequent Olympic Project for Human Rights (OPHR) were birthed out of the Black Power movement, which itself was an extension of the international Black Freedom and Pan-Africanism struggles (Blackman, 2021).

As an activist scholar Edwards's political philosophy was heavily influenced by Malcolm X,[11] the Organization of Afro-American Unity (OAAU), and the broader Black Power movement.[12] Specifically, Malcolm X helped Edwards understand the internationalization of the Black freedom struggle (Edwards, 1969/2017). Edwards embodied Black Power and Nationalism via his militant rhetoric, his donning of a black beret, afro, and goatee as part of his physical appearance, and his organization of grassroots and mass mobilization protests (Blackman, 2021; Cooper, 2021; Edwards, 1969/2017). Therefore, even when mainstream media tried to ignore or mince his words, he communicated the message of Black Power in a multitude of ways so it would be understood by international audiences that his efforts were part and parcel of a broader Black freedom struggle and human rights movement.

Moreover, Edwards not only understood leveraging the power of sport and Black participation in athletic industrial complex, but he was also cognizant of the importance of aligning the OPHR's efforts with broader social movements (Cooper, 2021). In his seminal book *The Revolt of the Black Athlete*,

Edwards (1969/2017) explained the intentionality of connecting his efforts with the Black Power movements across the world: "A substantial part of the S.J.S.C. [San Jose State College] and O.P.H.R. efforts involved propagating the ideological framing and definition of these struggles as legitimate and necessary components and manifestations of the broader society-wide civil rights and Black power movements" (p. xvii).

As a former athlete and at the time a sociology instructor at San Jose State College, now known as San Jose State University (SJSU), Edwards possessed a critical consciousness about the power of sport to stimulate broader social change. Prior to the Olympic boycott plans, Edwards organized SJSU football players to boycott a game against the University of Texas at El Paso to express their demands to the SJSU administration for addressing the insidious campus racial climate for Black students (Edwards, 1969/2017). The partial success of this boycott revealed to the nation that Black athletes were ready and willing to exercise their power to advance racial justice locally and nationally (Bass, 2002; Blackman, 2012, 2021; Cooper, 2021; Edwards, 1969/2017; Hartmann, 1996).

Building on this momentum, Edwards's OCHR group shifted its focus to using national and international sporting events as platforms to protest ongoing racial discrimination.[13] In concert with the broader Pan-African movement, the OCHR demanded the banning of South Africa and Rhodesia from the 1968 Olympics in Mexico City, Mexico, to force those countries to end their decades-long regime of apartheid (Blackman, 2012, 2021; Edwards, 1969/2017).[14] African American athletes who were in support of the Olympic boycott included basketball superstar Lew Alcindor (later known as Kareem Abdul-Jabbar), tennis standout Arthur Ashe, basketball legend Wilt Chamberlain, baseball pioneer Jackie Robinson, basketball superstar Oscar Robertson, and basketball standout Len Wilkens (Bass, 2002; Edwards, 1969/2017). In a resolution drafted at the Black Youth Conference that was read by Edwards on November 22, 1967, the following remarks were expressed:

South Africa
Whereas the United States has seen fit to allow the travel within the political borders of this country of persons from countries where black people can neither enter nor escape the slavery thereof.
And whereby the presence of these foreign persons, their participation in any aspect of social, political, or economic activity in this country, and the complicity of the United States functions in conjunction with such persons all represent an affront to the basic humanity of black people in this country,
Black men and women athletes have voted unanimously to boycott any meet where participants from two countries in particular might be in participation. These countries are: 1. South Africa 2. Rhodesia. (Edwards, 1969/2017, p. 51)

The communication of this strategy reflected media activism, while the enactment of the boycott by several Black athletes and their allies personified mass mobilization and the protests exhibited at the 1968 Olympics illustrated symbolic activism. Each of these efforts constituted political activism, and cumulatively they represented hybrid resistance in and through sport.

Moreover, the internationalization of this Black sporting resistance was evident in transnational support from various African, Latin American, South American, Asian, and European countries. Countries that expressed their support for the Olympic boycott prior to the 1968 National Black Power Conference included China, Cuba, Czechoslovakia, the United Kingdom, France, Guatemala, Guinea, Ireland, Mexico, Nigeria, Russia, Tanzania, Uruguay, Yugoslavia, and Zambia (Edwards, 1969/2017). An example of the mounting international pressure against South Africa following the OCHR's media activism was the expressed support from thirty-two nations who were a part of the Organization of African Unity (OAU) (Edwards, 1969/2017).[15] In an OCHR press release, Edwards explained the diasporic connection between African Americans and continental Africans regarding the South Africa boycott efforts:

> We shall work to establish a bond of communication between Black America and Black Africa based upon our mutual descent and problems growing out of the genocidal policies of certain white racist societies (i.e., United States of America, the Union of South Africa, Southern Rhodesia, etc.).
>
> We shall initiate a movement to establish a second set of games preferably held in an African Nation during the late summer.... These games will be financed by a co-ordinated effort around the world to raise funds in order that 1968 will in fact be a year of athletic competition in the true Olympic spirit. (Edwards, 1969/2017, p. 78)

Edwards's astute use of media activism was a major reason why international coverage and support of the Olympic boycott was achieved. Later, the African National Congress (ANC), American Committee on Africa (ACOA), and several communist and politically neutral nations also offered their support for the Olympic boycott (Edwards, 1969/2017).[16] The threat of economic activism via a boycott of the Olympics along with the mass mobilization activism idea of creating of a separate African Olympic Games demonstrated a *radical imagination of Black sporting resistance* and the power of Black unification against neocolonial ideologies and systems. As such, I argue that the OPHR's efforts alongside their comrades embodied the activation of historical and revolutionary consciousness, which is central to the Black radical tradition (Robinson, 1983/2000).

The combination of hemispheric and international pressure, particularly economic implications, forced the IOC to reverse its decision to admit South

Africa. In an emergency IOC vote, forty out of the seventy-one members approved the suspension of South Africa (Bass, 2002).[17] The collective efforts of the OCHR and other anti-apartheid groups resulted in the IOC banning South Africa from participation in the Olympics until 1992 (Donnelly, 2008).[18] The leadership of SASA and other African organizations who forced the IOC to uphold its ban on South Africa and Rhodesia led Blackman (2012) to conclude the following reality: "The developing African-led international and anti-apartheid in sports movement was a product of continental Pan-Africanism" (p. 6). The activation of Pan-Africanism via mass mobilization, economic, media, political, sports-based, and societal-centric activism illustrated Edwards's (2016a) proclamation about the unique power of sport to galvanize human rights activists and advocates across different geopolitical contexts.[19]

In addition, the unification of the OAU, African Americans, and allies across Asia and Eastern Europe served as a major victory for newly independent African nations who were seeking to gain international legitimacy in their postcolonial existence (Bass, 2002). Hence, revolutionary consciousness (Robinson, 1983/2000) through sport, as well as in non-sporting spaces, inherently involves the establishment and sustainment of *inter-diasporic relationships* grounded in converging interests, shared values, and common adversaries. Accounting for multilevel factors such as chrono-, macro-, meso-, and microsystem factors is a primary aim of the current text in terms of understanding how, when, where, and why Black sporting resistance manifests. The chronosystem factor of the interplay of Cold War politics during the postwar era reflected the uniqueness of this time and global context. The emergence of the Pan-Africanism and Afro-Asian solidarity movements during the mid-twentieth century is an example of a macrosystem factor influencing internationalists' efforts. Mesosystem factors include Black athletes' interactions with their allies across sports, nationalities, and political ideologies. Micro-system factors analyzed here are the increased salience of Black radicalism among Black sportspersons' identities in concert with concurrent anti-fascist, anti-capitalist, anti-colonial, anti-imperialist, and anti-war movements.

Relatedly, Bass (2002) highlighted how one of the primary fears of the United States was a political unification of African nations and the Soviet Union. In addition to socialist and communist philosophies, the solidarity on the issue of anti-apartheid strengthened the alignment of these nation-states. This relationship intensified during the postwar period (Bass, 2002). At the end of the *Information Booklet* that was disseminated to Black athletes interested in learning more about the proposed 1968 Olympic boycott, Edwards (1969/2017) expressed the broader internationalist and anti-colonial aim of the OPHR's efforts: "It's time that Africa, Asia, and Latin America unite to form a new conference conceived and dedicated in the spirit of freedom, justice, and equality—and not representative of nations which practice slavery and the destruction of its Black populations while piously preaching "democracy"... the medal of honor humanity will bestow upon those noble and advanced Black athletes, who sacrifice for a better world by their protest, will be emblazoned in the minds of mankind forever" (p. 154).

The most prominent Black internationalists were so powerful because of their political understanding of international anti-capitalist alliances.[20] The ties between African Americans, Cubans, Russians, Chinese, and continental Africans have been the most effective and most feared force against the United States and European imperialists such as Great Britain, France, Spain, Italy, Portugal, Belgium, and Germany (Horne, 2020b).[21] In an analysis of twentieth-century international politics, Williams (2012) surmised that communism, Asiatic nationalism, and Black nationalism were viewed as major threats to the United States and Western powers during the Cold War. The threat of an Olympic boycott and subsequent ending of apartheid in South Africa signified a victory for Pan-African, Pan-Asian, and Soviet unification efforts within and beyond sport.[22] In 1985, the United Nations Human Rights Commission (UNHRC) created an International Convention against Apartheid in Sports (Donnelly, 2008). A crowning achievement of the OPHR as a Black internationalist sporting organization was its ability to internationalize the issue of racial oppression and human rights violations in and through sport.

It is important to note here that although the OCHR (and later the OPHR) and related anti-apartheid efforts were not explicitly seeking to eliminate racial capitalism, they did pursue the disruption of this system of oppression to achieve tangible gains in terms of racial justice. I posit their focus on anti-colonialism, anti–White supremacy, and anti-imperialism within the context of South Africa was still effective insofar as it disrupted the ideological hegemonic outpost of the Olympics. The transformation of the Olympics from a routine reproductive site of colonial relations into a site of revolutionary anti-apartheid resistance was and remains a major victory for human rights activists worldwide. Notwithstanding, I argue there were two missed opportunities for this resistance movement. First, the lack of intentional focus on eliminating global racial capitalism meant that even with the end of apartheid, racial and class oppression could still be maintained, albeit in an evolved form. The election of President Nelson Mandela was a progressive step, but by the time he assumed his role in office much of his radical political views associated with the pre-1994 African National Congress (ANC) and South African Communist Party (SACP) had shifted to a more moderate centrist stance (Horne, 2019).[23] In concert with historical Black internationalists such as Paul Robeson and W.E.B. Du Bois, I surmise that nothing short of the total replacement of racial capitalism with a more egalitarian political and economic system such as socialism will remedy systemic oppression across and within borders.

A second and related missed opportunity was the lack of follow-through on the idea of creating a separate African Olympic Games. In concert with the foundations of Black Nationalism and Pan-Africanism, creating separate institutions, organizations, programs, and spaces that reify African cultural values and sociopolitical systems is emblematic of the Black radical tradition (Robinson, 1983/2000). A collective boycott of the Olympics would have not only created a significant economic disruption to the international sporting arm of racial capitalism, but it also would have signified a maturation of Black sporting resistance to an unprecedented level in the neocolonial era. However, because anti-capitalism was not explicit in the anti-apartheid movement, the mass mobilization effort was limited in terms of its transformative impact. Another idea expressed by Edwards (1969/2017) was the possibility of creating an Afro-Asian Olympic competition. If this idea had been executed, it would have initiated yet another blow to global racial capitalism. More specifically, Afro-Asian international sporting collaborations that embodied internationalist political philosophies would have aligned with revolutionary socialist and communist movements of the era. As such, the anti-apartheid movement embodied three of the key elements of Black internationalism (anti-colonialism, anti–White supremacy, and anti-imperialism), but the lack of full integration of all six tenets which resulted in a less-than-optimal impact temporally and in perpetuity.[24]

Beyond the OPHR, Arthur Ashe was one of the high-profile African American athletes in the United States during the late 1960s to the early 1990s. He was the first African American to win three major singles tennis tournaments (U.S. Open in 1968, Australian Open in 1970, and Wimbledon in 1975) (Ashe & Ramperstad, 1993). In 1969 and 1970, Arthur Ashe unsuccessfully attempted to secure a visa from the South African government to participate in the South African Open. His visa application was not approved until 1973, at which time he broke the color barrier at the South Africa Open. In this instance, Ashe's pioneering act was a form of *agentic participatory sporting resistance* whereby instead of boycotting South African sporting events altogether as a stance against apartheid, Ashe sought to use his agency to challenge the status quo. He was the singles runner-up to Jimmy Connors and doubles champion with Tom Okker that year. His visits to South Africa were highly polarizing and he received the most intense criticism from Black South Africans who felt he was being complicit with the government by participating in the South Africa Open rather than by following in the footsteps of other Black athletes who boycotted all international sport participation opportunities in and against South Africa. In 1970, his leadership contributed to South Africa being banned from the Davis Cup, which reflected his activation of agentic and mass mobilization (organizational) activism in and through sport. Later, in 1989, he convinced the Association of Tennis Professionals (ATP) to disapprove two tennis tournaments that were scheduled in South Africa due to the country's apartheid practices, which again reflected his initiation of agentic, mass mobilization, and economic activism in and through sport.

During his time in South Africa, Ashe witnessed firsthand the visceral and ubiquitous impact of apartheid. He described the ethnic racism he witnessed: "I saw the rigid divisions between the black and Colored and Asian and Jewish and English and Dutch peoples, with the Dutch holding the highest ground of apartheid" (Ashe & Ramperstad, 1993, p. 105).[25] In 1974, Ashe had a conversation with a young Black South African boy named Mark Mathabane,[26] which left an indelible impression on him. Mark shared with him that Black South Africans were not truly free, and he longed to know what freedom felt like. From that point on, Ashe committed himself to the anti-apartheid movement. Ashe would later say that his "core opposition to apartheid was undoubtedly my memory of growing up under segregation in Virginia" (Ashe & Ramperstad, 1993, p. 111). In other words, through an African diasporic connection via shared experiences, a collective identity, and common adversary, Ashe was able to connect his local experiences of growing up in Richmond, Virginia, in the United States with the global pervasiveness of anti-Black racism across the neocolonial world. Thus, Ashe moved from being a passive observer to an active participant in *the struggle that must be* for global African freedom from racial oppression (Ashe & Ramperstad, 1993; Cooper, 2021; Edwards, 1969/2017).

Ashe's hybrid resistance in the anti-apartheid movement in the 1970s included the activation of agentic resistance, advocacy, symbolic activism, mass mobilization activism, media activism, economic activism, and political activism. One of his most influential forms of resistance came through his advocacy involvement with the TransAfrica organization, which was formed by the Congressional Black Caucus (CBC) to advocate for African and Caribbean affairs. As a major leader with the TransAfrica Forum, the fundraising arm of the organization, he engaged in economic activism on behalf of African people globally. He also cofounded the Artists and Athletes Against Apartheid and cochaired the organization with Harry Belafonte, which was an example of mass mobilization and economic activism with sportspersons and supporters beyond sport. The organization encouraged athletes and entertainers to boycott performing in South Africa and worked to ensure the enforcement of U.N. sanctions against the apartheid nation (Ashe & Ramperstad, 1993). In 1985, Ashe was arrested for participating in an anti-apartheid protest in Washington, D.C. Following this protest, three Black community leaders including Randall Robinson organized a sit-in at the South African Embassy as a part of the national Free South Africa Movement. Along with Harry Belafonte, Coretta Scott King, and other Black leaders, Ashe participated in picket line demonstrations outside of the embassy in another example of symbolic and mass mobilization activism. He would later engage in media activism by using Black publications such as *Jet* magazine as well as White mainstream presses such as the *Washington Post* to amplify the message of ending South African apartheid and its connection to racism in the United States. Throughout the 1980s, he would also engage in scholarly activism by speaking at college campuses about the importance of student engagement in the international crisis (Ashe & Ramperstad, 1993).

The unification of anti-apartheid efforts extended across the globe. In the 1970s, West Indian cricket teams boycotted invitations to compete in South Africa. Despite economic incentives to participate in these matches, prominent West Indian cricketers such as Sir Isaac Vivian Richards were steadfast in declining these invitations (Davis, 2009). The West Indian cricketers of the 1960s through the 1980s were heavily influenced by the broader anti-colonial and West Indian independence social movements. Davis (2009) highlighted how Richards was openly supportive of and influenced by Bob Marley and Ethiopian emperor Haile Selassie (also referred to as Jah Rastafari), which reflected the connection between sport and broader Black social movements such as the Rastafarianism movement. The Pan-Africanism ethos and anti-apartheid position adopted and exhibited by Black sportspersons across the African diaspora in the mid- to late twentieth century highlighted the power of Black internationalism in and through sport.

Anti-War Movements and Hybrid Black Sporting Resistance

The twentieth century was defined by international wars between nation-states who promoted fascism, communism, socialism, and capitalism. The two most prominent wars of the century were World War I (WWI) between 1914 and 1918 and World War II (WWII) between 1939 and 1945. During these periods nearly all international sporting events were halted, including two of the quadrennial Olympic events. Another major conflict that lasted longer than both world wars combined was the Cold War, which stretched from 1947 to 1991. During this period, nation-states, particularly the Soviet Union and the United States, engaged in international propaganda campaigns to win the favor of the global audience. Both countries strategically recruited, developed, and deployed elite athletes to showcase their skills and promote the political aims of their respective governments. These international trips with athletes were called "goodwill diplomacy" or "ambassador visits" (Thomas, 2012). Despite the widespread nature of these ambassador visits, not all athletes were in support of their government's actions. Within this section, I will highlight instances where Black athletes engaged in political activism and hybrid resistance to challenge the contradictory actions of imperialist governments. In these instances, Black athletes embodied internationalist sporting resistance, which refers to the use of sport and international coalition building to engage in counter-hegemonic efforts centered on anti-colonialism, anti-imperialism, anti-capitalism, anti-sexism, and/or anti-war/militarism.

The range of Black internationalist sporting resistance efforts over the twentieth century included the use of agency, advocacy, political activism, economic activism, legal activism, media activism, and mass mobilization activism. For example, in 1959 the U.S. State Department sent National Basketball Association (NBA) player Bill Russell to Africa to promote American diplomacy efforts (Davis, 2018; Thomas, 2012). This trip was part of the United States Information Agency's (USIA) effort to use sport as a propaganda tool for American imperialist aims. Russell's trip included visits to Libya, Liberia, Côte d'Ivoire, Sudan, and Ethiopia. Although he was sent to promote a U.S. political agenda, he engaged in agentic resistance by using the trip to connect with his African roots and strengthen African American and continental African relationships (Thomas, 2012). When asked by a young Liberian boy why was he visiting Liberia, Russell offered the following response: "I came here because I believe that somewhere in Africa is my ancestral home. I came here because I am drawn here, like any man, drawn to seek the land of his ancestors" (Thomas, 2012, p. 2). Russell's ulterior motive for participating in the trip served as a means to undermine the United States' hegemonic political agenda. His actions in this instance personify agentic resistance. As a form of resistance, agency refers to "the use of personal choice and/or group actions to express a sense of individuality and/or sociocultural disposition within a specific context" (Cooper, 2021, p. 76). Russell was resolute in his beliefs about Black people deserving human and civil rights and the notion that all Black people have the right to be authentically themselves whether their views align with mainstream social movements or not. Russell's resistance underscore the heterogeneity of Black resistors based on their personalities, political identifications, and the distinctiveness of their respective positionalities within time, space, and context. Black sportspersons throughout history have used agentic resistance as a primary form of counter-hegemonic action because it is subtle and less likely to be reprimanded compared to more pronounced expressions of activism such as through protests or boycotts.

Another prominent African American who engaged in Black sporting resistance after participating in the U.S. goodwill ambassador and cultural diplomacy program was Mal Whitfield. As a goodwill ambassador, Whitfield traveled to Liberia, Libya, Kenya, Tunisia, Uganda, Nigeria, and Sierra Leone (Thomas, 2012; Whitfield, 1964). Similar to Russell, Whitfield's willingness to participate in these trips highlights how Black sportspersons, even those who engage in resistance at times, are susceptible to engaging in actions that strengthen rather than weaken imperial and colonial arrangements.[27] As a track and field Olympic champion, military veteran, and conservative political supporter, Whitfield embodied the desired characteristics of an African American who could represent the values of Americanism (Cooper, 2021; Thomas, 2012). However, in a shocking move, in 1964 Whitfield engaged in media activism when he published an article titled, "Let's Boycott the Olympics," wherein he called for African American Olympic athletes to boycott the 1964 Olympic Games (Cooper, 2021; Thomas, 2012; Whitfield, 1964). The core of Whitfield's article was emphasizing the hypocrisy of the United States' international efforts when compared to its domestic treatment of African Americans. The intentional framing of this issue as an international human rights issue within the context of anti–White supremacy and anti-imperialism accentuated how and why it represented Black internationalism. The actions of these two highly visible African American athletes, Russell and Whitfield, along with Jackie Robinson's shifting support for Black Power philosophies, signaled that the mid- to late 1960s in the United States marked a pendulum swing toward increased internationalist consciousness and sporting resistance among African American athletes.

Eroseanna Robinson was another Black internationalist athlete and an often overlooked activist athlete pioneer who courageously chose to oppose U.S. militarism in the late 1950s and early 1960s (Davis, 2018; Moore, 2017). In 1958, in an act of symbolic and political activism, Robinson declined to participate in a U.S.-sponsored track meet in Moscow, Russia, to express her discontent with her country's hypocritical political behavior (Davis, 2018). Robinson, like many athlete activists, understood the power of agentic bodily control in terms of deciding when, where, and how her body would be used. Thus, Robinson leveraged both her *agentic participatory sporting resistance* and *agentic refraining sporting resistance*. From the enslavement period to the mid-twentieth century, U.S. power wielders exploited Black bodies for their own political and economic purposes. The initiation of the goodwill ambassador campaign in the 1950s and 1960s was no different in that Black athletes were being used to offset international criticism about American race relations (Davis, 2018; Douglas, 2018a; Thomas, 2012).[28] By declining to participate in this campaign as a form of *agentic refraining sporting resistance* and symbolic and political activism, Robinson's absence signaled to the world and particularly the Soviet Union that all African Americans did not endorse U.S. militarism and imperialism. In the same spirit of athlete boycotts, Robinson's symbolic and political activism was manifested in her *absence* from a sporting space rather than her presence. In previous work, I argued that the first and second halves of the twentieth century were distinguished by their different sporting resistance tactics: the former period involved *fighting to be present/included in athletic spaces* whereas the latter period involved *being absent from these same spaces* with the shared intent of advancing broader Black freedom struggles (Cooper, 2021).

By both her presence and her absence and the expressiveness of her political views as a Black woman athlete, Robinson also embodied anti-sexism

(Burden-Stelly & Horne, 2020) in a highly visible sporting space. Black women in general and Black women athletes have historically and contemporarily been deemed as invisible and deposable and their primary purpose has been to serve patriarchal desires (Brown, forthcoming; Davis, 2018). However, when a strong and politically conscious Black woman athlete like Rose Robinson unapologetically uses her international platform in and through sport to engage in political activism, by proxy she signifies scores of Black women international freedom fighters who face intersectional oppressions. Her actions in concert with these Black women activist counterparts express the stance that Black women specifically will not be silenced. Hence, Black sporting resistance illuminates how the actions of one can represent and align with the feelings, beliefs, values, and radical imagination and power of many. More specifically, *Black internationalist sporting resistance* reflects how the championing of radical humanism inherently involves the concomitant dismantling of multiple forms of oppression including racism, sexism, militarism, imperialism, colonialism, and capitalism.

Moreover, Robinson did not support the Cold War or the Vietnam War on the grounds that the United States did not live up to its own professed creed of freedom, liberty, and justice for all by continuing to oppress its African American citizens (Cooper, 2021; Davis, 2018; Moore, 2017; Thomas, 2012). In 1959, in another act of symbolic activism, Robinson declined to stand for the national anthem at the Pan American Games to further heighten the visibility of her critique against the United States (Davis, 2018; Douglas, 2018a; Moore, 2017). It is important to note here that Robinson's historic symbolic activism *preceded* Tommie Smith and John Carlos's iconic Black Power protests at the Olympics by nine years (1968), Mahmoud Abdul-Rauf's famous anti-war protest before NBA games by thirty-seven years (1996), and Colin Kaepernick's renowned take-a-knee gesture during the Black Lives Matter (BLM) movement by fifty-seven years (2016). Stated differently, Robinson, a Black woman, was a pioneer of symbolic activism through sport and this text is intended to pay her the proper respect for her valor, sacrifice, and impact on human rights efforts within the United States and internationally. Her legacy should be known and revered as much if not more than her Black male activist athlete successors.

The combination of boycotting an international athletic event in 1958 and then protesting at an international athletic event in 1959 reflected the diverse ways in which Black athletes can and did leverage their power through sport (Cooper, 2021; Edwards, 2016a). In addition to her athletic boycotts and protests, Robinson also engaged in economic activism when she refused to pay taxes to the U.S. government to express her discontent with the country's military actions abroad (Douglas, 2018a). After being arrested and jailed, Robinson engaged in another act of symbolic activism by going on a hunger strike while incarcerated (Cooper, 2021; Douglas, 2018a). Robinson's hybrid resistance embodies an exemplary of *Black internationalist sporting resistance* because she was willing to risk her health and livelihood to stand in solidarity with anti-war, anti-imperialism, and anti–White supremacy activists. Instead of pledging allegiance to a racist, capitalist, and imperialist country, Robinson honored the legacy of freedom fighters and upheld the banner of Black internationalism.

The representation and the reality of racial conditions facing African Americans was a primary political tool for both the United States and the Soviet Union. For the United States, African American athletes were selectively utilized as representatives of racial progress in the country that professed to be the global leader of democracy, freedom, and opportunity (Cooper, 2021; Davis, 2018; Thomas, 2012). In contrast, the Soviet Union focused *on the realities* facing the critical mass of African Americans who were subjected to discrimination, violence, and oppression. These conflicting messages were at the core of the political messaging to African diasporic groups who were being targeted for their allegiance to either the capitalist United States or communist Soviet Union. In an examination of the racial propaganda promulgated through sport during the mid-twentieth century, Thomas (2012) offered the following assessment: "By overemphasizing the extent to which social mobility was achievable for African Americans, the State Department sought to influence diasporic political alignments during the Cold War. The U.S. government tried to show that American policies were supportive of the liberation and rise of all people of color worldwide, and the touring athletes were depicted as symbols of America's commitment. Hence, sports were at the forefront of American propaganda efforts" (p. 8).

President Eisenhower's 1959 Committee on Information Activities Abroad, also known as the Sprague Committee, created the ambassador tours to undermine pre-WWII Black internationalist efforts centered on anti-colonialism, promote the illusion of racial inclusion as a by-product of the U.S. democracy experiment, and offset criticisms of African Americans being racially oppressed (Thomas, 2012). These deceptive aims illuminate how hegemonic governments strategically use popular culture such as music, art, entertainment, and sport to expand their ideological domination. In 1949, at a House of Un-American Activities Committee (HUAC) hearing, Paul Robeson testified against the U.S. government and cited examples of ongoing racial oppression against African Americans and the unjust nature of U.S. imperialism (Robeson, 1958/1998). At the same testimony, Jackie Robinson accused Robeson of being associated with the Communist Party and misrepresenting the state of racial progress in the United States.[29] Following this hearing, Robeson had his passport revoked and he experienced a steady decline from the height of his popularity and influence in the 1930s and 1940s (Horne, 2014a). Notwithstanding,

Robeson's legacy as a Black internationalist continues to inspire generations of activists in and beyond sport.

A notable strength of Robeson's activism revealed a glaring limitation of other anti-war activists during this era. For example, in addition to championing anti-militarism, Robeson was outwardly anti-capitalist. His communist-leaning political views enabled him to foster harmonious alliances with anti-capitalist countries and groups across the world. In fact, it was Robeson's socialist and communist political views that primarily led to his targeting by the U.S. government. In other words, it is my contention that his anti-capitalist views posed a larger threat to galvanizing a revolution within the United States rather than his anti-militarism views. Compared to other Black internationalist sportspersons such as Muhammad Ali and Eroseanna Robinson, Robeson was unique in his direct condemnation of capitalism. Given the pernicious impact of the Red Scare in the United States during the Cold War, any person regardless of race who supported communist governments was subjected to intense surveillance and punishment. Thus, embodying an anti-capitalist view has been less common among Black sporting resistors (diasporic, transnational, and internationalist) precisely because a focus on this central axis of domination constitutes the greatest threat to the current social order. It is worth noting that any anti-imperialism, anti-militarism, and anti-colonial efforts inherently disrupt capitalistic systems. However, without a precise condemnation of racial capitalism and a clear support for alternative economic systems such as socialism or communism, any revolutionary efforts are subject to reproducing oppressive arrangements, albeit in an evolved form.[30]

In addition to the Cold War, another major military conflict that carried global implications in the twentieth century was the Vietnam War. The war coincided with growing African American alignment with African and Third World liberation efforts (Williams, 2012). After March 16, 1968, when a U.S. strike at Mỹ Lai killed five hundred unarmed Vietnamese including two hundred children, international outrage was directed at the United States (Saeed, 2002). In contrast to the start of the war, by the spring of 1968 a majority of Black Americans opposed the Vietnam War (Saeed, 2002). The most visible Black internationalist athlete who stood against the war was Muhammad Ali. In a famous interview in Miami, Florida, in 1966, Ali expressed the following sentiments regarding his stance: "I ain't got no quarrel with the Vietcong.... *Keep asking me, no matter how long, On the war in Viet Nam, I sing this song, I ain't got no quarrel with the Viet Cong...*" (Marqusee, 2017, p. 124). Later in 1967, at a fair housing event in Louisville, Kentucky, with Dr. Martin Luther King Jr., Ali offered the following remarks regarding his stance on the Vietnam War: "No, I am not going 10,000 miles from home to help murder and burn another poor nation simply to continue the domination of white slave masters of the darker people the world over.... If I thought going to war would bring freedom and equality to twenty-two million of my people, they wouldn't have to draft me, I'd join tomorrow" (Thomas, 2012, pp. 145–146). In concert with the core tenets of Black internationalism (Burden-Stelly & Horne, 2020), Ali did not differentiate racism against Black people in the United States and racist militarism against Vietnamese abroad. This sophisticated framing and articulation of global relations was a major weapon against U.S. ideological propaganda efforts, which sought to convince African Americans to adopt a nationalist orientation during the Cold War rather than an anti-colonial internationalist identity.

Ali was also famously quoted for saying that a Vietcong "never called me n——" (Farred, 1995, p. 37). These remarks were publicized internationally in London, Paris, Berlin, Zurich, Madrid, Hong Kong, Rome, and Amsterdam (Farred, 1995). Ali's astute ability to use witty and provocative rhetoric to convey the hypocrisies of neocolonial regimes as well as to communicate the interconnectedness of multiple forms of oppression (racism, militarism, and imperialism) enabled his message to resonate with oppressed people worldwide. It is also why his message continues to have implications for generations after his initial activism. Reflecting on Ali's activist legacy, Gorsevski and Butterworth (2011) offered the following articulation of his transnational impact:

> Ali's rhetoric demonstrates both the paradox of the violence and nonviolence in sports, which can often cause serious and sometimes fatal injury to athletes, while it conveys the violence in nonviolent activism, which likewise can injure or kill its adherents. . . . A clearer understanding of how Ali's social justice platform and ethos . . . enables critics to obtain more nuanced assessments of the intertwined rhetorics on civil rights, anti-colonialism, and anti-militarism. . . . Ali's forceful persona . . . represent[s] to the world the ideals, contradictions, sacrifices and necessity of performing civil disobedience. (p. 69)

Ali's conviction, along with his keen understanding of effective ways to combat U.S. hypocrisy, was exuded through his effective activation of media activism. My colleagues and I defined media activism as "the use of newspapers, journals, television, radio, and/or Internet (i.e., social media) to generate awareness and action related to social justice aims" (Cooper et al., 2020, p. 101). For decades, the United States strategically employed high-profile Black athletes such as Joe Louis, Jackie Robinson, Althea Gibson, Bill Russell, Wilma Rudolph, Mal Whitfield, and the Harlem Globetrotters to serve as goodwill ambassadors abroad (Cooper, 2021; Thomas, 2012). Similar to the framing of Jesse Owens's successes in the 1936 Olympics in Berlin, Germany, the United States sought to portray an illusion of racial inclusion and progress by parading these high-profile Black athletes around in international settings. However, Ali's anti–Vietnam War and anti–U.S. militarism stances served as a megaphone that revealed to the world the duplicity of U.S. domestic and foreign relation policies.

The apex of Ali's political activism occurred in 1967 when he declined to accept his drafting into the U.S. Army. Ali cited religious reasons along with his personal dissent toward militarism. Consequently, the government and international boxing authorities targeted Ali for his political resistance (Ali & Durham, 1975; Farred, 1995). Ali's refusing the draft and his outspoken opposition to the Vietnam War further internationalized the Black liberation struggle in the United States (Saeed, 2002). Ali spoke out about anti-militarism *before* Reverend Dr. Martin Luther King Jr. and other prominent Civil Rights leaders did so (Ali & Durham, 1975; Farred, 1995; Saeed, 2002). The significance of these efforts occurring at the height of Ali's boxing career should not be overlooked or minimized. The visibility and resonance of Ali's resentment was directly attributed to his success in the internationally popular sport of boxing. The history of pugilism and the modern-day framing of sport as a political battleground, both nationally and internationally, underscores the power of these spaces to amplify broader social movements and counter-hegemonic resistance efforts (Blackman, 2012, 2021; Carrington, 2010; Cooper, 2021; Cooper et al., 2019; Cooper et al., 2020; Edwards, 1969/2017).

Despite intense backlash and consequences, Ali remained convicted in not only his message about oppressed Black Americans, but also oppressed people who suffered from Pan-European racism, colonialism, imperialism, militarism, and capitalism (Ali & Durham, 1975; Farred, 1995; Saeed, 2002).[31] The fact that the most visible and one of the most financially successful Black men in the United States would speak out against racism and militarism signified that contrary the tenets of neoliberalism, no individual success can overshadow the perpetual degradation of millions. In response to a reporter, Ali expressed the core tenets of his faith: "All I want is peace. . . . Peace for myself and peace for the world. My religion is Islam. I am a follower of the Honorable Elijah Muhamad. I believe in Allah. I think this is the true way to save the world. There're five hundred million Muslims all over Asia, Africa and the Middle East. I'm one of them. And proud of it" (Ali & Durham, 1975, p. 138).

Ali's sentiments reflect his desire for durable peace and radical humanism, which aligns with Black internationalists' primary goal for the world. Religious identification/membership has also been an integral feature of internationalist efforts for centuries. Religious persecution is akin to racial, gender, and class persecution. Social psychologist scholars refer to these categories as *arbitrary sets* in their articulation of social dominance theory (Sidanius & Pratto, 2001). Aside from religion, one common feature people across Asia, Africa, and the Middle East share is experiences with immeasurable harm and anger as a result of European colonialism and imperialism. Ali's astute de-emphasis of his American nationality and heightened focus on his religious affiliation and identity as a member of globally oppressed people enabled his message to transcend traditionally divisive social identity categories such as race, ethnicity, and nationality. Among Ali's greatest strengths was his ability and willingness to not view himself as separate from a collective, thus embodying a core component of the definition of activism (Cooper et al., 2019). His well-being was inextricably bound by the condition of Black people and oppressed people globally. This characteristic is central to all forms of diasporic, transnational, and internationalist efforts (within and beyond sport) grounded in human rights and social justice.

Ali's Black internationalist sporting efforts also inspired Black athletes who came after him. In 1992, Craig Hodges of the National Basketball Association (NBA)'s Chicago Bulls engaged in Black internationalism when he expressed his opposition to U.S. militarism abroad and racism domestically in a list of grievances that he gave to President George H. W. Bush (Cooper, 2021; Hodges, 2017). As a member of a two-time NBA championship team and a teammate of the iconic Michael Jordan, Hodges' political and symbolic activism received increased media coverage. Four years later in 1996, another NBA player, Mahmoud Abdul-Rauf, generated international attention toward U.S. militarism and imperialism when he refused to stand during the playing of the national anthem before games (Cooper, 2021; Grewal, 2007). Abdul-Rauf described the United States as a tyrannical government that violated human rights by initiating unjust wars and invading Middle Eastern and African countries against their will. Both Hodges and Abdul-Rauf cited Ali and Malcolm X as major influences on their political consciousness and activism (Cooper, 2021; Grewal, 2007; Hodges, 2017). As African American athletes who were influenced by the Black Power movement, Hodges and Abdul-Rauf possessed and continue to possess a Black internationalist mindset for how to redress anti-Black racism in the United States because they understood the connection between domestic oppression and international imperialism.

Afro-Latino athletes' anti-war and anti-colonial protests have been largely overlooked in previous literature as well. In 1971 at the Pan American Games, Amado Morales declined to stand for the national anthem in protest of U.S. colonialism in Puerto Rico (Davis, 2018). In the 1990s another Puerto Rican and Afro-Latino, Carlos Delgado, then a Major League Baseball (MLB) player, was an outspoken activist against U.S. militarism in Puerto Rico. More specifically, Delgado voiced his dissent with the United States' decision to establish a naval base on the island of Vieques, Puerto Rico (Rhoden, 2004). Between 1943 and 2003, the United States used the small Afro-Latino island as a bombing practice site, which led to immeasurable environmental and health harms including high cancer rates on the island. The grassroots and media activism by Delgado and his fellow activists contributed to the naval base being closed in 2003.[32] In 2002, a year after the infamous 9/11 terrorist attack on New York

City, Delgado engaged in another act of symbolic activism by not standing on the field during the seventh inning when the song "God Bless America" was played. His reason for not being on the field was that he opposed U.S.-imposed wars in Iraq and Afghanistan (Rhoden, 2004). In an interview, Delgado succinctly stated his stance: "I am not pro-war; I'm antiwar, I'm for peace" (Rhoden, 2004, p. 1). This position exemplifies the anti-war and durable peace element of Black internationalism.

Another instance of activism by a Black athlete from a Caribbean island occurred in 1993 when NBA player Olden Polynice, a Haitian, went on a hunger strike against the U.S. government to express his solidarity with 230 Haitian refugees who were infected with human immunodeficiency virus (HIV) while being detained at a prison at Guantanamo Bay, Cuba (Bryant, 2018). Polynice was also a vocal critic of the anti-immigration policy promoted by U.S. president Bill Clinton's administration, which discriminated against immigrants of African descent (Bryant, 2018). Anti-war, anti-militarism, anti-colonialism, and anti-imperialism involve not only challenging the unjust invasion of nation-states and guerilla warfare, but also condemning carceral state practices such as inhumane imprisonment. The stances of these African diasporic athletes reflect the essence of Black internationalist sporting resistance with their political and military activism against imperialist governments.

International Black Sporting Resistance for the Black Lives Matter (BLM) Movement

A long-standing tradition in the United States is the imposition of lethal violence against Black people, particularly at the hands of law enforcement. The killing and unjust treatment of unarmed Black people was not unique to the twenty-first century, but a distinct feature of this era from previous generations was the viral dissemination of these harms via social media (Anderson, 2023; Cooper, 2021; Edwards, 2016a). On February 26, 2012, a 17-year-old African American male named Trayvon Martin was targeted, harassed, and killed by a civilian in Sanford, Florida. This case generated nationwide attention and attracted support from NBA superstar LeBron James and his then–Miami Heat teammates. Less than a month after Martin's killing, on March 24, 2012, James and his teammates posted a powerful image on Twitter (now known as X) with them wearing hoodies and their heads bowed with the hashtags, #WeAreTrayonMartin #Hoodies #Stereotyped #WeWantJustice (L. James, 2012). The social media activism from a globally iconic athlete such as James heightened the visibility of Martin's case both within the United States and internationally. A year later, the #BlackLivesMatter (BLM) movement was created by Alicia Garza, Patrisse Cullors, and Opal Tometi to increase awareness of gross injustices against African Americans and generate support to demand justice from the U.S. criminal justice system (BLM, 2023). It is important to acknowledge the timeline of James and his teammates' social media activism and the subsequent international mass mobilization movement of BLM that roused the support of millions of people across the world largely through social media (BLM, 2023). Even prior to the inception of the formal BLM movement, Black athletes and Black sporting resistance broadly played an integral role in elevating attention toward the vulnerable plight of African Americans.

On August 26, 2016, Colin Kaepernick, then quarterback of the San Francisco 49ers of the National Football League (NFL), intentionally sat down on the bench during the playing of the national anthem before a preseason football game against the Green Bay Packers. After the game, Kaepernick offered an explanation for his symbolic and political activism: "I am not going to stand up to show pride in a flag for a country that oppresses black people and people of color.... To me, this is bigger than football and it would be selfish on my part to look the other way. There are bodies in the street and people getting paid leave and getting away with murder" (Haislop, 2020, p. 1). Later, on September 1, 2016, after meeting with former NFL player and U.S. Army Green Beret Nate Boyer, Kaepernick modified his protest from sitting on the bench to taking a knee (Haislop, 2020). It was this second protest gesture that became the iconic symbol of twenty-first-century Black athlete activism, or what Edwards (2016a) refers to as the fourth wave of Black athlete activism. Kaepernick's public demonstrative activist action (PDAA) became one of the symbols of the BLM movement (Cooper et al., 2019).[33]

James and his teammates' social media activism and Kaepernick's symbolic and political activism built upon what Bryant (2018) described as *The Heritage* and what I refer to as *A Legacy of African American Resistance and Activism through Sport* (Cooper, 2021). Following the Black athlete activism during the Civil Rights and Black Power movements, there was a period of stagnation in terms of mass mobilized activism in and through sport (Edwards, 2016a). The BLM movement revived the internationalization of the Black Freedom Struggle. Similar to previous Black social movements, Black sportspersons were integral actors in demanding justice. The BLM movement shifted attention toward a range of intersecting oppressions including police brutality, voter suppression, the abuse and marginalization of women and people who identify as transgender and queer, educational neglect, and economic deprivation (Anderson, 2023; Cooper, 2021; Farred, 2022). Between 2013 and 2021, the BLM movement garnered international support for not only African Americans who were unjustly killed, but also for Black people and all oppressed people globally who suffered from racism and intersecting forms of oppression at the hands of the state and vigilantes. The documentation of BLM protests in sport in the United States has been widely discussed and thus I will not reiterate these examples here.³⁴ Given the focus of this text, however, I will highlight select instances of sporting examples that intensified international support for the BLM movement.

In 2013, the Fédération Internationale de Football Association (FIFA) created its Task Force Against Racism and Discrimination (Hylton, 2020; Obayiuwana, 2017).³⁵ Members of this task force included a politician, media personnel, a union leader, a referee, and a handful of players. It is important to note that a majority of the members of this task force were not of racially marginalized backgrounds, which highlights the lack of value placed on having representation from groups who possess a distinct perspective and experience with anti-Black oppression and marginalization. The task force was disbanded in 2016 despite ongoing concerns regarding racism within FIFA, including at the 2018 World Cup in Russia (Harris, 2016; Obayiuwana, 2017). Although this attempt at creating an infrastructure to address racial equality reflected a form of advocacy and allyship on the surface, as is the case with many racial justice efforts that are not created or led by those who are most disproportionately impacted by White racism, this effort fell short of its espoused goals (Obayiuwana, 2017).

Related to the point about disingenuous efforts among sport organizations, Boykoff (2022) defines *sportswashing* as "a phenomenon whereby political leaders use sports to appear important or legitimate on the world stage while stoking nationalism and deflecting attention from chronic social problems and human-rights woes on the home front" (p. 342). Even though FIFA is technically not a representative of a single nation-state, scholars have noted the unscrupulous behavior of its leaders, such as Sepp Blatter's bribery actions regarding the bid process for the 2022 World Cup in Qatar and the organization's subsequent favoritism toward certain nation-states due to political relationships and economic arrangements (Boykoff, 2022). As such, this organization serves as a powerful hegemonic mechanism for neocolonial and imperialist governments. According to Boykoff's (2022) sportswashing typology, FIFA would represent an authoritarian political context in conjunction with the host nations for its events. FIFA's sportswashing involves masking corruption and neoliberal capitalistic motives with the illusion of promoting sport for social change and the public good. Contrarily, in an act of media activism, Nigerian journalist and former member of the task force Osasu Obayiuwana offered a scathing critique of FIFA's lack of investment and serious support for anti-racism. He disclosed how the task force only met three times in a three-and-a-half-year period. He also highlighted how FIFA did not implement any substantive efforts to sanction or change the cultures of football associations across Europe that had a history of racism, particularly anti-Black racism. An important aspect of media activism in sport is to heighten the accountability of organizations who espouse that they are serious about addressing racism within their spheres of influence.

Obayiuwana's media activism toward FIFA in concert with scholarly analyses and journalistic exposés of the organization's corrupt business practices is noteworthy (Boykoff, 2022, Harris, 2016; Hylton, 2022; Obayiuwana, 2017). However, similar to the limitations of the anti-apartheid and anti-war movements highlighted earlier in this chapter, an anti-capitalist tenor was a conspicuous omission from the BLM movement within and beyond sport. For example, the creation and economic growth of FIFA is directly connected to colonial, imperial, and racial capitalist actions across the globe. Thus, although the BLM movement championed anti-racism in a laudable manner, without a concurrent attack on racial capitalism, any reform efforts that could be achieved would fall short of the Black internationalist vision for a radical humanist world. Since modern-day sport is a by-product of European imperialism, colonialism, and racial capitalism, sportspersons engaging in anti-capitalist resistance also fundamentally challenge a system that benefits them in material and nonmaterial ways (Carrington, 2010; Danylchuk, 2012; Mwaniki, 2017)—hence the paradox of being a Black sporting resistor within a neoliberal capitalist system where sport serves as a formidable ideological outpost for sustained hegemony (Cooper, 2021; Coakley, 2018; Sage, 1998). As I describe in greater detail in chapter 5, I argue that a revolution for sustained cultural empowerment requires indissoluble strategic coordination of Black internationalist efforts whereby an apparatus of protection and support is established for all revolutionaries.

In addition to media activism for the BLM movement, individual athletes also engaged in Black sporting resistance during this period. In 2019, Gwen Berry, U.S. Olympic hammer thrower, won gold at the Pan American Games in Lima, Peru. As an ode to Tommie Smith and John Carlos's famous protest at the 1968 Olympics, Berry raised her fist and lowered her head on the podium while the national anthem was playing. She offered the following reason for her symbolic and political activism:[36]

> I just couldn't stand by and listen to that song that didn't represent Black Americans and so many Black Americans are being killed under the flag of America. And I just decided to raise my fist in solidarity with those people. Here I am with this big USA across my chest representing this country that says freedom and justice for everyone. And I know I'm living in that very same country that systemic racism and oppression, honestly led me down this path and you know, and made my life what it is . . . so how can I be proud in that moment to represent that very country that does not care and exploit people like me. (HuffPost Video, 2023, 00:20–00:52)

Following her protest, Berry was reprimanded by the USA Track and Field (USATF) Foundation, who in Berry's words told her to never "do anything like that again and they will not support it" (HuffPost Video, 2023, 1:33–1:36). Her $30,000 USATF Foundation grant was reduced to $5,000. She also received numerous death threats for her activism, which underscores the severity and sacrifices that come with engaging in counter-hegemonic actions, particularly in international sporting spaces. In 2020 it had been recorded that BLM protests were organized across five continents in countries including Mexico, Colombia, Brazil, Nigeria, South Africa, Spain, Poland, Ukraine, Iran, India, Japan, Indonesia, and Australia (WBUR, 2020).[37] Berry's support of the aims of the BLM movement and her use of international sporting platforms to voice her opinion illustrates her Black internationalist sporting resistance against White supremacy and sexism as a Black woman athlete. Although Berry's symbolic and political activism through sport was enacted individually, her actions were a part of the mass mobilization activism occurring within the BLM movement from the early 2010s to the early 2020s.

In concert with Berry's symbolic and political activism, in 2020 at the Tokyo Olympics, Raven Saunders, a U.S. silver medalist in the shot put and a Black woman who identifies as lesbian, raised her arms in the form of an X on the medal podium (Morse, 2021). The 2020 Tokyo Olympics were watched by over 3 billion viewers and included participants from over 220 countries (IOC, 2021). A distinct feature of Saunders's activism compared to her Olympic activist predecessors was the presence and visibility of her activism on social media platforms. This courageous symbolic activism reflected her expressed support for intersectional oppressed people worldwide, particularly those who deal with mental health issues. Her activism was deeply connected to her personal experiences as a Black person who identifies with the lesbian, gay, bisexual, transsexual, and queer (LGBTQ) community and deals with corresponding mental health challenges that are stigmatized and marginalized in the broader society; hence, through her activism she demonstrated the interconnectedness between the personal and the public political spheres and the individual experience and the collective condition. Saunders explained the significance of her X protest via an X (formerly Twitter) post: "It's the intersection of where all people who are oppressed meet" (Morse, 2021, para. 2). This statement personifies the spirit of Black internationalism sporting resistance. Saunders's protest was aligned with the BLM movement, which was started in response to the unjust killing of unarmed Black people in the United States, but which over time evolved to represent various oppressed groups globally including those whose identify as LGBTQ and experience unjust violence and oppression (BLM, 2023). The intersectional emphasis of the BLM movement enabled it to attract supporters across a wide spectrum of backgrounds and geopolitical spaces whereby all people who were oppressed by racism, sexism, heterosexism, militarism, and capitalism galvanized to eliminate these interconnected systems of domination (BLM, 2023; Collins, 1990, 2008; Crenshaw, 1991).

Both Berry's and Saunders's symbolic and political activism was grounded in what Collins (1990) described as confronting a matrix of domination. In an effort to shift the dominant discourse away from additive models of oppression, Collins (1990) described the benefit of using an intersectional analysis: "Such an approach fosters a paradigmatic shift of thinking inclusively about other oppressions.... Placing African-American women and other excluded groups in the center of analysis opens up possibilities for a both/and conceptual stance." (p. 543). As Black women, Berry and Saunders embodied what intersectionality scholars describe as *double jeopardy*, whereby they were keenly aware of the interplay of racism and sexism in society (Collins, 1990, 2008; Crenshaw, 1991). These lived experiences informed their activism. Utilizing their international platform through sport, they drew attention to the ongoing oppressions facing Black people and other racially marginalized groups across geopolitical contexts.

In a similar vein, Black athlete support for the BLM movement expanded to the sport of tennis when Naomi Osaka used her platform to engage in agentic, symbolic, political, and media activism. At the 2020 U.S. Open tennis tournament, Osaka wore face masks with the names of seven African Americans who were unjustly killed by law enforcement to show her solidarity with the broader BLM movement (Razack & Joseph, 2021): Breonna Taylor of Louisville, Kentucky; Elijah McClain of Aurora, Colorado; Philando Castile of Falcon Heights, Minnesota; Ahmaud Arbery of Brunswick, Georgia; Tamir Rice of Cleveland, Ohio; George Floyd of Minneapolis, Minnesota; and Trayvon Martin of Sanford, Florida. Each of these deaths were highly publicized and served as clarion calls for mass mobilization activism during the BLM movement. Through ESPN, the U.S. Open is broadcasted internationally to six continents (ESPN, 2023). During the two-week event, over 600,000 spectators attended in person and 1.8 million viewers tuned into the championship match between Osaka and Victoria Azarenka of Belarus (Nagle, 2021). Thus, Osaka's symbolic activism through sport reached a global audience. As a person of Haitian and Japanese descent with dual citizenship in the United States and Japan, Osaka's strategic use of an international sporting event to draw attention to the gross injustices facing African Americans reflected her African diasporic alliance and inter-diasporic allyship as well as her hybrid resistance. In poetic fashion, Osaka won the 2020 U.S. Open, which symbolized her victory for the Black internationalism on and off the court.

Even though the BLM movement originated in the United States, its impact extended beyond national borders and resonated with Black sportspersons across the world. Another notable Black internationalist sportsperson who joined the BLM movement was British Formula One racer Lewis Hamilton, who is of Grenadian and British descent. His pioneering sporting resistance occurred in 2007 when he became the first Black racer to participate in

Formula One. In the same year, he won the Canadian Grand Prix. Over the next decade, Hamilton would ascend to the heights of success in the sport by recording more than one hundred victories and winning seven championships. His meteoric rise in the sport did not quell his racial conscious and commitment to improving Black lives in England and beyond. Following the infamous summer of 2020, where the publicity surrounding the murder of George Floyd sparked international unrest against racial injustice, Hamilton was moved by witnessing Floyd's unjust killing via recordings posted on the internet. He was subsequently inspired to engage in the BLM protests in London (Katwala, 2021). Hamilton's involvement in these efforts reflected his activation of grassroots, mass mobilization, political, and symbolic activism.[38] As a member of the African diaspora and a person who has experienced anti-Black racism throughout his life, Hamilton's shared identity of being Black and his experiences with anti-Black racism in connection to George Floyd's mistreatment compelled him to join the movement. During the 2020 race season, Hamilton took a knee and wore BLM inspired T-shirts to show his support for Colin Kaepernick's symbolic and political activism and the BLM movement's call for racial justice against unjust state violence via police brutality (Katwala, 2021).

After a victory at the Tuscan Grand Prix event, Hamilton donned a T-shirt that read "Arrest the cops that killed Breonna Taylor." The specific demand expressed on Hamilton's shirt exemplified one of the core criteria of activism, which differentiates this type of resistance from borderline activist actions such as agency, advocacy, allyship, and pioneering (Cooper, 2021; Cooper et al., 2019). As a Black British citizen, Hamilton's demand for justice for an African American woman who was killed in the United States illustrates his *Black internationalist sporting resistance*. In concert with Gilroy's (1993) concept of the Black Atlantic, Hamilton did not view himself exclusively in national citizenship or ethnic terms, but rather as a part of a global Black racial and African diasporic group that continued to be subjected to racial oppression across the globe.

Furthermore, in true Black internationalist form, Hamilton called attention to interrelated injustices affecting the global community. In analysis of Hamilton's multifaceted activism, Farred (2022) offered the following conclusion: "Hamilton ... identified the Black Lives Matter movement as the raison d'etre of his 2020 triumph ... as that athlete who can help us think beyond a single issue—as important as, say, racism—in order to propose ways in which racism, the threat to environmental devastation, and growing economic inequality brought about by the ravages of late-capitalism be taken up together—that is, as equally important issues, bound together in a nonhierarchical relationship. Issues interlinked, issues that demand simultaneous address" (p. xviii).

Black internationalists understand that oppressive forces are interconnected, and thus addressing one form of oppression without targeting another manifestation of oppression simultaneously is not a prudent option. In the case of Hamilton, his hybrid resistance as a Black internationalist sportsperson highlighted the cumulative harm to humanity and the earth as a result of the anti-Black racism, racial capitalism/social inequality, and environmental destruction that are the by-products of neoliberalism (Farred, 2022). Although African (Black) diasporic and transnationalism sporting resistance often involve the targeting of multiple forms of oppression, Black internationalist sporting resistance is distinct in that it inherently involves a multifaceted assault on interlocking systems of repression.

Another example of Black internationalism in sport during the BLM movement occurred when the Cricket West Indies (CWI) and South African Cricket teams wore BLM logos on their uniforms during a three-test series in England in 2020 (Reuters, 2020). Jason Holder, a West Indies cricketer, said in a statement, "We believe we have a duty to show solidarity and also help raise awareness.... We have come to England to retain the Wisden Trophy but we are very conscious of happenings around the world and the fight for justice and equality" (Reuters, 2020, p. 1). The solidarity of West Indian cricketers with the BLM movement mirrors the Black internationalist relationships that facilitated West Indian independence efforts during the mid-twentieth century (James, 1963). Scholars such as Joseph (2012a, 2017) have highlighted how Gilroy's (1993) conception of the Black Atlantic has been evident in Afro-Caribbean transnational and diasporic sporting experiences. The example of the CWI teams showing support for the BLM movement further highlights how the Black Atlantic is also embodied through Black internationalist sporting resistance.

Along the same lines, Lungi Ngidi, a standout South African cricketer,[39] initiated a nationwide conversation about the BLM movement by stating his opinion in a press conference that South African sport federations needed to engage in substantive dialogue and change regarding the experiences of Black South African athletes (Moonda, 2020a). Ngidi offered a statement regarding his sports-based agentic and media activism: "As a nation, we have a past that is very difficult, with racial discrimination, so it's definitely something we will be addressing as a team and if we are not, it's something I will bring up.... It's something that we need to take very seriously and like the rest of the world is doing, make the stand" (Moonda, 2020a, p. 1).

One of the strengths of Black internationalism is not only does it increase international support for issues in nation-states outside of one's homeland,[40] but it also inspires resistance and demands for change within one's homeland, such as Ngidi's demands for eradicating racism in South African sports. In other words, Black internationalists do not separate injustices, particularly anti-Black racism, in one setting from another. For Black internationalists, anti–White supremacy requires challenging this insidious ideology and its manifestations wherever it rears its ugly head, which largely remains in nation-states that continue to wrestle with the residue of neocolonialism.

As a Black internationalist sportsperson, Ngidi connected the injustices associated with the unsolved murders of unarmed African Americans in the United States, which started the BLM movement, with the ongoing pervasive structural racism in South African sports such as cricket and rugby, which is a by-product of the legacy of apartheid. This sophisticated connection underscores the Black internationalist analytic lens whereby structural inequalities and ideological hegemony are identified as the core sources of oppression in both pronounced and subtle ways.[41] In a summary of the interplay between the BLM movement and South African activism through cricket, Swart and Maralack (2021) offered the following synopsis: "The BLM movement has served as a catalyst for the voices of black cricketers to be heard and has created a platform for institutionalized racism and transformation in South African cricket to be addressed" (p. 727). Thus, the BLM movement not only garnered international attention toward and support for redressing ongoing anti-Black racism and state violence and police brutality in the United States, but it also amplified the consciousness of activists internationally to hold their own nation-states and homeland organizations more accountable for their racist policies, practices, and outcomes.

Through his sporting resistance leadership, Ngidi was able to galvanize the support of thirty-one former and current South African players and administrators of color to demand change from the Cricket South Africa (CSA) organization (Moonda, 2020b). The collective resistance by this group of South African sportspersons, as a form of mass mobilization activism, led the CSA to express its support of the BLM movement and subsequently establish a "Transformation Charter" to redress ongoing racism in the sport, among other structural issues (Dhyani, 2020). Following the agentic and media activism of Ngidi, a group of Black South African professional rugby players including Springboks captain Siya Kolisi met with Sport Minister Nathi Mthethwa to express their support of the BLM movement and the need for more systemic change in South African sport and society (Botton, 2020; Tshwaku, 2020).

The South African athletes and administrators who express support for BLM received significant backlash not unlike their counterparts in the United States. As noted earlier, the disruptive nature of activism, particularly in and through sport, incites fear and discomfort among those who prefer and benefit from the status quo. However, it is precisely this disruption or rupture that ignites seismic change in societies in terms of law and policy reforms and cultural norm shifts. The activism of the South African rugby players led South African Rugby (SAR) chief executive officer Jurie Roux to initiate a process whereby the grievances of Black players would be addressed and a stronger commitment to combating and preventing anti-Black racism in the sport would be pursued (Tshwaku, 2020). This timeline of events highlights how the power of agentic activism to stimulate mass mobilization and legal activism, insofar as the CSA and SAR are concerned, should not be underestimated and more importantly underscores the benefit of engaging in strategic hybrid resistance in concert with broader social movements.

Another example of Black sporting resistance in the BLM movement is found in Australia. As noted in chapter 1, the connection between the struggle of African Americans in the United States and Aboriginals in Australia dates back to at least the early 1900s with Jack Johnson and the communication between the Universal Negro Improvement Association (UNIA) under the leadership of Marcus Garvey and Fred Maynard and members of the Coloured Progressive Association of New South Wales and Australian Aboriginal Progressive Association (AAPA) (Maynard, 2005). In 2020 during the BLM era, Australian women cricketers led by First Nations standout player Ashleigh Gardner performed a barefoot circle and engaged in a moment of silence to honor Australian First Nations and Indigenous people in this region (Litchfield et al., 2022).[42] Gardner, her teammates, and the Australian women's cricket league acknowledged the influence of the BLM movement on their heightened awareness of ongoing injustices toward First Nations peoples in Australia (Litchfield et al., 2022).

Related to Gardner's and her teammates symbolic activism via allyship, Osmond and Klugman (2022) explored the connections between activism in Australian sport during the BLM movement and the famous protest of Nicky Winmar in 1993. In the summer of 2020, several sportspersons associated with the Australian Football League (AFL) took a knee before matches to show their support of the international BLM movement (Osmond & Klugman, 2022). Accompanying their gesture, league representatives issued a statement affirming their solidarity with Indigenous people and people of color in Australia. The term *Indigenous* in this context refers to Aboriginal peoples and Torres Strait Islanders who are the First Nations groups who are indigenous to what is now known as Australia (Osmond & Klugman, 2022). The following description summarizes the anti-colonial connections between First Nations people of Australia and the African Americans who started the BLM movement: "In fact, First Nations peoples in Australia embraced Black Lives Matters not simply as an act of solidarity with African Americans and Black people globally also because the movement resonated with their own histories, circumstances, and lives.... In Australia, as elsewhere, the worldwide movement catalysed communities and extended opportunities for 'community-led activism'" (Osmond & Klugman, 2022, p. 369).

These Indigenous groups experienced the most devastating impacts of settler colonialism. Chattel slavery and Jim Crow practices in the United States, apartheid in South Africa, and blackbirding in Australia are all practices of oppression grounded in settler colonialism (Horne, 2007; Swan, 2020, 2022). Hence, the current work builds upon previous Black internationalist scholarship by centralizing Black resistance in and through sport in understanding global connections between African (Black) diasporic groups across the Pacific and the Atlantic.

Aboriginal activists of the past and present have expressed solidarity with Black Power movements in the United States and beyond (Horne, 2007; Maynard, 2005; Osmond & Klugman, 2022; Swan, 2020, 2022). For example, Nicky Winmar is an Aboriginal man of the Noongar people and a legendary Australian footballer who engaged in symbolic activism in 1993—ironically or rather poetically, deemed the International Year of Indigenous Peoples—against anti-Aboriginal racism in Australia (Osmond & Klugman, 2022).[43] Winmar's 1993 protest involved him lifting his uniform and pointing to his chest while saying aloud, "I'm black and I'm proud to be black," in a match between Saint Kilda and Collingwood (Osmond & Klugman, 2022, p. 367).[44]

In their analysis of Winmar's activism, Osmond and Klugman (2022) offered the following reflection: "It was an act of sovereignty thousands of miles from his homeland, Noongar country. In that moment, no one could lay claim to Nicky Winmar. No one could possess him. He had refused the colonial terms of engagement. Refused to simply accept what was being said to him. It was at once an embodied statement of pride and a demand for change. And it remains arguably the most powerful image of Australian sport, if not of Australia more generally" (p. 372).

Winmar's symbolic activism reflects the three core components of Black sporting resistance, which involves the epistemological, ontological, and axiological embracing of Blackness and simultaneous fracturing of Whiteness. Winmar's knowledge and embracement of his Noongar roots and values along with his physical presence and dominance as an Australian footballer illuminated how resistance manifests in and through sport. One year after Winmar's iconic protest, in 1994, another Aboriginal athlete named Cathy Freeman wrapped herself in a First Nations flag along with an Australian flag after her victory in the 200 meters at the Commonwealth Games in Victoria, British Columbia, to signify her activism for Aboriginal sovereignty and rights (Amnesty International, 2018).[45] While running her victory lap with these flags she also ran barefoot to symbolize her connectivity with her Aboriginal cultural roots. Both Winmar's and Freeman's activism reflects the anti-colonialism ethos of Black internationalism in and through sport. The iconic representation of sport activism across time, space, and context has consistently included a Black athlete,[46] thus illuminating intergenerational Black internationalist sporting resistance across geopolitical spaces.

Nearly three decades after these protests, Winmar wore a T-shirt with George Floyd's face on it and took a knee during a nationally televised broadcast on *Yokayi Footy* in 2020 to express his support of the BLM movement (Osmond & Klugman, 2022). Winmar would later demand for the First Nations flag to be hoisted in front of the AFL headquarters. Later that year, the team captain for the 2020 Australian Olympic men's basketball team, Patty Mills, echoed the sentiments of Winmar by stating that the issues raised by the BLM movement were not isolated to the United States and racism must be addressed in Australia, with its history of perpetual mistreatment of Aboriginal First Nations people (Osmond & Klugman, 2022). Within Australia, the primary issues around anti-colonialism include sovereignty, nationhood, and broad-based social justice (Osmond & Klugman, 2022). Specifically, Aboriginal First Nations people experience the same issues oppressed Black people experience globally, which include police violence, mass incarceration, miseducation, lack of access to health care resources, economic deprivation, land theft, and political underrepresentation. The spirit of the BLM movement remains necessary internationally, and sport has served as a conduit for the broader social change the movement seeks to achieve across geopolitical contexts.

Summary

Within this chapter, I have highlighted how Black internationalism has been activated in and through sport. Drawing inspiration from the broader Black internationalist movement in the interwar years, twentieth- and twenty-first-century Black sportspersons have utilized their platforms to champion anti–White supremacy/continental unity, anti-colonialism/self-determination, anti-imperialism/revolutionary transformation, anti-capitalism/socialism, anti-sexism/radical Black humanism, and anti-war/durable peace (Burden-Stelly & Horne, 2020). The most prominent example of *Black internationalist sporting resistance* occurred with the anti-apartheid movement in the mid-twentieth century. Groups such as the OCHR (and later the OPHR) and star athletes such as Arthur Ashe of the United States and Sir Isaac Vivian Richards of Antigua played an integral role in heightening and sustaining awareness about the need to eliminate apartheid in South Africa. Although sport was not the primary factor in ending apartheid in South Africa, it played in an instrumental role in generating awareness and support for the effort.

In addition to anti-apartheid efforts, anti-war/militarism in the mid-twentieth century was another major area where *Black internationalist sporting resistance* was present. Specifically, the Cold War and Vietnam War were focal points for sport activism led by individuals such as Muhammad Ali and Eroseanna "Rose" Robinson, who redefined what true U.S. patriotism means.[47] Lastly, the recent BLM movement was the largest international racial justice movement in world history largely due to the impact of social media. Black sportspersons such as Gwen Berry and Raven Saunders of the United States, Osasu Obayiuwana and Lungi Ngidi of South Africa, Naomi Osaka of the United States as well as of Haitian and Japanese descent, Lewis Hamilton of the United Kingdom as well as of Grenadian and British descent, and Nicky Winmar of the First Nations of Australia galvanized support for the BLM movement in their respective sports and countries. In summary, *Black internationalist sporting resistance* has a rich legacy, and current world conditions indicate its presence and strength are needed now more than ever.

5

A Radical Imagination of Future Black Sporting Resistance

• • • • • • • • • • • • • • • • • • • •

> The extent to which sport as a racial project can once again be used for progressive purposes will rest, in large part, on the ability of those invested in sports cultures to hold on to, develop and articulate critical consciousness that goes beyond the sports boundary. (Carrington, 2010, p. 177)

Black sporting resistance has a rich legacy, and these actions represent an extension of broader Black social movements. Sport has never just been a mere leisure activity for entertainment purposes void of political implications. For Black people, sport has always served specific political, cultural, and spiritual purposes. In colonial and neocolonial spaces, Black sport participation represented and continues to represent an effort to experience an elusive sense of humanity and social upward mobility in the face of oppressive realities. Beyond athletic performances and representation in various sport positions, Black sporting resistance has involved using the platform of sport to advance racial justice struggles outside of the arenas, fields, stadiums, rings, and rinks. Instead of conceding to the notion that sportspersons are apathetic entertainers disconnected from the plight of the critical mass of Black people, those who exhibit

Black sporting resistance understand the inextricable bond between themselves and the broader communities they represent. This book outlines how Black sportspersons across generations and geopolitical contexts have utilized their agency and resources to challenge oppressive beliefs, policies, practices, and systems. Within this chapter, I will highlight key insights from previous Black sporting resistance efforts and present ideas for a radical imagination of future Black sporting resistance that can contribute to sustained empowerment and the eradication of all forms of oppression.

African (Black) diasporic sporting resistance was presented as distinct counter-hegemonic actions that have galvanized international support intra- and intergenerationally. Within the sport of boxing, African (Black) diasporic sporting pioneers such as Jack Johnson and Joe Louis emerged as racial icons for broader social movements such as the intergenerational Black Liberation Struggle, Pan-Africanism, anti-fascism, the New Negro movement, and the nascent Civil Rights movement. During this period, the pervasive racist belief promulgated by White proponents of Jim Crow was that Black people were innately inferior and lacked the intellectual and physical skills to compete against White opponents. Johnson's victories against the likes of Tommy Burns of Canada and Jim Jeffries of the United States and Louis's victories against Primo Carnera of Argentina and Max Schmeling of Germany carried international significance. Race leaders such as W.E.B. Du Bois, Marcus Garvey, and C.L.R. James all referenced their historic performances as evidence that the Black race was not inferior to Whites and, more importantly, that their success foreshadowed the imminent liberation of African people globally. Johnson's and Louis's *stealth racial empowerment* did not require that they serve as the spokespersons for the movements, but rather they were expected to excel at the highest level possible in their highly publicized sporting contests. In other words, their resistance was embodied in their boldness and skillful performances in the ring and simultaneously they were positioned as racial icons for international activist groups such as the Universal Negro Improvement Association (UNIA), National Association for the Advancement of Colored People (NAACP), Coloured Progressive Association of New South Wales and Australian Aboriginal Progressive Association (AAPA), Carrancistas of Mexico, West Indian independence organizations, and other anti-colonial and anti-fascist groups across the world. These African (Black) diasporic and inter-diasporic connections converged with the belief that both Johnson and Louis served as sources of collective identity and political empowerment to advance their respective causes of upending racial and political oppression (Horne, 2005; James, 1963; Maynard, 2005).

Notwithstanding the benefits of *stealth racial empowerment*, one limitation of this approach involves when Black sportspersons do not explicitly communicate messages of solidarity with specific social movements, then their identities and actions are susceptible to being co-opted by oppositional forces. With

Johnson, his actions outside of the ring such as intimate relationships with White women and lack of consistent explicit connectivity with Black social movements throughout his life and career led to oppositionists such as the U.S. government manipulating his actions to further advance their claims that Black people were deviant and threats to society rather than serious political actors deserving of respect and equal citizenship rights. In Louis's case, his quiet and polite demeanor was co-opted by the U.S. government to advance its own political propaganda goals that prioritized imperialism, militarism, and nationalism over addressing racism domestically and eliminating fascism and imperialism abroad. As such, my analysis of stealth racial empowerment suggests this type of resistance yields positive and negative outcomes as it relates to advancement of broader Black freedom struggles. From a resistance perspective, it is considered a lower-level counter-hegemonic action that is necessary under certain conditions, but its effectiveness is optimized when strategically aligned with the aims of broader social movements. In addition, it is my contention that stealth racial empowerment should not be exercised in perpetuity because eventually the goal is to activate a critical mass of Black internationalist resistance whereby this type of diasporic resistance will not be necessary. Stated differently, I contend the ultimate aim of our efforts should be to engage in stealth approaches of resistance only until collectively we can be committed to a range of coordinated overt resistance efforts across time, space, and context.

Like Johnson and Louis, Muhammad Ali was another prominent African (Black) diasporic pugilist, but unlike them he did not engage in stealth racial empowerment. Ali's diasporic influence involved his outspoken support for anti-colonial, anti–White supremacy, anti-imperialism, and anti-war efforts. As a proud converted Muslim, a major aspect of Ali's international resonance was the combination of his racial, ethnocultural, and religious identifications. The multiplicity of these identities enabled him to resonate with various oppressed groups across the world. His unapologetic and unwavering commitment to his race and the international struggle for challenging White racism, imperialism, and militarism underscores his uniqueness as an African (Black) diasporic sporting resistor. Even as the U.S. government and its allies sought to discredit and defame Ali, his reputation continued to grow. His affiliation with the Nation of Islam (NOI) and race leaders such as Malcolm X further amplified his message and platform. Ali's intentional scheduling of fights in African and Asian countries during the decolonialization era in the mid- to late twentieth century as well as his meetings with African heads of state reflected his keen understanding of the power of African-Asian solidarity, or what I refer to as *inter-diasporic alliances*, against European imperialism. Ali's legacy as an African (Black) diasporic sporting resistor highlights how racial empowerment through sport can also be manifested in overt ways (in contrast to stealth racial empowerment), albeit not without sacrifices.

Another sport where African (Black) diasporic sporting resistance was prevalent throughout the twentieth century was fútbol. The modern-day sport of fútbol has European origins and thus it was spread throughout the world during the colonization period (Foster, 2003). Similar to other aspects of social decorum, celebrated styles of play and tactics were grounded in Eurocentric norms. Thus, when Pelé and his Brazilian teammates, many of whom were Afro-Brazilians, utilized a creative, spontaneous, and free-flowing style of play described as *brasilidade* to defeat European powerhouses in the 1958, 1962, and 1970 World Cup events, it signified a shifting of the guard in the most popular sport in the world (Andrews et al., 2016). In his analysis of the distinct playing styles, Foster (2003) described the Afro-Brazilian style of play as Dionysian, whereas the Apollonian style of play was exhibited by Europeans. Not only did the Afro-Brazilians demonstrate on a global stage that the European style of play was not superior, but Pelé's masterful performances also revealed that the greatest fútbol player in the world was African. Similar to Johnson, Louis, and Ali, Pelé's historic achievement of being the undisputed best player in his respective sport, one in which White athletes were supposed to dominate in perpetuity, operated in concert with international decolonization efforts and thus signified the power of African (Black) diasporic sporting resistance, particularly in the case of pioneering and agentic efforts. The success of Pelé, his African diasporic counterparts, and their successors represents the epistemological, ontological, and axiological fracturing of White supremacy in and through sport.

Relatedly, African footballers on the continent engage in *native homeland sporting resistance* when they choose to represent African countries in international competition. Players such as Didier Drogba of Côte d'Ivoire and Jay-Jay Okocha of Nigeria activate their agentic resistance by declining to use dual citizenship to represent a non-African country. Even though many African footballers play for professional teams outside of their native homelands, African diasporic sporting resistors who decide to represent their African lineage in events such as the FIFA World Cup and Olympic Games reflect their deep cultural ties and commitment to African empowerment. This embracement of African identity illustrates the Black Nationalism tenor of the mid-twentieth century during the decolonization era, whereby African countries were literally and figuratively breaking the challenges of decades of colonial oppression. These African diasporic sporting resistors in fútbol used their agency to embrace their African national identities when they had the choice to represent a European nation where they migrated for professional career opportunities. African players who either migrate to or were born in non-African countries and remain there to compete still generate a level of diasporic resonance via *stealth migrant sporting resistance*, albeit in a different way from their counterparts who engage in native homeland sporting resistance. The creation of African fútbol leagues and events such as the All African Games, as well as the hosting of mega-events such as the 2010 Fédération Internationale de Football Association (FIFA) World Cup in South Africa, are examples of African (Black) diasporic sporting resistance via mass mobilization activism and efforts to achieve sustained cultural empowerment by centering the growth and health of the countries and communities on the continent.

Capoeira is a sport that was popularized in Brazil by Afro-Brazilians, and it also represents a source of *African (Black) diasporic sporting resistance*. Originating in Angola and then evolving through cultural hybridity, the martial arts practice of capoeira bridged the gap between African generations who lived on the continent and the diasporic groups who persevered through enslavement and oppression on lands beyond their homelands. The key components of capoeira include the enactment of movements, rhythms, songs, and purpose that embody African history, cosmology, and cultural values such as discipline, harmony, and protection of one's body, familial bonds, and communalism. Capoeira not only literally served as a form of military activism against European colonizers during slavery but it also later served as a form of *collective cultural resistance* for *capoeiristas* and their protégés worldwide (Aula, 2017; Dossar, 1992; Joseph, 2012b; Lindsay, 2019). Collective cultural resistance involves the preservation of African virtues through performative actions that are grounded in spirituality and communalism.

Black transnationalism is another key component of Black sporting resistance. The West Indian cricket players and teams of the twentieth century reflected localized mobile transnational formations whereby ethnicity, culture, and reciprocity were centralized (Dahinden, 2010; James, 1963). The teams' matches against colonial countries such as England, South Africa, and Australia carried heightened significance given the backdrop of West Indian independence efforts. As a transnational community (Faist, 2010), the teams were composed of cricketers from Trinidad, Jamaica, Barbados, Antigua, and the region then known as British Guiana (Davis, 2009; James, 1963; Marqusee, 1994/2016). West Indian cricket teams also personified symbolic and economic activism by boycotting matches in South Africa to express their support for the anti-apartheid movement of the 1970s (Davis, 2009). The players and teams engaged in hybrid resistance within the Caribbean region as well as internationally. Pioneering feats such as the 1975 International Cricket Cup (ICC) victory over Australia and subsequent tour match wins against England in 1976 typified West Indian athletic prowess and political power via sport (James, 1963; Wilde, 1994). Hence, cricket served as a proverbial battleground of colonialism versus anti-colonialism; thus, as C.L.R. James stated, the victories on the cricket pitch were serious politics indeed with epistemic and material consequences for Black West Indians and the African (Black) diaspora more broadly.

Moreover, *agentic* and *collective cultural resistance* were performed via distinctive styles of cricket play that included fast-paced test cricket, aggression, trash talking, and performative creativity as well as spectators' creation of a *liming* atmosphere at the games, all of which stood in stark contrast to European cultural norms of acceptability (James, 1963; Joseph, 2017; Marqusee, 1994/2016). Grassroots and mass mobilization activism were reflected in the creation of local, national, and transnational teams such as Shannon Club of Trinidad, West Indian Cricket, and Mavericks Cricket and Social Club (MCSC), as well as with leagues such as the Quaid-e-Azam and events such as the Clive Lloyd Cup (James, 1963; Joseph, 2014, 2017; Marqusee, 1994/2016). Key to the success of these teams, leagues, and events was the presence of reciprocal transnational networks (Faist, 2000). The economic, political, and cultural flows of resources and relationships served as examples of the process of transnationalization (Faist, 2000). Furthermore, the multi-territory effort to demand the inclusion of the West Indian team in the Imperial Cricket Conference also illustrated mass mobilization activism (James, 1963; Marqusee, 1994/2016). Black sporting resistance was exhibited outside of the cricket pitch with C.L.R. James's seminal book *Beyond a Boundary* (1963) serving as an example of scholarly activism.

In the sport of baseball, the Negro (now known as African American) and Afro-Latino players, teams, and leagues of the United States, Mexico, Cuba, and Puerto Rico were examples of transnational circuits (Faist, 2000). Between 1885 and the early 1960s, these transnational circuits produced some of the most talented players in the history of the game, innovative businesses, and invaluable cultural bonding experiences (Bruce, 1985; Burgos, 2007, 2011; Holway, 1988, 1989; Lanctot, 1994, 2004; Lomax, 2003, 2014; Peterson, 1970; Rogosin, 1985; White, 1995). Mass mobilization and economic activism were reflected in the creation of the National Association of Colored Baseball Clubs of the United States and Cuba (NACBC) and the International League of Colored Baseball Clubs in America and Cuba (ILBCAC) in 1906 and the subsequent Negro Leagues that existed until the mid-twentieth century (Lomax, 2003). The formation of teams such as the Chicago American Giants and Homestead Grays in the United States and Cuban Giants and Cuban Stars in Cuba was an example of grassroots and mass mobilization (organizational) activism (Burgos, 2007; Lomax, 2003, 2014). These teams and leagues also practiced political/civic activism via collaborations with Black political organizations and leaders, media activism via reciprocal relationships with the Black press, and pioneering and economic activism via the establishment of the Colored World Series. The environments at these sporting events typified *collective cultural resistance* by creating a habitus where Black humanity, excellence, and communalism were uplifted despite the ubiquitousness of anti-Black racism in the broader society.

As a transnational kinship group, the Colored Hockey League of the Maritimes was created by descendants of the Maroons of Jamaica and Africans who were enslaved in the United States (Fosty & Fosty, 2008; Lawson, 1972). The creation of Africville in Nova Scotia and this all-Black hockey league in partnership with Black social institutions such as Black churches, schools, businesses, and social organizations was an illustration of a transnational space. Leaders such as Henry Sylvester Williams, James A. R. Kinney, James Robinson Johnston, and James Borden were Pan-Africanists who used sport as a means to foster the healthy development of the Black community in Canada. The pioneering league created the Colored Championship in 1898. Team names were grounded in culturally empowering memories and symbols such as the Mossbacks of Hammond Plains, whose team name was a reference to the moss growing on the trees that Africans who were escaping slavery would seek to verify that they were heading northward (Fosty & Fosty, 2008). In addition, players engaged in the creation of new moves such as the slap shot, originated by Eddie Martin, and the flopping save, pioneered by Henry "Braces" Franklyn (Fosty & Fosty, 2008). The hybrid resistance of the transnational kinship group exemplified Black resolve, persistence, and resistance in and through sport.

The Harlem Renaissance basketball team of the 1920s–1940s (also known as the Black Rens) constituted a localized diasporic transnational formation (Dahinden, 2010). The team founder, Bob Douglas, was a migrant from Saint Kitts (Rayl, 1996). The relationships between the Rens and the transnational African diasporic communities in Harlem during the early twentieth century resulted in the creation of one of the greatest basketball teams in the history of the sport. Douglas's economic activism as a team owner served as a precedent for future Black sport team owners (Cooper, 2021). The team won 87.1 percent of its games between 1923 and 1939 (including 88 consecutive wins during the 1932–1933 seasons) and defeated teams such as the all-White Original Celtics in 1935 and 1937, with the latter victory coming in the first interracial professional basketball game in U.S. history (Rayl, 2017). As pioneers, the Rens were the first all-Black team to become champions of the World Championship Tournament for Basketball (doing so in 1939) and to be members of the National Basketball League (NBL) (joining in 1948) (Rayl, 1996). The transnational formation of the Rens in Harlem, New York, during the height of the New Negro era, Harlem Renaissance, and Black nationalism movement facilitated the success and long-term impact of this Black sporting resistance organization. As an offspring of these broader social movements, the Rens' success personified *Black transnationalism sporting resistance*.

The Shadow Riders of the Subterranean Circuit were another localized diasporic transnational formation (Dahinden, 2010) that exhibited Black sporting resistance. The modern-day sport of rodeo was born as a by-product of the

Mexican pastime *charrería* and the cultural hybridity of African Americans, Mexicans, and Native Americans (Blanchard, 1995; Pearson, 2021). Consistent with other Black transnational sporting formations, Black cowboys and cowgirls activated their pioneering, economic, grassroots, mass mobilization, and economic activism by creating their own rodeo circuits, events, museums, and businesses such as the Boley Rodeo, Southwestern Colored Cowboys Association (SCCA), Okmulgee Colored Round-Up Club, Prairie View Trail Riders Association, Southwestern Colored Rodeo Association (SCRA), Latting Rodeo Company (LRC), Black Rodeo Association (BRA), American Black Cowboy Association (ABCA), Cowboys of Color Rodeo Series, Black World Championship Rodeo, Bill Pickett Invitational, Real Cowboys Association (RCA), C91 Ranch and Livestock Rodeo Productions, National Multicultural Western Heritage Museum and Hall of Fame (NMWHMHF), and, more recently, the U2 Rodeo Cowboys of Color Rodeo Series (Cartwright, 2021; Ford, 2020; Pearson, 2004, 2021). The historical and contemporary *charrería* events involve cultural celebrations and artifacts, which reflects what I refer to as *collective cultural resistance* in sport. In the face of racial discrimination, the transnationalization of Black rodeo illustrates the ingenuity of African Americans and their *inter-diasporic alliances*.

Distinct from African (Black) diasporic and Black transnationalism sporting resistance, *Black internationalist sporting resistance* centralizes political activism. Black internationalist sporting resistors align closely with anti-colonial, anti–White supremacist, anti-war/militarism, anti-sexist, and anti-imperialist entities to amplify the freedom struggle of the oppressed. Examples of Black internationalist sporting resistance include the anti-apartheid movement, anti-war movements, and the Black Lives Matter (BLM) movement in and through sport. Each of these movements involved political, symbolic, grassroots, mass mobilization, economic, agentic, legal, and military activism. Standout Black internationalist sporting resistors were Harry Edwards, Tommie Smith, John Carlos, Muhammad Ali, Eroseanna Robinson, Arthur Ashe, Gwen Berry, Raven Saunders, Osasu Obayiuwana, Lungi Ngidi, Naomi Osaka, Lewis Hamilton, and Nicky Winmar, to name a few. These courageous sportspersons sacrificed their safety and careers to champion Black internationalism in and through sport.

Future of Black Internationalist Sporting Resistance

In 2022, the exemplar African diasporic historian Robin D. G. Kelley celebrated the twentieth anniversary of his seminal book *Freedom Dreams: The Black Radical Imagination*. In this text, Kelley (2002) explored the historical developments of various Black social movements including Back to Africa, Black Nationalism, Pan-Africanism, Black Communism, Black Socialism, the Civil

Rights Movement, Black Power, Surrealism, and Radical Black Feminism. Throughout the book, he highlighted the significance of Black people's imagination of a better future and the various ways in which they pursued these visions over time. The power of dreaming while experiencing oppressive conditions cannot be understated, because racial oppression is designed to stagnate all hope for freedom, justice, and prosperity. More specifically, Kelley (2002) emphasized how "the most radical elements of the black freedom movement, the movements and activists that spoke of revolution, socialism, and self-determination... looked to the Third World for models of black liberation in the United States" (p. 62). In a similar vein, the recommendations outlined in the remainder of this chapter embody a commitment to Black internationalism in and through sport whereby "revolutionary transformation" is sought, and it is "inextricably linked to the struggles of colonized people around the world" (Kelley, 2002, p. 63).

Using previous Black resistance efforts within and beyond sport as a guide, I offer proposals for future Black sporting resistance. First, I recommend that Black political activists and social organizations and movements incorporate sporting resistance more in their counter-hegemonic efforts. Organizations such as the African Union, UNIA, NAACP, BLM, and others should work more closely with Black sportspersons to craft comprehensive resistance strategies to optimize collective impact. Similar to the Bandung Conference in 1955, the Pan-African conference in 1960, and Black Power Conferences in 1967 and 1969, future conferences, programs, and events can include sport on the agenda to explore ways to utilize these spaces and activities as a vital sources for advancing the struggle. The OPHR is one example of this effort, but learning from their missteps and expanding the breadth and reach of this type of organization is recommended. We have seen the power of the anti-apartheid boycott and more recently the power of the BLM movement and the recent international pressure levied to release Brittney Griner from Russian imprisonment (Brown, forthcoming). In February 2022, Griner was arrested for possessing less than a gram of cannabis oil at an airport customs checkpoint, which violated Russian drug laws. Her arrest came amid mounting tensions between Russia and Ukraine, the latter of which was being supported the U.S. government. Griner's supporters in the United States viewed her arrest and sentencing of nine years imprisonment as excessive and more about political posturing between the Russian and U.S. governments rather than an appropriate decision based on the alleged offense. Furthermore, Griner's intersectional identity as a Black lesbian woman was also cited as major reason why she was targeted in Russia, which has a history of anti–lesbian, gay, bisexual, transsexual, and queer (LGBTQ) laws and customs (Boykoff, 2022). We must harness this same energy for political prisoners via a wider range of Black internationalist efforts. Along with Pan-Africanism, I recommend promoting the adoption of scientific socialism/

African communalism as promulgated by former Ghanian revolutionary and president Kwame Nkrumah and revolutionary Black Power leader Kwame Ture (Carmichael, 1971; Nkrumah, 1973), but given the heterogeneity of political and economic philosophies among the African (Black) diaspora I do not suggest that a global movement start with this proposition. I recommend identifying areas of agreement first, such as anti-colonialism, anti–White supremacy, and human rights, or what Mwaniki (2017) refers to as "antiracist humanism," and then as progress is made more substantive discussions about revolutionary political and economic systems can ensue.

There is also a need for increased political education in Black sporting spaces from the youth to the adult level. This political education would achieve the vision postulated by Kelley (2002), who advocated for the "unleashing of the mind's most creative capacities, catalyzed by participation in struggles for change" (p. 191). Political education grounded in Black radicalism facilitates the deconstruction of colonial ways of thinking, being, and doing while simultaneously igniting the manifestation of liberatory and empowering minds, actions, institutions, and world-making.[1] In my previous work, I proposed a resistance socialization model that would involve educating all Black sportspersons about the history of Black sporting resistance (Cooper, 2021). The seminal works of C.L.R. James, Harry Edwards, Ben Carrington, Munene Franjo Mwaniki, and Janelle Joseph, among others, should be required reading whereby young Black sportspersons' critical and diasporic consciousness can be cultivated from an early age and nurtured throughout their development and into adulthood (Cooper, 2019, 2021). I reiterate this recommendation here with the added emphasis on African (Black) diasporic, transnational, and internationalist resistance. There are multiple ways this type of political education through sport can be delivered. One way to deliver this content is by embedding it in existing community service efforts that are common among interscholastic, intercollegiate, and even professional sports teams. Instead of only volunteering at a local charity, there can be organized political education sessions that highlight connections between resistance efforts in sport and broader social movements locally, nationally, and internationally. If organizations do not acquiesce to this idea, then a grassroots approach separate from the sport organizations, in partnership with non-sport activist groups, can be pursued.

Another way to infuse this political education is to change the names of youth and interscholastic program teams in predominantly Black communities to those of Black sport activists. Team names can reflect traditional African tribes, cultural values, memories, achievements, and any sources of African (Black) empowerment. After his ascension as president of Ghana and as a Pan-African revolutionary, Kwame Nkrumah facilitated the establishment of the Ghanaian Football Association and named the national team the Black Stars to symbolize Ghanaian nationalism and Pan-African pride (Dankwa, 2022).

In concert with Nkrumah, I surmise that the naming of teams and leagues in this manner could centralize African collectivism and communalism versus neoliberal individualism and exceptionalism. Relatedly, a number of Black high schools in the United States such as Paul Laurence Dunbar in Washington, D.C., and Booker T. Washington in Atlanta, Georgia, are named after famous Black luminaries.[2] I propose a similar approach across athletic programs; before, during, and after games there could be specific messages that share information about the courageous actions and impacts of these individuals and groups. Examples of team names could be the Black Internationalists, Black Nationalists, Pan-Africanists, Black Liberation Struggle, Black Radicalists, Black Transnationalists, Black Stars, Shadow Riders, North Stars, Paul Robeson Resistors, C.L.R. James Justice Advocates, Henry Sylvester Williams Freedom Fighters, Eroseanna Robinson Revolutionaries, and Muhammad Ali Activists, to name a few. Sporting resistance and activism typology concepts can be utilized for team names and events as well. Relatedly, I recommend these same athletic programs include sporting resistance education as an eligibility requirement, particularly for predominantly Black schools. In my previous work, I proposed the establishment of sporting resistance certificates that could be earned by completing a set of modules (Cooper, 2021). These certificates could be incorporated into the athletic eligibility requirements for participants.

Another space where political education and inter-diasporic alliances could be fostered is building on the existing historically Black colleges and universities (HBCUs) homecomings and annual classics in the United States. These events already celebrate Black excellence across a multitude of industries. Building on this practice, sport activism feats could be highlighted more throughout these events, and awards could even be provided to athletes and coaches who exhibit the spirit of sport activism through their actions. Along the same lines, I recommend HBCU athletic programs establish and/or strengthen international sporting ties with programs and institutions across the Caribbeans, Latin America, South America, Asia, Australia, and Africa, including those in socialist countries. These partnerships could involve collaborative tournaments and exhibitions that incorporate political education through sport. For example, imagine an HBCU–Pan-African sport classic hosted in Washington, D.C., with college teams from across the African diaspora and the continent. These events could include a tour of the National Museum of African American History and Culture as well as panels, engaging workshops, and case study projects for participants that center on learning and applying sporting resistance concepts. These events can be sponsored by Black internationalist groups and their allies. Along with schools, community centers, and athletic organizations, I recommend the dissemination of sporting resistance content via social media, flash cards, and other marketing materials to hubs in Black communities such as Black faith centers, barbershops, salons, and other social venues. Institutes and centers such as the Institute for Innovative Leadership in Sport at the University of Massachusetts Boston, and the San Jose State University Institute for the Study of Sport, Society, and Social Change, along with the Black Student Athlete Summit, can amplify their programming to include more current and former activist sportspersons and collaborate with African diasporic and continental institutions.

Collectively, this resistance socialization can emphasize the message of Professor Acklyn Lynch during his session at the 1969 Black Power Conference in Bermuda, in which he promoted anti-colonialism and African-centered education as keys to sustained empowerment for the race and continent (Swan, 2009). This resistance education must also include an intense focus on "global African liberation struggles against 'Western capitalist domination'" (Swan, 2009, p. 82). This political education can also resemble the trainings offered by the Black Panther Party for Self-Defense of the 1960s and 1970s (Horne, 1997). Lynch also advocated for changing the names of artifacts from those of colonialists to those of African leaders and agents of change (Swan, 2009). I echo this sentiment and suggest that in addition to sport team names, buildings and their related organizations adopt and promote Black sporting resistors such as Paul Robeson, Muhammad Ali, Eroseanna "Rose' Robinson, Sir Isaac Vivian Richards, Cathy Freeman, and Nicky Winmar. Elevating the contributions and political positions of these individuals will help bridge gaps between the past and present as well as between the global or international and the local.

The adoption of a common African language such as Swahili for team names, media coverage, and related communications could also signify a systemic shift toward decolonization and the redemption of African empowerment. Related to the naming of sport organizations, I recommend an international economic movement to secure land and resources to increase Pan-African/Black collective ownership of sport organizations, facilities, and related industries such as tourism, hospitality, and food. In this proposal, resources would be viewed within a scientific socialist paradigm and no land would be privatized.[3] These land procurement efforts would be established in concert with Indigenous activists' aims to reclaim their lands from settler colonizers. In other words, these land procurement efforts would not reproduce exploitative relationships and outcomes, but rather embody the spirit of African communalism. For example, in concert with Kelley (2002) I support the position that lands such as the modern United States should be returned to Native Americans and managed by a council elected among this group. African-governed lands on the continent and in places such as the Caribbean region would exist harmoniously and reciprocally with Indigenous populations, thus exhibiting inter-diasporic alliances that embody an internationalist spirit. The purpose of this economic approach would be grounded in scientific socialism and radical humanism rather than neoliberalism and racial capitalism.

There is also a need for creating Black sporting resistance scholarly and media networks internationally. These platforms could serve as conduits for mobilizing efforts, transmitting information, controlling and debunking mainstream narratives, and applying political and economic pressure on colonial institutions and leaders. Archives at the local, national, and international levels, research symposiums, curriculum creation, news publications, and a host of other empowerment efforts could be developed throughout these networks. A proposed title for one or more of these publications or events is *Ujima*,[4] which is Swahili for "collective work and responsibility." Research can be conducted and disseminated on African (Black) diasporic, transnational, and internationalist efforts of the past and present and can include proposals for the future. These Black sporting resistance institutes, centers, and universities could also partner with other Black political, social, cultural, educational, economic, legal, and religious institutions and groups as well as allies to advance the collective plight of oppressed people worldwide.

Consistent with Edwards's (2016a) five waves of Black athlete activism framework, I propose that the use of innovative technologies is essential for optimizing Black sporting resistance and the success of broader Black freedom struggles. The use of artificial intelligence, social media, and other emerging technological tools must be integrated with tactfulness and critical consciousness to achieve future success against sophisticated anti-Black forces. For Black sporting resistance to be optimized there is also a need for more Pan-African sport partnerships. Given the tremendous success of African American athletes, there should be a concerted effort for these individuals to form partnerships with African continental and diasporic groups to build brands, leagues, events, businesses, schools, hospitals, banks, political organizations, and related entities. The strengthening of these partnerships would optimize anti-colonial and anti-Black racist efforts. The combination of political education and Pan-African partnerships can lead to the optimization of various types of activism and resistance efforts (Cooper, 2021).

In concert with Horne (2005, 2014a, 2020b), I recommend Black sportspersons and organizations mobilize with national and international labor unions to situate the struggle as a human and labor rights issue. Along with the Black political organizations referenced earlier, working with labor unions could create strategic cross-cultural leverage points. Moreover, Horne (2005, 2014a, 2020b) and Burden-Stelly and Horne (2020) recommend that African Americans work more closely with global left, Pan-African, Tricontinental, Third World, and Afro-Asian solidarity groups. I support this recommendation and suggest that sportspersons and organizations be intentionally welcomed and supported as serious political actors. Related to political education among existing sport unions, I recommend all these groups incorporate the sport resistance and activism typology and its examples presented in this text and related works at their annual meetings. Given that these unions were established to champion labor rights, these spaces are primed to be sources of education and empowerment on more effective ways to leverage their influence in concert with counterparts in industries beyond sport and transnationally.

Similar to the successful efforts that resulted in the banning of apartheid-era South African teams from the 1968 Olympics, future global sporting resistance must involve optimal unification efforts among the African (Black) diaspora with Asian, Latino/a/x, Indigenous, and select groups of European allies. Historically, the previous Soviet Union has been a strong ally of African independence and empowerment efforts. A commitment to Black internationalism is essential for global liberation from colonial oppression. In summary, Burden-Stelly and Horne (2020) described Huey P. Newton's vision for the future:

> Revolutionary intercommunalism emplaced the struggles of African descendants amongst other "unemployables" of the world, including Third World and poor peoples. Together, the historical task of the dispossessed was to seize power, redistribute wealth, socialize labor, and realize communism as the highest stage of development. Likewise, these communities should determine their own destinies and develop cultures that were human-centered as opposed to dehumanizing and destructive.... Revolutionary intercommunalism, then, held intact the dynamic between the historical and material conditions of African descendants, international cooperation, intercontinental solidarity, and inter-ethnic affinity—a relationship that was key to the revolutionary transformation of humanity. (Newton, 1973, as cited in Burden-Stelly & Horne, 2020, p. 72)

In concert with this position, I recommend Black sporting resistance be an integral part of manifesting several of the key tenets of revolutionary intercommunalism, but with a focus on scientific socialism. Sport inherently is not exploitative, but it must be reimagined and enacted in spaces where neoliberalism and racial capitalism are not the foundational systems in which they exist. Lastly, since military activism is essential for any substantive revolution, future sport organizations can serve as mobilizing sources that serve both practical and psychological aims.[5] The end goal must be Black internationalism, Pan-Africanism, sustained cultural empowerment, global radical humanism, and a world free of oppression and environmental destruction, achieved through durable peace.[6] Sport has played and will continue to play an important role in remaking the world to be more equitable, safe, and environmentally sustainable for all people and future generations.

Summary

Within this chapter, I provide a summary of previous Black sporting resistance across international spaces in order to inform future steps for sustained freedom and empowerment. I highlighted examples of African (Black) diasporic, transnational, and internationalist sporting resistance across diverse geopolitical milieu during the nineteenth, twentieth, and twenty-first centuries. I then presented my recommendations for how sport can be utilized in the future to optimize the Black freedom struggles and broader internationalist efforts. It is my hope and inclination that sport plays a more prominent role in the strategies and activation of counter-hegemonic efforts within and across African (Black) human rights, labor rights, and social and environmental justice movements. Revolution and sustained cultural empowerment are not only possible, but they are inevitable so as long as the will of those who have been oppressed remains steadfast. The struggle continues, and victory will be won. TOGETHER WE RISE!!!

Acknowledgments

First and foremost, I thank, honor, and praise my Lord and Personal Savior Jesus Christ for His infinite love, grace, mercy, and blessings. Everything I am and everything I do is to glorify God, Jesus Christ, and the Holy Spirit that dwells within me. Thank you to my mother (Dr. Jewell E. Cooper), my father (Dr. Armah J. Cooper), and my brother (Adam Cooper) for their love and support from the day I was born. Thank you to my grandparents (Josephine Johnson Egerton Wilkins, Rev. Walter Eugene Egerton Sr., Izetta Roberts Cooper, and Dr. Henry Nehemiah Cooper) and extended family for your love and support. Thank you to the love of my life, my amazing wife and the mother of our children, Dr. Monique S. Cooper. You are a wonderful blessing to my life, and I love you more every day! To Nia, Natalie, Naomi, and Nehemiah, Daddy loves you more than words can express, and I am honored and blessed to be your Father and Dad. To Marcus and Nathaniel, I love you both and I am proud of the men you are becoming. Keep growing and trusting in the Lord. To all my Collective Uplift mentees, you already know. I love you all and I am proud of your growth and the impact we continue to have on the world. To all my mentors, friends, classmates, students, colleagues, and all my supporters, thank you for being an inspiration to me in multiple ways. To my ancestors and all Black freedom fighters, thank you for courage, sacrifice, and commitment. We will emerge victorious! TOGETHER WE RISE!!!

Notes

Introduction

1. The term *West Indian* refers to Anglophone Caribbean people (including those of Guyana) regardless of Asian, Indigenous, or African descent. For the purposes of this text, I focus on West Indian people of African descent who were formerly enslaved in the region on the coast of North and South America, including in Jamaica, Antigua, Turks and Caicos, the Virgin Islands, Trinidad and Tobago, Barbados, Saint Kitts and Nevis, the Bahamas, Puerto Rico, Cuba, the Dominican Republic, Haiti, the Cayman Islands, Anguilla, Montserrat, Dominica, Saint Lucia, Grenada, Aruba, Curaçao, Bonaire, Saint Vincent, and Margarita. After the 1960s these territories became known as the Caribbeans (as well as those from Guyana). Hence, throughout the book I will use the term *Black West Indian* to delineate those who lived in the West Indies and were viewed as African or Black versus those who were viewed as non-African or non-Black (e.g., Asian or White European). The terms *West Indies* and *West Indian* were misapplied to the people of this region because European colonizers thought they traveled to India instead what later became known as the Americas. During the anti-colonial era, several countries changed their names as part of an effort to reclaim their cultures and identities (e.g., British Guiana became Guyana) (see Davis, 2009; Marqusee, 1994/2016; and Wilde, 1994, for expansive discussions on this topic). The term *Caribbeans* is used to refer to these same lands post-decolonization (Williams & Bunkley-Williams, 2021).
2. James's home country of Trinidad did not secure independence until 1962.
3. A common feature of colonialism involves the land theft and exploitation of the Indigenous and enslaved populations from other regions of the world such as Africa. Within these arrangements, a numerical minority group of Europeans impose their domination through a range of oppressive tactics, not the least of which being violent terrorism (Fanon, 1952/2008, 1961/2004; Hartman, 1997; Rodney, 1972; Williams, 1974/1987).
4. From its inception to the present day, sport remains a highly gendered space whereby men and boys are prioritized over women and girls as well as

non-gender-binary-conforming groups (Coakley, 2017; Cooky, 2017; Maguire, 1999; Messner, 2010; Sage, 1998).

5 It is important to note that African, Asian, and Indigenous groups engaged in physical activities and versions of sport dating back to ancient times, but modern sports have been largely European projects either by invention or co-optation (Lindsay, 2019; Pearson, 2004, 2021; Wiggins, 2018; Yehudah, 2020).

6 Regarding the false notion of European colonization representing advancement in human civilizations, I support the following statement from renowned anti-colonial poet Aimé Césaire (1955/2001), one of the pioneers of the Négritude movement: "And I say that between colonization and civilization there is an infinite distance; that out of all the colonial expeditions that have been undertaken, out of all the colonial statutes that have been drawn up, out of all the memoranda that have been dispatched by all the ministries, there could not come a single human value" (p. 34). Stated differently, the imposition of global imperialism and colonialism that evolved into modern racial capitalism has undermined rather than reified the best traits of human existence. Greed, theft, injustice, and immoral violence (distinct from moral revolutionary violence and armed self-defense—see the work of Franz Fanon (1961/2004) and Robert F. Williams (2013) for a deeper discussion on these topics—are emblematic of imperialism, colonialism, and racial capitalism. In concert with Black internationalists, I champion anti–White supremacy, anti-capitalism, anti-militarism, anti-sexism, and anti-colonialism.

7 I delineate the working class from the enslaved class because although both represent labor groups, the former was provided with a resemblance of human treatment (i.e., wages) whereas the latter was subjected to dehumanizing conditions and codified as property (Fanon, 1952/2008; Rodney, 1972; Robinson, 1983/2000; Wallerstein, 1961/1967/2005; Williams, 1974/1987).

8 Throughout the book, I explore Black sportsmen and sportswomen albeit to varying degrees. Given the prevailing sexism in sport from the nineteenth to the twenty-first centuries, there were more documented instances of Black sportsmen being overrepresented in sporting spaces internationally (Coakley, 2017; Sage, 1998). Notwithstanding this, and consistent with my previous work (Cooper, 2021), I aim to be more gender inclusive in my scholarly analyses, particularly in chapters 2 and 4. I also acknowledge that I do not include analyses of Black sportspersons who identify as non-gender-binary-conforming or transgender. I believe the scholarly examination of their experiences and resistance efforts is important. However, a limitation of the sources I analyzed for this study is the lack of explicit description of Black sportspersons' gender identification beyond *man* and *woman*. Given the relatively new usage of these terms such as *non-gender-binary conforming* and *transgender* in the twenty-first-century nomenclature, I surmise this will be a growing area of inquiry for future research.

9 My colleagues and I use the term *in and through* sport to delineate resistance efforts that focus on changing conditions within sporting spaces (*in* sport) and those that use sport as a platform to redress broader cultural, social, political, legal, and/or economic changes in society (*through* sport) (Cooper, 2021; Cooper et al., 2019).

10 Consistent with my previous work, the term *Black sportspersons* is used to refer to athletes, coaches, media, spectators, and any individual or group connected to sport who uses this platform to champion social change (Cooper, 2021; Cooper et al., 2019; Cooper et al., 2020).

11 The term *Black* is used to refer to people of African descent who have been subjected to racialized oppression. Although race is a social construct rather than a biological fact, the historical and social reference of the term *Black* is more as a political point rather than a perpetuation of racist hierarchal conceptions.

12 An example of resistance through participation is capoeira Angola (Dossar, 1992). An example of resistance through achievements is Althea Gibson's pioneering success at the 1956 French Open and 1957 Wimbledon and U.S. Open events (Cooper, 2021). An example of resistance through resource mobilization is the creation of Black-owned and -managed sport organizations such as the Afro-Caribbean cricket teams and leagues in the Caribbeans, United States, Canada, and Europe (James, 1963; Joseph, 2017). An example of resistance through innovation is the creative sport strategies and maneuvers such as the creation of the hockey slap shot and flopping save by descendants of formerly enslaved Africans in Jamaica (later known as Maroons) and the United States (later known African Americans) in Africville, Nova Scotia (Fosty & Fosty, 2008). An example of resistance through dignified dispositions in the face of intense racism is African-descendant French footballers' (Kingsley Coman, Randal Kolo-Muani, and Aurelien Tchouameni) noble responses to the racist vitriol they received after missing penalty kicks at the 2022 Fédération Internationale de Football Association (FIFA) World Cup final versus Argentina (Graham, 2022).

13 It has been widely cited that Nicky Winmar embraced his darker skin as well as his Black racial identity as an Aboriginal person. The racial construction of Black has hybrid meanings across time, space, and context (Osmond & Klugman, 2022; Swan, 2022). For the purposes of this text, I will highlight select Aboriginal groups who have been categorized and subjugated as Black or Colored (see the work of Swan, 2022, for an extensive discussion on Black internationalism in the Pacific regions of the world). The use of *savage* to describe both Blacks and Indigenous populations underscores how both groups were subjected to racial oppression and how in many instances they were either grouped together or, through intercultural relationships, they created a hybridized identity—and in all instances they experienced racist treatment. Ogbar (2020) also highlighted how Black people in the United States and Canada includes those who have mixture of African heritage with additional heritage groups such as Indigenous, Latinx, Asian, and European.

14 Nichols's (1974/1987/2004) philosophical aspects of cultural difference provides a useful framework for understanding historical patterns across diverse groups of human beings.

15 The focus on the empowerment of Black humanity, cultural heritages, political ideologies, and spiritual beliefs in and through sport is central to my broader scholarly project, which includes varying explorations such as ecological analyses of Black male holistic athlete socialization experiences in the United States (2019), African American sportspersons' engagement in resistance and activism (2021), and the current examination of Black sportspersons' enactment of resistance and activism across international contexts.

16 Additional typology categories that have emerged that are not explored in this text include fashion and environmental activism in and through sport.

17 The term *black* is lowercase here to be consistent with the cited source (Mwaniki, 2017). Because race is a social construct, several authors use lowercase when including a racial term and uppercase when referring to a cultural or political group.

18 Ben Carrington, Janelle Joseph, Munene Franjo Mwaniki, and C.L.R. James are not the only Black international and critical sport scholars; I cite numerous others throughout this book. However, they are singled out for their exemplary contributions focused on the impact of sport on the African diaspora. In my opinion, their texts are seminal in the bourgeoning subfield of African diasporic sport studies.

19 I also explore Muhammad Ali's sporting resistance in Asian countries such as the Philippines, Indonesia, and Malaysia as well as African countries such as Zaire (now known as the Democratic Republic of Congo) (Ali & Durham, 1975; Marqusee, 2017).

20 Examples of my efforts to avoid ethnic essentialism are my distinct analysis of Muhammad Ali's decision to decline to enlist in the U.S. Army for the Vietnam War in the late 1960s and his scheduling of a boxing match in Zaire (now the Democratic Republic of Congo) during the mid-1970s, in contrast to examinations of the West Indian cricketers competing against colonial nations such as England and Australia during the 1980s (Ali & Durham, 1975; Marqusee, 1994/2016).

21 It is noted that Africans faced adversaries aside from Europeans such as Arabs. However, given the extent of the transatlantic atrocity, the colonization of Africa post–Berlin Conference of 1884, and the impact on the current state of African people globally in the twenty-first century, Europeans are centralized as the primary antagonist to African holistic development (Rodney, 1972; Williams, 1974/1987). Jacqueline Battalora's (2021) book *Birth of a White Nation: The Invention of White People and Its Relevance Today* is a useful resource for understanding the social construction and implications of Whiteness.

22 Aboriginals, Indigenous people, and Asians were also targeted for violence and resource extraction during various points between the fifteenth and twentieth centuries (Dunbar-Ortiz, 2014; Horne, 2020a, 2020b). Resource extraction included the enslavement and labor exploitation of human beings, the taking of land resources via genocide and theft, and intellectual and cultural theft (Carruthers, 1999; Rodney, 1972; Williams, 1974/1987). European imperialism sought to dominate the world, hence the prevalence of English-, Spanish-, French-, and Portuguese-speaking countries throughout the Americas, Africa, and various regions throughout the globe. Indigenous people's land was seized through genocide in what is now known as North America (Dunbar-Ortiz, 2014).

23 Scholars have also noted how modern capitalism was built off the international enslavement system (Rodney, 1972; Wallerstein, 1961/1967/2005; Williams, 1974/1987). Industries such as insurance, the stock market, the entertainment industry, and banking were all significantly financed by this heinous system.

24 Primarily Black men and adolescents are the economic laborers for the athletic industrial complex (AIC) (Hawkins, 2010; Smith, 2009). However, Black women and girls are also exploited through national and international sporting systems (Davis, 2016; Brown, forthcoming).

25 *Outlayers* refers to Africans who were formerly enslaved in the United States in the eighteenth and nineteenth centuries and escaped from slavery and created their own territories with Indigenous groups (Ogbar, 2020). *Maroons* refers to people of African descent who were formerly enslaved in the Americas and Caribbeans and who migrated to other parts of these areas during the antebellum era to establish their own settlements. The most well-known Maroons of the

Caribbean region were from Jamaica (Ogbar, 2020). There were also Maroons across Mexico (*palenques*), Brazil (referred to as *quilombos*), Venezuela, Colombia, Cuba, Guiana, and throughout North America (e.g., the Carolinas, Georgia, Florida, and Virginia) (Robinson, 1983/2000). *Cimarrons* is a Spanish term used to describe African people who were formerly enslaved who fought European colonizers and subsequently established their own settlements in partnership with Indigenous groups throughout the Americas and Caribbeans (Ogbar, 2020; Robinson, 1983/2000). The Geechies are African people who were formerly enslaved in the present-day Carolinas and Georgia region of the United States and created settlements and a hybridized/creolized African culture amid the harsh antebellum conditions (Ogbar, 2020).

26 Horne (2018a, 2020a) highlighted in his historical research how at different times the Spanish, French, and British served as context-specific allies for African people in the Americas and Caribbean region due to intra-European conflicts and interest convergence with the latter group.

27 For an expansive analysis on militant strategies exhibited by African diasporic groups in the Western Hemisphere, I recommend the works of C.L.R. James (2012), Cedric Robinson (1983/2000), and the volumes of publications by Gerald Horne (2015, 2018a, 2020a) for a more detailed discussion on this phenomenon.

28 Emigrationism was supported by many Europeans as well because the notion of creating separate societies was preferred by them rather than creating a society where Africans were equal citizens (Ogbar, 2020). An example of this intersecting interest was the creation of the American Colonization Society (ACS) and the subsequent founding of the country of Liberia (Beyan, 1989). It is worth noting that emigrationism was not a consensus among all Africans and in the instances where these efforts were initiated they were also accompanied by inter- and intragroup tensions (see Beyan, 1989, for a discussion of the conflict with the founding and subsequent [under]development of Liberia).

Martin R. Delany is prominent Black nationalist of the nineteenth century who promoted the establishment of a Black nation in Africa where Africans who were formerly enslaved in the Americas could seek refuge (Ogbar, 2020). In his book *The Condition, Elevation, Emigration, and Destiny of Colored People of the United States, Politically Considered*, published in 1852, Delany advocated for the establishment of a free African nation that was not associated with the ACS. In 1859, he visited an African region, now known as Nigeria, to create a treaty between the Native Africans and the Africans seeking to leave the Americas (Ogbar, 2020).

29 Kwame Ture is formerly known as Stokely Carmichael. He was a member of the Student Nonviolent Coordinating Committee (SNCC), one of the pioneers of the Black Panther Party in Lowndes County, Alabama, and a renowned Black Power and Pan-Africanist leader (Carmichael, 1971).

30 Agozino (2014) presented an insightful argument about how Marx referenced the enslavement of Africans and their subsequent revolutionary efforts as foundational to his seminal critiques of capitalism. Notwithstanding these references, it is widely understood that the central unit of analysis in Marx's work was working-class people in industrial European societies, with implications for similar social class groups worldwide. Thus, I agree that Marx drew inspiration from African contributions, namely their liberation efforts to inform his political economy analysis for oppressed working-class people, but along with Robinson (1983/2000) and Carmichael (1971) my primary assertion is African revolutionary efforts must be grounded in their

unique experiences throughout human history (particularly prior to colonization, as outlined in Nkrumah's [1970] Consciencism concept) and incorporate their specific cultural orientations (e.g.,, the role of spirituality and relationship to the environment). Another glaring omission from Marx's (1867/1887) analysis is the lack of attribution of socialist and communist foundations to ancient African communal systems. Beyond focusing on the labor exploitation and revolution, it is important to centralize how Africans for generations engaged (and continue to engage) in communal practices that foster harmonious cross-cultural relations as well as respect for the environment (Rodney, 1974; Williams,1974/1987). In other words, I do not view scientific socialism and Black radicalism as mutually exclusive from Marxism and Leninism, but I also do not attribute their origins to these thinkers and philosophies. Rather, I attribute the origins of scientific socialism and Black radicalism to ancient African communalism; hence I identify as a Pan-Africanist guided by a scientific socialist ethos (Carmichael, 1971).

31 The term *Negro* refers to African people who were formerly enslaved in the Americas throughout the eighteenth and nineteenth centuries. It was used as a synonym for terms such as *Black* and *Colored* during the late nineteenth and early twentieth centuries. It is important to acknowledge that the term *Negro* has been and remains viewed as a pejorative by certain groups within and beyond the African diaspora. As an African American, I do not view the term *Negro* in a pejorative manner but rather interpret it as racial and ethnic descriptor for African people in the United States during the early to mid-nineteenth century. In my previous work, I highlighted how the New Negro movement (Early, 2008) was largely viewed as a progressive period that embraced the resolve and persistence of the group that would later be labeled as African Americans (Cooper, 2021).

32 Swan (2009) noted how a year later, in 1970, the Congress of African People (CAP) conference was held in Atlanta, Georgia. This gathering was intended to be the second annual Black Power Conference (BPC), but due to pressures from colonizing forces the event not only had to be relocated from Barbados, but the name of the conference had to change as well to avoid including the words *Black Power*.

33 The BPC in 1969 in Bermuda was sponsored by the Progressive Labour Party (PLP) Youth Wing (Swan, 2009). The international support for BPC included telegrams from the Palestinian Liberation Organization (PLO), the Japanese Red Army, Guyana's People's Progressive Party (PPP), the Black Panther Party, the South African National Liberation Front, and the Cuban Revolutionary Committee, among other revolutionary groups. This connection underscores how race-based efforts within the African diaspora have consistently been intersectional whereby issues of class, gender, and other social categories and conditions have been integral parts of political resolutions. For example, there was a session on Black women led by Queen Mother Moore (founder and president of the Universal Association of Ethiopian Women, Inc.) and Thelma Morgan of Bermuda. Additional issues discussed at the conference included technology, education, communications, economics, religion, history, and politics (Swan, 2009).

34 Organizations such as the Chicano Brown Berets, Puerto Rican Young Lord Party, Asian American Hardcore, Yellow Brotherhood, American Indian Movement, Polynesian Panther Party, the Sephardic Black Panthers in Israel, and Dalit Black Panthers in India were all inspired by the Black Panther Party for Self-Defense, which underscored the international and inter-cultural resonance of the freedom struggle (Newton, 1973; Ogbar, 2020).

Chapter 1   Black Sporting Resistance

1. Diaspora and internationalism often involved political aims such as cultural preservation in the face of hegemonic conditions, whereas transnationalism does not inherently include political aims and can involve activities such as sharing goods and/or services for economic livelihood and/or personal enjoyment.
2. See Horne (2014, 2015, 2018a, 2020b) for an expansive analysis of international and intercultural political alliances.
3. See Safran (1991), Cohen (1997), and Bruneau (2010) for extensive discussions of different types of diaspora typologies.
4. Gilroy (1993) refers to this condition as the state of being an infrahuman, which refers to the ontology of a species who is denied human rights yet viewed as possessing partial humanity.
5. Arabs are another notable group that enslaved Africans prior to the nineteenth century (Williams, 1974/1987).
6. I do not subscribe to the term *White supremacy*, as noted in my previous work (Cooper, 2019). My rationale then and now is that supremacy is not an accurate description of the actions or state of being of the groups of people who identify themselves as White. More accurate descriptions would be evildoers, oppressors, colonizers, and violators of human rights.
7. Related terms referenced here include Afro-, African American, West Indian, Caribbean, Geechee (also known as Gullah), Maroon, Moor, Negro, and so forth. *Afro* is an abbreviation to refer to people of African descent who explicitly embody African cultural features. African American refers to descendants of African people who were formerly enslaved in the United States from the late 1500s through the late 1800s (Hine et al., 2006). This term was introduced into mainstream nomenclature in the late twentieth century. *African American* is another term to refer to the group that was formerly referred to as *Negro* in the late nineteenth and early twentieth centuries in the United States. See the notes in the introduction for definitions of West Indian, Caribbean, Maroon, and Negro. Moor refers to an eighth-century term that referred to African people who practiced Islam in the northern part of the continent (Ogbar, 2020). The term later was applied to any Arab or person with dark brown skin. Geechee or Gullah refers to African people who were formerly enslaved in the modern-day regions of South Carolina, North Carolina, Georgia, and Florida in the United States and who established their own territories and cultural system beginning in the early sixteenth century (Ogbar, 2020). Although distinguished by geography, all aforementioned groups share a common experience with racialized oppression and engaged in resistance via the preservation and adaptation of ancient African cultural practices.
8. Examples of historically situated events include colonization and the transatlantic enslavement atrocity. Sociological conditions include the perpetual transnational anti-Black racist systems, policies, practices, and outcomes in neocolonial contexts.
9. Scholars largely trace African American lineage to modern-day Angola, Nigeria, Ghana, Liberia, Sierra Leone, Mali, Chad, and Niger (Franklin, 1947/1974; Horne, 2018a, 2020b; Rodney, 1972; Williams, 1974/1987).
10. The use of Black sporting resistance is akin to Gilroy's (1993) application of Black Atlantic creativity when examining the influence and evolution of music and artistic expression.
11. Bruneau (2010) also refers to this process as the condensation of social networks.

12 Establishment of networks in settled lands is also referred to as grassroots or cross-border social formation (Bruneau, 2010; Dahinden, 2010; Faist, 2010).
13 See Horne (1985) for an in-depth analysis of the different eras of the NAACP's political philosophies throughout the twentieth century.
14 See Horne (2019) for an expansive analysis of the pre- and post-1994 ANC political orientation and actions.
15 European countries who met at the Berlin Conference in 1884 are examples of imperialism in action (Burden-Stelly & Horne, 2020).
16 Robinson (1983/2000) used the term *racial capitalism* to emphasize the inherent racial oppression and stratification embedded in modern capitalism.
17 Although a key tenet of Black internationalism, this focal area is not explored in great depth within the current book. The lack of in-depth focus on anti-sexism is not intended to communicate a lack of importance, but rather to indicate that the scope of the examples in the book connected more with the other five elements of Black internationalism. I acknowledge this limitation and encourage readers to review my previous work to see how anti-sexism was highlighted in African American sporting resistance (Cooper, 2021).
18 History has revealed there were notable limitations to the different ideologies, political perspectives, and social movements. In an analysis of diverse political philosophies among African Americans, Birt (1997) delineated race-centric versus classic liberal approaches.
19 See the post-activism life experiences of Paul Robeson, Muhammad Ali, Tommie Smith, John Carlos, Wilma Rudolph, Craig Hodges, and Mahmoud Abdul-Rauf as examples of the risk and consequences associated with engaging in high-stakes activism.
20 I intentionally insert the gender demarcation term here to call attention to the sexism embedded in common sport nomenclature. Disrupting the male-centric nature of sport is consistent with my anti-sexist and post-structuralist orientation.
21 Resistor refers to any person that engages in resistance/counter-hegemonic actions. All activists are resistors, but all resistors are not activists.
22 It is worth noting reparations have not been secured for all Africans whose lineages were enslaved and exploited through the transatlantic atrocity. However, notable gains have been made in settler colonial states such as the United States and in newly independent African nations (James, 2012).
23 An example of a non-sporting political system or governing body is the International Criminal Court (ICC). An example of sport political system or governing body is the International Olympic Committee (IOC).
24 One notable exception is Horne's (2020a) book on boxing, racism, and racketeering in the United States, *The Bittersweet Science: Racism, Racketeering, and the Political Economy of Boxing*.

Chapter 2   A Collective Consciousness

1 Kiswahili is an example of a language that as served as a cultural symbol. Hip-hop, reggae, calypso, jazz, gospel, and rhythm and blues (R&B) music are examples of African (Black) cultural symbols. The Pan-Africanism red, green, and black flag is an example of an African cultural symbol. Yoruba is an example of an African spiritual and religious system that has served as cultural symbol. Black Nationalism is an example of a political ideology that has served as a cultural symbol.

Ethiopia and Egypt are examples of real and imagined homelands for African people, constituting an example of a cultural symbol.
2. The term often is used here to delineate instances where Black icons have been used by the colonial structure to create an illusion of inclusion or serve as an opiate for the masses while status quo racial and class inequality is maintained. See Andrews (2001) and Leonard and King (2012) for a more in-depth analysis of this phenomenon.
3. Gilroy (1993) defined *infrahuman* as being in an ontological state of partial humanity, which involves being denied human rights.
4. The term *continent* is used here to delineate African independence efforts in other parts of the world including the Caribbean region, Americas, and Pacific region (James, 2012; Swan, 2009).
5. Negroes [*sic*] was another common label for people of African descent in the colonized settings in the Americas (Horne, 2014b).
6. Later in the cases of fighters such as Max Schmeling, racists such as Adolf Hitler would use sports as sites where Aryan superiority (different from all White or European people) would be proven (Erenberg, 2006).
7. See Mao Tse-tung (1965/1967/2016) for an extensive analysis on universality and particularity of contradictions and their connections to anti-capitalism and communist struggles.
8. See the work of Swan (2020) and Horne (2018b) for an in-depth analysis of international Black power alliances particularly throughout the Pacific regions.
9. As noted earlier, the terms *Negro*, *Colored*, or *Black* were more common during the early twentieth century, but I use the modern-day term *African American* to delineate African diasporic people who have a lineage in the United States dating back to the transatlantic atrocity or the *maafa* in contrast to their diasporic and continental counterparts whose lineage is connected to other parts of the globe (Cooper, 2021).
10. During his exile in Mexico, it is important to note that Jack Johnson was more vocally critical of the U.S government and promoted African American migration to Mexico to align with Mexican revolutionaries (Horne, 2005). These actions later in his career reflect agentic and political activism.
11. Jack Johnson's agentic resistance involved personal motivations such as his desire to be the best fighter in the world, his individual disposition involving his contempt for mainstream White social norms and laws, and his athletic accomplishments such as his victories over White opponents (Cooper, 2021). Each of these actions served as threats to the White social order.
12. Jack Johnson was born and grew up in Galveston, Texas (Johnson, 1927). According to Horne (2022), Texas is the vanguard of fascism in the United States and internationally. Thus, Johnson's emergence in Texas further elucidates the power of his ascension and global impact on people across the African diaspora.
13. Later these conflictive forces were described as Allies (United States, Great Britain, and Soviet Union) versus Axis (Germany, Italy, and Japan) powers. However, this framing includes nationalistic and political biases; see the extensive work of Gerald Horne for an expansive analysis on these topics (Horne, 2005, 2014a, 2015, 2018b, 2019, 2020a, 2020b).
14. In addition to Owens, other notable African American Olympians included Archie Williams, Mack Robinson, Fritz Pollard Jr., Ralph Metcalfe, Cornelius Johnson, and Dave Albritton (Erenberg, 2006).

15 An example of a conflicting nationalism movements is that of Black Nationalism in the United States versus White mainstream nationalism. An example of conflicting political ideologies and international movements is that of Pan-Africanism movements compared to anti-fascist movements in European countries.

16 The anti-German sentiments were evident in the media coverage of the event. Dawson (1938) wrote the following description in his *New York Times* article after the fight: "On the third knockdown Schmeling's trainer and closest friend, Max Machon, hurled a towel into the ring, European fashion, admitting defeat for his man.... The German was thoroughly 'out.' It was as if he had been poleaxed. His brain was awhirl, his body, his head, his jaws ached and pained, his senses were numbed from that furious, paralyzing punching he had taken even in the short space of time the battle consumed ... the punches which dazed him were thundering blows to the head, jaw and body, in bewildering succession, blows of the old Alabama Assassin reincarnate last night for a special occasion" (p. 1).

17 See Cooper (2019) for an expansive discussion of the ecological system that influences Black athletic experiences (sub-, chrono-, macro-, exo-, meso-, and micro-).

18 Heywood and Dworkin (2003) introduced the concept of stealth feminism, and my reference here is connected to their concept. They described how many female athletes did not overtly identify as feminists and thus they embodied what the authors coined as *stealth feminism*. Heywood and Dworkin (2003) further explained the symbolic role of female athletes: "Female athleticism gives us one story of bodies that fought back" (p. 54). Stealth feminism is similar to the concept of agentic resistance (Cooper, 2021) whereby individuals and groups do not have to explicitly identify with activist causes in order to advance their agendas. Moreover, the authors argued that female athletes of the late twentieth century needed the aid of activists and advocates of feminist movements to create conditions for them to have access to quality sport opportunities (Heywood & Dworkin, 2003). However, the authors surmised that the second and third waves of feminism needed female athletes to assist with heightening the visibility of their causes via the athletes' cultural iconic status.

19 The accuracy of the story of Muhammad Ali throwing his Olympic medal into the Ohio River has been debated for years. Whether the story is true or not, the fact that Ali expressed that an Olympic medal means less to him than his love for Black people is the essence of Black sporting resistance from an axiological standpoint and thus why this story is referenced in this section.

20 A few examples of successful African independence efforts during this era include the Gold Coast becoming Ghana, Belgian Congo becoming Zaire, Bechuanaland becoming Botswana, Northern Rhodesia (later Rhodesia) becoming Zimbabwe, and South-West Africa becoming Namibia (Farred, 1995).

21 Additional African and Asian countries that invited Ali to visit were Nigeria, Saudi Arabia, Libya, Mali, Kuwait, Somali, Uganda, Pakistan, Indonesia, Sudan, and Morocco (Ali & Durham, 1975; Marqusee, 2017). Farred (1995) emphasized how Ali's fight in Zaire publicized the newly liberated country to the world as a free African nation no longer under European colonial rule. Zaire is now known as the Democratic Republic of Congo.

22 Prior to then–Cassius Clay winning his 1960 Olympic gold medal in Rome, he was cited as being supportive of the American dream and believed African

Americans could advance economically and socially as long as they worked hard and did not overemphasize racial differences (Ali & Durham, 1975). This view was opposite from his post–Nation of Islam (NOI) conversion when his politics were very critical of the White racist social order of the United States and more explicitly pro–Black power domestically and internationally.

23 In his article, Saeed (2002) mentioned how the term "black" in Scotland was used to refer to all ethnic minorities. The malleability of the term to refer to multiple ethnic groups underscores the diasporic appeal of the concept and its various political applications under the banner of anti-colonialism.

24 Muhammad translates to "worthy of all praises" and Ali translates to "the most high" (Saeed, 2002).

25 As a Christian, I denounce the hypocritical and anti-Christ behaviors of colonizers who have misused the Bible to support their inhumane endeavors. Thus, I refer to these groups as *masquerading Christians* to delineate them from those who are true believers and followers of Jesus Christ.

26 It is important to note that masquerading Muslims have also engaged in imperial efforts and human rights violations throughout history as well; see Horne (2014a) for a more expansive discussion on the religious conflict throughout the sixteenth to eighteenth centuries.

27 A basic premise of Gerald Horne's (2014a, 2018a, 2020b) scholarship includes the emphasis on religious conflicts and oppression preceding colonial-imposed racial domination. Thus, it is important to understand the malleability of certain social categories that have been used as proxies for imperial and colonial aims.

28 During the late 1960s, the Nation of Islam (NOI) was labeled as a terrorist organization by the U.S. government (Ali & Durham, 1975).

29 Scholars have noted how Islam is closely associated with British South Asians and British Pakistanis (Marqusee, 1995; Saeed, 2002).

30 It is worth noting that the multiple sects of Islam, as with all world religions, have at times conflicted with one another across time, space, and context (Ali & Durham, 1975).

31 The term *Ummah* refers to the global Islamic community (Ali & Durham, 1975; Saeed, 2002).

32 Among ancient African tribes, the tribal leaders who oversaw the sport and physical activities were members of the same tribal group as the participants (Yehudah, 2020).

33 da Silva (2014) also pointed out how Pelé's political views were highly contested by activists in the 1970s in Brazil. Thus, there was not a consensus among Black social movement participants regarding his symbolic status, but he was internationally heralded as a champion for Black people and working-class people based on his humble beginnings and subsequent athletic success.

34 The word *many* is intentionally used here to indicate that not all African (Black) diasporic athletes engage in borderline activist actions. As noted earlier in the chapter, Muhammad Ali is a notable African (Black) diasporic athlete who engaged in hybrid activism. Notwithstanding this example, because of the significant sacrifices that come with being a sport activist, many African (Black) diasporic athletes embody stealth racial empowerment as their preferred mode of resistance. This approach yields benefits and detriments due to its ambiguous posture.

35 I acknowledge the presence and harmful impacts of African fútbol trafficking (Esson, 2015). However, my focus here is on the voluntarily migration of African

footballers for economic, visibility, and athletic competitive purposes while retaining a strong sense of connection to and reciprocal relationship with their homelands.
36 If European superiority was an innate fact, then there would be no need or desire to recruit African players.
37 Supreme Council of Sport in Africa met in Brazzaville, Congo, in 1968 prior to the Mexico City Olympics to discuss the Organization of African Unity (OAU) plans to boycott the international event in support of the anti-apartheid movement (Bass, 2002).
38 The OAU remained in existence until 1993 (Harris, 1994).
39 Although the World Cup in South Africa was historic, it also carried problematic aspects including the fact that it was associated with the corrupt FIFA organization and there were widespread criticisms of displacement, discrimination, exploitation, and human rights abuses associated with hosting this mega-event (Boykoff, 2016).
40 Aula (2017) traces the origin of capoeira to the Bantu people of Luanda, Angola.
41 Dossar (1992) also noted how capoeira has spiritual connections to the Kongo culture and cosmology and Bakongo worldview.
42 See Dettman (2013) for a detailed overview of the Angolan combat game called engolo.
43 In addition to Vincente Ferreira Pastinha, Jośe Tadeu Carneiro Cardoso was another popular *Mestre* (*Master*) of capoeira Angola in the mid-twentieth century in Bahia and Rio de Janeiro (Assuncao, 2005).
44 Key terms associated with capoeira include: a) *Mestre* (Master), b) Angloeiros and Regionalistas (adepts who wear white pants; only Angloeiros shoes to honor the outdoor roots of the game, whereas Regionalistas are barefoot to honor the game's slave roots), c) roda (dance circle), d) berimbau (musical bow that directs the music and movements of the performance), e) atabaque (wooden drum with metal rings and wooden wedges), f) pandeiro (tambourine made of goatskin, wood, and metal jingles, g) agogô (two metal bells played with the striking of wood), h) reco-reco (a bamboo wood), i) axé (the invisible energy of the roda), j) batizado (baptism), k) bateria (instruments used to distract onlookers), l) dobrão (metal instrument used to honor orixas), m) bananeira (a position involving a person standing on their hands with their feet in the air—translates to "banana tree"), n) antiphony (call-and-response), o) floreio (acrobatic flourishes), p) n'golo (zebra dance), q) ladainha (prayer or invocation for supplication), r) golpes (strikes), s) counter glopes (counterstrikes), t) saidas (evasive movements), u) chamada (a call represented through upright arms extended to form a cross), v) volto da mundo (walk counterclockwise around the circle) (Assunção, 2005; Dossar, 1992; Joseph, 2012b; Lindsay, 2019).
45 Delamont and colleagues (2017) highlighted how Angola groups do not have strict uniforms or uphold hierarchy meanings for belts whereas the contemporary groups tend to engage in these practices—other differences include the use of speed and power with kicks and the use of moves in formal settings such as trainings or classes or informal settings such as public venues.

Chapter 3 They Lived on Their Own Terms

1 I recognize the limitation of this continental-centric approach, but I purport that it is a benefit for diasporic scholars to embrace their positionality in terms of

ethnicity, familiarity based on lived experiences, and, in my case, scholarly expertise. This approach is a part of a genealogy of African diasporic scholars who use a North American focus to engage in international analyses, such as W.E.B. Du Bois, Paul Robeson, Gerald Horne, Cedric Robinson, and Robin D. G. Kelley.

2 *Transnational syncretism* refers to cross-border reciprocal relationships and cultural distinctiveness (Faist, 2010).

3 European influence on West Indian society extended to areas such as education, politics, economy, religion, law, music, art, and sport (James, 1963).

4 It is beyond the scope of this text to engage in a more in-depth philosophical debate about the racist underpinnings of European-imposed epistemological, axiological, and ontological claims that have pervaded aspects of religion, education, and culture more broadly. However, suffice it to say I self-identify as Pan-Africanist who supports scientific socialism and I am a person who embodies the Black radical tradition. In concert with Horne (2014a), I argue that the use of terms such as *the Enlightenment period* and *Modernity* are highly problematic because they presuppose European advancement constitutes progress for all humanity and dismisses centuries of human advancements for and by African and Indigenous populations. In addition, the supposed Enlightenment and Modernity eras ignores the inhumane systems of oppression imposed upon African, Indigenous, and Asian people worldwide that occurred prior to and during these periods.

5 Several Afrocentric intellectuals have posited that fear of White European genetic annihilation is a primary reason for the demonic imposition of European colonialism and imperialism (Cress-Welsing, 1991; Peck, 2021). This point is important because the violations of human rights are often attributed to economic motives, but the acknowledgement of deeper psychological and physiological responses to the possibility of one's own extinction provides a more comprehensive understanding of historic and contemporary intercultural relations.

6 Lawrence George "Yagga" Rowe is another prominent Jamaican cricketer of the twentieth century, but due to his role in one of the rebel tours in South Africa during the apartheid era his reputation has been tarnished (Davis, 2009).

7 In a system of oppression, the notion of true agency is always compromised to a certain extent.

8 I would argue that even prior to the twentieth and twenty-first centuries that any African (Black) participation in sports governed by Europeans reflects a compromised position whereby their talents and performances are more likely to be exploited for purposes that benefit groups outside of their native communities.

9 The extent to which African (Black) sport participation benefits and challenges racial capitalism varies by context.

10 I refer to the public displays of excellence as external realities that led to reorientations of psychological mental models, which include internal beliefs and attitudes.

11 I acknowledge that cognitive dissonance first involves a level of denial of new information or ideas and is then followed by resentment or backlash before the possibility of accepting new ways of thinking, being, and doing.

12 British Guiana became known as Guyana after achieving independence in 1966.

13 Scholars have noted how many African diasporic intellectuals and artists experience a political transformation after traveling to Europe and/or Africa, including W.E.B. Du Bois, Paul Robeson, Malcolm X, C.L.R. James, and James Baldwin (Horne, 1985, 1997, 2016).

14. See table 4.1 on page 90 of Swan (2009) for a detailed overview of these Black power organizations.
15. *Cricket and I* is a book on the life of Learie Constantine (James, 1937).
16. *Modern Politics* is a book on the importance of anti-colonial political resistance (James, 2013).
17. The term *displaced homeland* is used to emphasize that Africans in the United States were largely displaced from their African homelands during the *maafa* or transatlantic atrocity (Asante, 2003; Rodney, 1972; Williams, 1974/1987). This is not to ignore the fact that there were Indigenous Africans in the Americas prior to colonization, but even these Africans were largely displaced once European colonizers arrived and pursued genocide, land theft, and enslavement.
18. See Horne (2018a, 2020a, 2020b) for an expansive discussion about the distinct mistreatment of African (previously referred to as Colored or Negro) Americans compared to their diasporic comrades outside of the United States. According to Horne (2018a, 2020b, 2020b) this intense bigotry toward African Americans in rooted in the fact that they were once viewed as property that economically sustained the creation of White capitalist groups and, throughout their existence under enslavement conditions, they forged alliances with adversaries of the United States to spite the latter group. Since the White Americans won the counterrevolution of 1776, they have intergenerationally sought to punish African Americans for their lack of loyalty to the settler colonial project (Horne, 2018a, 2020a, 2020b).
19. Some scholars have referred the integrationist hope of excelling in sport leading to full citizenship rights and better treatment of Black people as the myth of the Black athlete (Blackman, 2012, 2021; Edwards, 1969). This approach adopts a critical perspective on the collective outcomes (and limited benefits) for Black people as a group despite the success of Black athletes across multiple sports.
20. Lomax (2014) highlighted how not all Negro League owners were in agreement with the integrationist aim of leaders such as Rube Foster. In fact, it was this issue, among other financial allocation disputes, that led to the dissolution of expansive success for these leagues (Lomax, 2003, 2014).
21. The Double V campaign communicated victory abroad against fascism and victory at home against racism (Cooper, 2021).
22. I use the term *universal justice* to refer to racial, economic, environmental, religious, sociocultural, political, gender, and ability justice across the world.
23. José "The Black Diamond" Méndez was born in Cardenas, Cuba (NBHF, 2022).
24. It has been documented that numerous Negro League owners were connected to the numbers-running business and other forms of illegal gambling (Lomax, 2003, 2014). I do not condemn these individuals and actions wholesale because in a system of oppression groups are forced to pursue economic sustainability in any way possible, whereas if society was governed in a more equitable manner these actions would be less likely to take place.
25. Both groups were excluded from mainstream opportunities, including baseball, by American and Spanish colonizers during the later 1800s (Burgos, 2011).
26. Hybrid resistance efforts of African American and Afro-Latino baseball players included grassroots, mass mobilization, economic, agency, media, and pioneering activism.
27. The abolition and decolonial independence efforts are examples of societal resistance; the creation of separate teams, leagues, and championships is an example of sport-based resistance.

28. The Underground Railroad is one example of a route utilized by African Americans seeking freedom. The First Maroon War of 1730, Counterrevolution of 1776, Second Maroon War of 1795, and the War of 1812 are the revolutionary conditions mentioned here (Horne, 2020a).
29. Henry Sylvester Williams was the lead organizer of the 1900 Pan-African conference in London (Fosty & Fosty, 2008; Ogbar, 2020).
30. The term *homesite* is intentionally used here instead of *homeland* because I argue for all African diasporic people that our homelands are on the continent of Africa. Thus, places such as the Americas, Caribbean region, and other geographies outside of Africa can and have served as homesites where African diasporic people reimagine, create, reproduce, and modify their cultural habitus, but these beliefs and practices are connected to ancient African cultural systems (Asante, 1990, 2003; Asante & Mazama, 2005; Carruthers, 1999; Franklin, 1947/1974; Gordon, 1996; James, 2012; Robinson, 1983/2000; Rodney, 1972; Swan, 2009, 2020, 2022; Williams, 1974/1987).
31. George Fosty and Darril Fosty are White men. Throughout history, several White scholars and journalists such as David K. Wiggins, Dave Zirin, Richard Lapchick, and Mike Marqusee have made laudable contributions to the study of African American and Afro-Caribbean athletes. As such, I describe their contributions as scholarly allyship because they are advocating for a racial group that is different from their own (Cooper, 2021). These authors are promoting humanism while retaining a level of race consciousness.
32. This notion of teamwork being a form of resistance is context specific. As noted throughout the book, some actions under certain conditions are deemed as resistance and even activism whereas these same actions in another context are neither resistance nor activism. Here, I am specifically referencing the Black hockey players' embodied resistance during the late 1800s when prevailing ethnological theories and mainstream ideologies viewed Black people as innately deficient and incapable of exhibiting desirable human behaviors.
33. George (1992) highlighted how the area between Seventh Avenue and 139th Street in Harlem was particularly concentrated with Black migrants from the southern United States and the Caribbean region.
34. Popular sporting events at the Renaissance casino included basketball, wrestling, and boxing matches (George, 1992; Rayl, 2017).
35. The legacy of these athletic entertainment spectacles is found today in historically Black colleges and universities' (HBCUs') annual homecoming and classic events (Cooper et al., 2014).
36. Hybrid resistance was reflected by the Rens via economic activism, mass mobilization activism, grassroots activism, pioneering activism, and advocacy. Economic activism was personified through cooperative economics with Black businesses and select White businesses. Mass mobilization activism involved interstate commerce, events, and partnerships. Grassroots activism was demonstrated through the team's existence and longevity in and impact on Harlem, New York. Pioneering activism was reflected in the breaking down of racial barriers in professional basketball in the United States. Advocacy was exhibited through the team's support for civic organizations and charities. Collectively, these efforts contributed to the team's historic success and the palpable impact of the team beyond sport (Cooper, 2021; George, 1992; Henderson, 1939; Rayl, 1996, 2017).
37. Douglas (owner of the Rens), Joe Lapchick (owner of the Original Celtics of New York), and Eddie Gottlieb (owner of the South Philadelphia Hebrew Association)

38. Major contributors of the Rens during the 1920s and early 1930s included Cum Posey, James "Stretch" Sessoms, William T. "Pimp" Young, William "Big Greasy" Betts, George Gilmore, "Lyss" Young, George Fiall, Specks Moton, Rock Anderson, Clarence "Fat" Jenkins, James "Pappy" Ricks, Eyre Saitch, Tarzan Cooper, Johnny Holt, Bill Yancey, Willie Smith, and Jackie Bethards (Rayl, 1996).
39. The impact of the lawsuits subsequent to Curt Flood's courageous legal activism in 1969 led to the desegregation of MLB (Cooper, 2021).
40. Spencer Haywood's lawsuit in 1971 resulted in the end of the age restriction that prevented talented players from entering the NBA unless they were four years removed from high school (Cooper, 2021).
41. Oscar Robertson's efforts alongside his peers led to a historic increase in players' rights via union-led collective bargaining agreements in the NBA (Cooper, 2021).
42. The transnational formation of the Rens included a transnational migrant team owner, transnational migrant media coverage, transnational partnerships with Black political and social organizations, and transnational entrepreneurship endeavors such as the Renaissance Casino (George, 1992; Rayl, 1996, 2017).
43. *Ro-day-o* is a derived from the Spanish *rodear*, which means to surround or encircle (Pearson, 2021).
44. See Pearson (2021) for an extensive discussion of innovations by Indigenous Mexicans and multiracial independent contractors such as *colear el toro* (tailing the bull), *manganas a caballo* (calf roping), *piales en lienzo* (roping the legs of a galloping horse), *cala de caballo* (horse reining), *jinetas de yeguas* (bareback bronc riding), and *jinetos de toros* (bull riding).
45. Pearson (2021) described hoolihanding as "where a rodeo cowboy leaps from his galloping horse onto the back of a bull, grabbing its horns, and riding the animal until it is tethered by its horns" (p. 36).
46. Dightman was awarded the opportunity after another participant was injured (Cartwright, 2021).
47. A unique aspect of Bill Pickett's bulldogging technique was his biting of the lip of the steer to wrestle it to the ground (Ford, 2020).
48. Notable Black cowboys include Bill Pickett, Herbert "the Bronze Buckaroo" Jeffries, Marvel Rodgers, Charles LeBlanc, Roy LeBlanc, Glynn Thurman, and Cleo Hearn (see Cartwright, 2021, and Ford, 2020, for a more extensive discussion). The hybrid resistance referenced here includes agentic, pioneering, grassroots, mass mobilization, and economic activism.
49. See Horne (2020a) for more expansive discussion on the myths associated with Juneteenth, although the underlying message of the holiday is embraced by the author.
50. This music form involves "a combination of Cajun, rhythm and blues, and country and western" music (Pearson, 2004, p. 194).
51. Pearson (2004) referred to Black rodeo cowboys as "Shadow Riders" to emphasize their historical marginalization in rodeo competitions compared to their White counterparts (Pearson, 2004, p. 190).
52. Examples of small Black rural towns in the Texas Gulf Coast region included Kendleton, Prairie View, Richmond, and Egypt (Pearson, 2004).

Chapter 4 Revolutionary Consciousness

1. The first Black African to win an Olympic gold medal was marathon runner Abebe Bikila of Ethiopia (Bass, 2002).
2. East and West Germany were unified for the 1964 Olympics. The IOC was viewed as playing an instrumental role in this effort in terms of sport participation (Bass, 2002).
3. In 1968, North Korea also withdrew from the Grenoble Olympic Games due to the IOC not recognizing the Democratic People's Republic of Korea (Bass, 2002).
4. Examples of this intergenerational inhuman treatment include systemic economic deprivation, police brutality, lack of access to quality health care, and political disenfranchisement (Ali and Durham, 1975; Cooper, 2021; Edwards, 1969/2017).
5. As noted in chapters 2 and 3, diasporic and transnational sporting resistance is often used by activist groups who are engaged in political activism, but the sportspersons themselves are not necessarily involved in the same oppositional behavior.
6. Blackman (2012) noted how the Sharpeville Massacre and corresponding media coverage of this tragic event, along with support from the Soviets, increased international attention on South African apartheid in the mid-1960s.
7. The following six demands were presented by the OPHR: "1) Restoration of Muhammad Ali's title and right to box in this country. 2) Removal of the antisemitic and anti-black personality of Avery Brundage from his post as Chairman of the International Olympic Committee. 3) Curtailment of participation of all-white teams and individuals from the Union of South Africa and Southern Rhodesia in all United States and Olympic events. 4) The addition of at least two black coaches to the men's track and field coaching staff appointed to coach the 1968 United States Olympic team. (Stanley V. Wright is a member of the coaching team but he is a devout Negro [sic] and therefore is unacceptable). 5) The appointment of at least two black people to policy making positions on the United States Olympic Committee. 6) The complete desegregation of the bigot dominated and racist New York Athletic Club" (Edwards, 1969/2017, p. 53).
8. The OCHR later evolved into the Olympic Project for Human Rights (OPHR) (Edwards, 1969/2017).
9. Black athletes who attended the Black Power Conference in Los Angeles on November 22–23, 1967, included Tommie Smith, Lee Evans, Otis Burrell, and Lew Alcindor (now known as Kareem Abdul-Jabbar) (Thomas, 2012). Other Black non-athlete supporters included Omar Ahmed and Chuck Stone of the National Black Power Conference, Callis Brown and Roy Innis of the Congress of Racial Equality (CORE), Lincoln Lynch of the United Black Front (UBF), and the Harlem Tenants' Rights Party (Blackman, 2021).
10. This conference attracted over twelve hundred attendees from across the United States, Bermuda, and Nigeria (Blackman, 2021).
11. Edwards's master's thesis at Cornell University focused on the Black Muslim family, which reflected his keen interest in the impact of the Nation of Islam on Black culture (Edwards, 1969/2017).
12. Additional influences on and supporters of Edwards's racial empowerment message included Dr. Martin Luther King Jr., the Honorable H. Rap Brown, Dr. Louis Lomax, Mr. Floyd McKissick, Stokely Carmichael (later known as Kwame Ture), Sam Skinner, and Dick Gregory (Edwards, 1969/2017).

13 The successful boycott of the New York Athletic Club (NYAC) track and field meet in 1968 was an example of the effectiveness of the OPHR's activism (Edwards, 1969/2017). The NYAC decided to hold the meet despite the threat of a boycott. Attendance fell by 50 percent, as track and field powerhouses Georgetown and Villanova, all the Ivy League schools, all the New York high school teams, and University of Southern California All-American Orenthal James (O. J.) Simpson boycotted. Additionally, the Russian team withdrew (Blackman, 2012).
14 The issue of South Africa participating in the 1968 Olympics was previously raised by Russian IOC delegate Alekski Romanov in 1959 (Blackman, 2012).
15 Some of the African countries who supported the boycott early were Algeria, Uganda, Ethiopia, Tanzania, Gambia, the United Arab Republic, Kenya, and Sudan (Edwards, 1969/2017). Later, when the Supreme Council of Sport in Africa (SPCA) approved the boycott, the following countries were included in the movement: Congo, Nigeria, Mali, Togo, Gabon, Uganda, Malagasy Republic, Tunisia, Ghana, Libya, Niger, and Guinea (Bass, 2002). African diasporic countries who supported the boycott included Trinidad, Cuba, and Jamaica. Non-African countries who either expressed concern about South Africa's inclusion in the Olympics or indicated their support of the boycott were Syria, Norway, Denmark, Sweden, India, Russia, Bulgaria, France, Czechoslovakia, Hungary, Japan, Mongolia (supported boycott), Cambodia (supported boycott), North Korea (supported boycott), and Belgium (Bass, 2002; Edwards, 1969/2017).
16 It has been argued elsewhere that the Olympic boycott was not executed in totality largely because of state-sanctioned repression via biased media coverage, as opposed to the mainstream narrative that the movement was not popular (Blackman, 2021). According to Blackman (2021), mainstream media outlets misrepresented the OPHR activists as "militant, unconventional, and/or unpatriotic" (p. 157). Black media outlets that supported the OPHR included the *New York Amsterdam News* and *Muhammad Speaks* (Blackman, 2021).
17 In 1970, the IOC implemented a complete banning of South Africa (Bass, 2002).
18 South Africa was banned from the 1964 Olympics in Tokyo as well for its noncompliance with eliminating its racist apartheid policies and practice. The Olympic ban continued until 1992 (Bass, 2002; Donnelly, 2008).
19 The following except from the OCHR Information Booklet captures the intra- and inter-diasporic spirit of the organization: "It's time that Africa, Asia, and Latin America unite to form a new conference conceived and dedicated in the spirit of freedom, justice, and equality—and not representative of nations which practice slavery and the destruction of its Black populations while piously preaching 'democracy.'" (Edwards, 1969/2017, p. 154).
20 Prominent Black internationalists included Paul Robeson, William Patterson, Claudia Jones, and Muhammad Ali (Burden-Stelly & Horne, 2020; Cooper, 2021; Horne, 2020a).
21 In addition to these various ethnic groups, various socialist and communist nations challenged neocolonial capitalist countries during the twentieth century (Horne, 2020b).
22 During the late 1960s, the Soviets created a program to provide coaching, equipment, and other sport development support to African nations (Bass, 2002). These efforts reflected the harmonious relationships between the Soviet Union and African nations, albeit ones that were grounded in anti-Western sentiments.

23 This shift from radical to moderate political views was due to the collapse of the Soviet Union and insurmountable anti-communist pressures from Western nation-states and their allies (Horne, 2019).
24 The additional three elements of Black internationalism are anti-capitalism, anti-sexism, and anti-war (Burden-Stelly & Horne, 2020).
25 In his memoir, Ashe discussed the influential role Nelson Mandela had on him and his political activism. Mandela's African diasporic influence on Ashe underscores the role of collective identity (Ashe & Ramperstad, 1993).
26 Mark Mathabane would later author the internationally acclaimed book *Kaffir Boy* in 1986. Mathabane would write about how Ashe's trips to South Africa and his tennis performances would inspire him to pursue freedom for himself and all Black South Africans (Ashe & Ramperstad, 1993). Mathabane's inspiration from Ashe is an example of the African (Black) diasporic sporting resistance that is highlighted in chapter 2.
27 The ambassador trips exploited Black sportspersons for political propaganda associated with U.S. nationalism and militarism (Cooper, 2021; Thomas, 2012).
28 Additional African American athletes who were vocally critical of the goodwill ambassador campaign included Wilma Rudolph and Earlene Brown (Davis, 2018). A common theme across all these athletes was their disenchantment with the message that the United States was the land of the free and a place of democracy, when in reality African Americans were continuously being discriminated against and denied full citizenship rights.
29 Jackie Robinson would later state he regretted his position against Paul Robeson, and he felt Robeson was a freedom fighter for human rights, particularly those of African Americans (Cooper, 2021; Thomas, 2012).
30 A major critique of post-decolonial efforts in the Caribbean region and across African nations is the lack of successful implementation of anti-capitalist governing systems (Burden-Stelly & Horne, 2020). Even critiques of certain forms of Black Nationalism and Pan-Africanism, such as the vision promulgated by Marcus Garvey, suggest that Black capitalism is not a solution for African oppression (Robeson, 1958/1988). I concur with these conjectures and purport that the implementation of all six elements of Black internationalism (Burden-Stelly & Horne, 2020) must be achieved for African decolonization and sustained cultural empowerment.
31 It is worth noting that later on February 2, 1980, Ali traveled to Africa (Tanzania, Kenya, Nigeria, Liberia, and Senegal) as an emissary of the president per the directive of President Jimmy Carter; his main purpose was to convince African nations to boycott the 1980 Olympics in Moscow (Thomas, 2012). At that time, the United States and Soviet Union were still in an intense cold war. Much to the chagrin of President Carter, the African leaders were disenchanted with the United States sending Ali instead of an official member of the president's cabinet who could negotiate arrangements for Cold War agreements (Thomas, 2012). Stated differently, Thomas (2012) described how the African leaders viewed Ali's visits as "a patronizing gesture rather than as a negotiation between sovereign nations" (p. 169).
32 Carlos Delgado also engaged in advocacy by donating thousands of dollars to support Puerto Ricans who were adversely impacted by the presence of the U.S. naval base in Vieques (Rhoden, 2004).

33 Additional powerful symbolic gestures associated with the BLM movement are the "Hands Up Don't Shoot" gesture in honor of the late Michael Brown, who was killed in Ferguson, Missouri, on August 14, 2014, and the phrase "I Can't Breathe" in honor of the late George Floyd, who was killed in Minneapolis, Minnesota, on May 25, 2020.

34 See Cooper (2021), Anderson (2023), and Brown (forthcoming) for an extensive overview of these sport examples.

35 Black members of the FIFA Task Force on Racism and Discrimination included Yaya Toure (Ivorian footballer), Osasu Obayiuwana (Nigerian journalist), and Tokyo Sexwale (former South Africa cabinet member) (Obayiuwana, 2017).

36 Later in 2021, at the U.S. track and field Olympic trials, Berry engaged in another act of symbolic and political activism after earning third place in the hammer throw event. Instead of standing at attention and facing the U.S. flag during the playing of the national anthem, she faced away from the flag, tilted her head, and placed her hand on her waist to signify her ongoing solidarity with the message of the BLM movement. Near the end of the song, she raised a black T-shirt that read "Activist Athlete" and placed it upon her head. According to Berry, she was told by the event officials that the national anthems would be played before the medalists walked out to the podium (Fischels, 2021).

37 For an expansive map of locations where BLM protests occurred, see https://www.creosotemaps.com/blm2020.

38 During the summer of 2020, Hamilton also exhibited scholarly activism by investing in the creation of the Hamilton Commission (Katwala, 2021). This purpose of this research project was to study why ethnic minorities were underrepresented in motorsports across all levels.

39 Given the fact that the apartheid regime in South Africa lasted from 1948 to 1994, many have viewed the country as one of the prime examples of how a nation can engage in racial healing. For example, the Truth and Reconciliation Commission in South Africa is cited internationally as a preferred method for how a country should seek to redress it historical wrongs, although this perspective has been largely conveyed by mainstream media outlets (Verdoolaege, 2005) versus grounded in the perspectives of Black South Africans (see Gready, 2010; Stanley, 2001; and Stein et al., 2008, for extended discussions on the limitations and shortcomings of the TRC).

40 Ngidi's social media activism was reflected in his use of the hashtag #BLM on X (formerly Twitter) (Moonda, 2020a).

41 Pronounced forms of oppression include murders, incarceration rates, and health disparities. Subtle forms of oppression include lack of equitable access and treatment of Black athletes, lack of accountability for racist actions from spectators, players, and administrators, and so forth.

42 These gestures are noteworthy but require a level of scrutiny based on their performative nature and lack of substantive engagement with structural reform to improve the conditions facing First Nations people of Australia.

43 Although there have been (and continue to be debates) about the racial identities of Aboriginal and Indigenous people across various continents, for the purposes of the current analysis I will focus on Aboriginal people who did self-identify as Black in racial and political terms. As noted earlier, the commonalities between setter colonialism and cultural practices as well as the connections between ancestral migrations informs how the terms *Aboriginal* and *Black* are viewed as

interchangeable within the current analysis (see Swan, 2022, for a more extensive analysis and discussion on this topic).

44 Winmar's activism inspired his fellow AFL members to advocate for policy changes that address racism in the sport of football (rugby), such as Rule 30 (racial and religious vilification laws) (Litchfield et al., 2022; Osmond & Klugman, 2022).

45 In 1995, Prime Minister Paul Keating officially made the Aboriginal flag a national flag, and it now sits proudly alongside the Australian national flag (Amnesty International, 2018). In 2007, Freeman founded the Cathy Freeman Foundation, which works with remote Indigenous communities to close the gap in education between Indigenous and non-Indigenous children in Australia (Amnesty International, 2018). This foundation is an example of sporting resistance via educational advocacy (Cooper, 2021).

46 Iconic Black activist athletes include Tommie Smith, John Carlos, and Muhammad Ali in the United States, Nicky Winmar and Cathy Freeman in the First Nations (Australia), and Sir Isaac Vivian Richards of the West Indies/Caribbean region (Cooper, 2021; Davis, 2009; Osmond & Klugman, 2022).

47 The point here regarding the redefinition of U.S. patriotism refers to a commitment to radical humanism rather than oppressive White supremacy, militarism, colonialism, capitalism, sexism, and imperialism (Burden & Stelly, 2020). In his seminal analysis of the founding of the United States, Horne (2014b) provided an extensive discussion on the distinction between a revolution and a counterrevolution, noting that the latter is more accurately associated with the façade of American exceptionalism.

Chapter 5 A Radical Imagination of Future Black Sporting Resistance

1 Kelley (2002) surmises that surrealism is the revolutionary approach that will yield desired outcomes for African diasporic people. My position here is not contradictory to Kelley's assertion, although I do not conceptualize my approach as surrealism. We agree that embodying the Black radical tradition (Robinson, 1983/2000) is essential, and his emphasis on love and poetry as revolutionary tools aligns with the aim of the sport activism and resistance typologies (Cooper, 2021; Cooper et al., 2019). Notwithstanding, Kelley's surrealist view places a higher emphasis on artists as visionaries, whereas I view all people seeking a world that reflects humanism as possessing and able to reify a radical imagination. I also believe sportspersons will play an important role in any revolutionary efforts, whereas sports are not largely emphasized in Kelley's conception of a surrealism revolutionary. We both share a radical imagination worldview centers on Pan-Africanism whereby African cultural systems are prioritized and exist harmoniously with non-African groups.

2 Several other cities, such as Tulsa, Oklahoma, Norfolk, Virginia, Pensacola, Florida, and Shreveport, Louisiana, have Booker T. Washington High Schools.

3 This perspective on no privatized land aligns in spirit, although not exactly in terms of specificity, with Kelley's (2002) land international territory idea.

4 This idea mimics the recommendation from the 1969 Black Power Conference in Bermuda that called for the development of a Bermuda-based Black Power publication called *Umoja* (the Kiswahili term for unity) (Swan, 2009). A goal for all the recommendations presented in this chapter is to optimize synergy and alignment with the recommendations proposed by previous and current Black

Power organizations who share similar political and sociocultural proclivities with Black internationalist, Pan-Africanist, and scientific socialist aims.
5 An example of a practical aim for future sport organizations is the hosting of political education and cultural empowerment trainings. An example of the psychological aim of future sport organizations is an increased sense of self-efficacy and schema adaptability to conflicting social situations.
6 It must also be understood that revolutionary violence will be a part of the movement, but it should be pursued in the spirit of armed self-defense and protection of human rights as opposed to reproduction oppressive arrangements.

References

Abdel-Shehid, G. (2005). *Who Da Man? Black Masculinities and Sporting Cultures.* Toronto: Canadian Scholars' Press.

Abrahams, R. D. (1983). *The Man-of-Words in the West Indies: Performance and the Emergence of Creole Culture.* Baltimore: Johns Hopkins University Press.

Acheampong, E. Y., Bouhaouala, M., & Raspaud, M. (2019). *African Footballers in Europe: Migration, Community, and Give Back Behaviours.* New York: Routledge.

Adi, H., & Sherwood, M. (2003). *Pan-African History: Political Figures from Africa and the Diaspora since 1787.* New York: Routledge.

African Union (2022). *Diaspora*. Retrieved from https://au.int/en/diaspora-division

Agozino, B. (2014). The Africana paradigm in *Capital*: The debts of Karl Marx to people of African descent. *Review of African Political Economy, 41*(140), 172–184.

Ali, M., & Durham, R. (1975). *The Greatest: My Story.* New York: Random House.

Amnesty International (2018, September 25). Seven athletes standing up for what they believe in. Freedom of Expression, Association and Assembly. Retrieved from https://www.amnesty.org.au/seven-athletes-standing-up-for-what-they-believe-in

Anderson, C. (2012). Rethinking radicalism: African Americans and the liberation struggles in Somalia, Libya, and Eritrea, 1945–1949. In N. Slate (Ed.), *Black Power beyond Borders: The Global Dimensions of the Black Power Movement* (pp. 13–34). New York: Palgrave Macmillan.

Anderson, S. (2023). *The Black Athlete Revolt: The Sport Justice Movement in the Age of #BlackLivesMatter.* Lanham, MD: Rowman & Littlefield.

Andrews, D. L. (2001). *Michael Jordan, Inc.: Corporate Sport, Media Culture, and Late Modern America.* New York: SUNY Press.

Andrews, D. L., Lopes, V. B., & Jackson, S. J. (2016). Neymar: Sport celebrity and performative cultural politics. In P. D. Marshall & S. Redmond (Eds.), *A Companion to Celebrity* (pp. 421–439). New York: John Wiley & Sons.

Andrews, V. (2020). *Policing Black Athletes: Racial Disconnect in Sports.* New York: Peter Lang.

Angelou, M. (1969/2009). *I Know Why the Caged Bird Sings.* New York: Random House.

Aninat, E. (2002). Surmounting the challenges of globalization. *Finance and Development, 39*(1), 3–11.

Arnaud, P. (1998). Sport—a means of national representation. In P. Arnaud & J. Riordan, *Sport and International Politics: Impact of Fascism and Communism on Sport* (pp. 3–14). London: Routledge.

Arnaud, P., & Riordan, J. (1998). *Sport and International Politics: Impact of Fascism and Communism on Sport*. London: Routledge.

Asante, M. K. (1990). *Kemet, Afrocentricity and Knowledge*. Trenton, NJ: Africa World Press.

Asante, M. K. (2003). *Afrocentricity: The Theory of Social Change*. Chicago: African American Images.

Asante, M. K., & Mazama, A. (2005). *Encyclopedia of Black Studies*. Thousand Oaks, CA: Sage.

Ashe, A., & Ramperstad, A. (1993). *Days of Grace: A Memoir*. New York: Alfred A. Knopf.

Assunção, M. R. (2005). *Capoeira: The History of an Afro-Brazilian Martial Art*. London: Routledge.

Aula, I. (2017). Translocality and Afro-Brazilian imaginaries in globalised capoeira. *Suomen Antropologi: Journal of the Finnish Anthropological Society, 42*(1), 67–90.

Bale, J., & Maguire, J. (1994). *The Global Sports Arena: Athletic Talent Migration in an Interdependent World*. Portland, OR: Frank Cass.

Barr, A. (1996). *Black Texas: A History of African Americans in Texas, 1528–1995*. Norman: University of Oklahoma Press.

Bass, A. (2002). *Not the Triumph but the Struggle: The 1968 Olympics and the Making of the Black Athlete*. Minneapolis: University of Minnesota Press.

Battalora, J. (2021). *Birth of a White Nation: The Invention of White People and Its Relevance Today* (2nd ed.). New York: Routledge.

Bauböck, R., & Faist, T. (2010). *Diaspora and Transnationalism: Concepts, Theories, and Methods*. Amsterdam: Amsterdam University Press.

Beyan, A. J. (1989). The American Colonization Society and the origin of undemocratic institutions in Liberia in historical perspective. *Liberian Studies Journal, 14*(2), 140–151.

Birt, R. (1997). Existence, identity, and liberation. In L. R. Gordon (Ed.), *Existence in Black: An Anthology of Black Existential Philosophy* (pp. 206–212). New York: Routledge.

Blackman, D. (2012). African Americans, Pan-Africanism, and the anti-apartheid campaign to expel South Africa from the 1968 Olympics. *The Journal of Pan African Studies, 5*(3), 1–25.

Blackman, D. L. (2021). Harry Edwards, Black Power, and countering the mainstream media's repression of the revolt of the Black athlete. *American Journalism, 38*(2), 150–176.

Blanchard, K. (1995). *The Anthropology of Sport: An Introduction*. Westport, CT: Bergin & Garvey.

BLM. (2023). Black Lives Matter website. Retrieved from https://blacklivesmatter.com

Bonilla-Silva, E. (2018). *Racism Without Racists: Color-Blind Racism and the Persistence of Racial Inequality in America* (5th ed.). Lanham, MD: Rowman & Littlefield.

Botton, W. (2020, July 24). "Cancer" in SA sport has been exposed by BLM—Nathi Mthethwa. The Citizen. Retrieved from https://www.citizen.co.za/sport/cancer-in-sa-sport-has-been-exposed-by-blm-nathi-mthethwa

Boykoff, J. (2016). *Power Games: A Political History of the Olympics*. New York: Verso.

Boykoff, J. (2022). Toward a theory of sportswashing: Mega-events, soft power, and political conflict. *Sociology of Sport Journal*, *39*(4), 342–351.

Brown, D. (2020). *Sports in African American Life: Essays on History and Culture*. Jefferson, NC: McFarland & Company.

Brown, L.E.C. (forthcoming). *Black Feminism, Black Women, and Sports*. Newark, NJ: Rutgers University Press.

Brown, L.E.C. (forthcoming). *Say Her Name: Centering Feminism and Black Women in Sport*. Newark, NJ: Rutgers University Press.

Brown-Vincent, L. (2020). The pandemic of racial capitalism: Another world is possible. *From the European South*, *7*, 61–74.

Bruce, J. (1985). *The Kansas City Monarchs: Champions of Black Baseball*. Lawrence: University Press of Kansas.

Bruneau, M. (2004). *Diasporas et espaces transnationaux*. Paris: Anthropos-Economica.

Bruneau, M. (2010). Diasporas, transnational spaces and communities. *Diaspora and Transnationalism: Concepts, Theories and Methods*, *3*(1), 35–50.

Bryant, H. (2018). *The Heritage: Black Athletes, a Divided America, and the Politics of Patriotism*. Boston: Beacon Press.

Burden-Stelly, C. B. (2022). *Organize, Fight, Win: Black Communist Women's Political Writing*. Brooklyn, NY: Verso.

Burden-Stelly, C., & Horne, G. (2020). From Pan-Africanism to Black Internationalism. In R. Rabaka (Ed.), *Routledge Handbook of Pan-Africanism* (pp. 69–86). New York: Routledge.

Burgess, M. (1993). Canadian "range wars": Struggles over Indian cowboys. *Canadian Journal of Communication*, *18*(3), 351–364.

Burgos, A. (2007). *Playing America's Game: Baseball, Latinos, and the Color Line*. Berkeley: University of California Press.

Burgos, A., Jr. (2011). *Cuban Star: How One Negro-League Owner Changed the Face of Baseball*. New York: Hill and Wang.

Bush, R. (2005). Reflections on Black internationalism as a strategy. *Socialism and Democracy*, *19*(2), 82–90.

Bush, R. (2009). *The End of White World Supremacy: Black Internationalism and the Problem of the Color Line*. Philadelphia: Temple University Press.

Butler, B. N., DeMartini, A. L., & Cooper, J. N. (2023). Athletes and activism, and the NBA: Through the lens of added value theory. *European Journal for Sport and Society*. https://doi.org/10.1080/16138171.2023.2298588

Byrd, B. R. (2020). Black internationalism from Berlin to Black Lives Matter. In C.R.W. Dietrich (Ed.), *A Companion to U.S. Foreign Relations: Colonial Era to the Present* (pp. 547–571). New York: John Wiley & Sons.

Carmichael, S. (1971). *Stokely Speaks: From Black Power to Pan-Africanism*. Chicago: Chicago Review Press.

Carmichael, S., & Hamilton, C. V. (1967). *Black Power: The Politics of Liberation in America*. New York: Vintage.

Carrington, B. (2010). *Race, Sport, and Politics: The Sporting Black Diaspora*. Los Angeles: Sage.

Carruthers, J. (1999). *Intellectual Warfare*. Chicago: Third World Press.

Cartwright, K. R. (2021). *Black Cowboys of Rodeo: Unsung Heroes from Harlem to Hollywood and the American West*. Lincoln: University of Nebraska Press.

Cavil, J. K. (2015). Early athletic experiences at HBCUs. In B. Hawkins, J. N. Cooper, A. R. Carter-Francique, & J. K. Cavil (Eds.), *The Athletic Experience at Historically Black Colleges and Universities: Past, Present, and Persistence* (pp. 19–57). Lanham, MD: Rowman & Littlefield.

Césaire, A. (1955/2001). *Discourses on Colonialism*. (J. Pinkam, Trans.). New York: Monthly Review Press.

Chen, C., & Mason, D. S. (2019). Making settler colonialism visible in sport management. *Journal of Sport Management, 33*(5), 379–392.

Coakley, J. (2017). *Sports in Society: Issues and Controversies* (12th ed.). New York: McGraw-Hill Education.

Cobb, C. E., Jr. (2016). *This Non-Violent Stuff'll Get You Killed: How Guns Made the Civil Rights Movement Possible*. Durham, NC: Duke University Press.

Cohen, R. (1997). *Global Diasporas*. Seattle: University of Washington Press.

Collins, P. H. (1990). Black feminist thought in the matrix of domination. *Black Feminist Thought: Knowledge, Consciousness, and the Politics of Empowerment, 138*, 221–238.

Collins, P. H. (2008). *Black Feminist Thought: Knowledge, Consciousness, and the Politics of Empowerment* (3rd ed.). New York: Routledge.

Cooke, N. (2014). *I Am America: The Chicago Defender on Joe Louis, Muhammad Ali, and Civil Rights, 1934–1975*. [Master's thesis, University of Western Ontario]. UWO Electronic Thesis and Dissertation Repository. https://ir.lib.uwo.ca/etd/2027

Cooky, C. (2017). Women, sports, and activism. In H. J. McCammon, V. Taylor, J. Reger, & R. L. Einwohner (Eds.), *The Oxford Handbook of U.S. Women's Social Movement Activism* (pp. 602–620). New York: Oxford University Press.

Cooper, J. N. (2019). *From Exploitation Back to Empowerment: Black Male Holistic (Under)Development Through Sport and (Mis)Education*. New York: Peter Lang.

Cooper, J. N. (2021). *A Legacy of African American Resistance and Activism Through Sport*. New York: Peter Lang.

Cooper, J. N., Cavil, J. K., & Cheeks, G. (2014). The state of intercollegiate athletics at historically Black colleges and universities (HBCUs): Past, present, & persistence. *Journal of Issues in Intercollegiate Athletics, 7*, 307–332.

Cooper, J. N., Macaulay, C., & Rodriguez, S. H. (2019). Race and resistance: A typology of African American sport activism. *International Review for the Sociology of Sport, 54*(3), 151–181.

Cooper, J. N., Mallery, M., & Macaulay, C.D.T. (2020). African American sport activism and broader social movements. In D. Brown (Ed.), *Passing the Ball: Sports in African American Life and Culture* (pp. 97–114). Jefferson, NC: McFarland & Company.

Corbett, D. R., & Stills, A. B. (2007). African Americans and the media: Roles and opportunities to be broadcasters, journalists, reporters, and announcers. In D. D. Brooks and R. C. Althouse (Eds.), *Diversity and Social Justice in College Sports: Sport Management and the Student-Athlete* (pp. 179–200). Morgantown, WV: Fitness Information Technology.

Crenshaw, K. W. (1991). Mapping the margins: Intersectionality, identity politics, and violence against women of color. *Stanford Law Review, 43*(6), 1241–1299.

Cress-Welsing, F. (1991). *The Isis Papers: The Keys to the Colors*. Chicago: Third World Press.

Dahinden, J. (2010). The dynamics of migrants' transnational formations: Between mobility and locality. In R. Bauböck & T. Faist (Eds.), *Diaspora and*

Transnationalism: Concepts, Theories and Methods (pp. 51–72). Amsterdam: Amsterdam University Press.

Dankwa, K. B. (2022). The history and development of football in Ghana. In *Football (Soccer) in Africa: Origins, Contributions, and Contradictions* (pp. 165–187). New York: Springer.

Danylchuk, K. E. (2012). The challenges of the internationalization of sport management academia. In A. Gillentine, R. Baker, & J. Cuneen (Eds.), *Paradigm Shift: Critical Essays in Sport Management* (pp. 149–161). New York: Routledge.

Darby, P., Akindes, G., & Kirwin, M. (2007). Football academies and the migration of African football labor to Europe. *Journal of Sport and Social Issues, 31*(2), 143–161.

da Silva, A. P. (2014). Pelé, racial discourse and the 1958 World Cup. *Soccer & Society, 15*(1), 36–47.

Davies, C.E.B. (2008). *Encyclopedia of the African Diaspora: Origins, Experiences, and Culture* (Vol. 1: A–C). Santa Barbara, CA: ABC-CLIO.

Davis, A. R. (2016). No league of their own: Baseball, Black women, and the politics of representation. *Radical History Review, 2016*(125), 74–96.

Davis, A. R. (2018, June 7). *Black athletes, anthem protests, and the spectacle of patriotism*. Black Perspectives. Retrieved from https://www.aaihs.org/black-athletes-anthem-protests-and-the-spectacle-of-patriotism/#:~:text=Robinson%20had%20no%20interest%20in%20helping%20the%20State,refused%20to%20stand%20for%20the%20national%20anthem.%202

Davis, D. H. (2009). Celebrating resistance: Articulating diasporan notions of celebrity in sport from Jack Johnson to King Pele and George Headley to Brian Lara. *Wadabagei, 12*(2), 121–135.

Dawson, J. P. (1938, June 23). Louis defeats Schmeling by a knock out in first. *New York Times*. Retrieved from https://www.proquest.com/historical-newspapers/louis-defeats-schmeling-knock-out-first-80-000/docview/102398515/se-2

Delamont, S. & Stephens, N. (2008). Up on the roof: The embodied habitus of diasporic capoeira. *Cultural Sociology, 2*(1): 57–74.

Delamont, S., Stephens, N., & Campos, C. (2017). *Embodying Brazil: An Ethnography of Diasporic Capoeira*. New York: Routledge.

Dettman, C. (2013). History in the making: An ethnography into the roots of "Capoeira Angola." *The World of Music, 2*(2), 73–98.

Dhyani, K. (2020, July 16). *Cricket South Africa releases statement in support of Black Lives Matter, and Lungi Ngidi*. Inside Sport. Retrieved from https://www.insidesport.in/cricket-south-africa-releases-statement-in-support-of-black-lives-matter-and-lungi-ngidi

Diop, C. A. (1974). *The African Origin of Civilization: Myth or Reality*. Westport, CT: Lawrence Hill.

Doidge, M. (2016). Racism and European football. In *Routledge Handbook of Sport, Race and Ethnicity* (pp. 174–185). New York: Routledge.

Donnelly, P. (2008). Sport and human rights. *Sport in Society, 11*(4), 381–394.

Dossar, K. (1992). Capoeira Angola: Dancing between two worlds. *Afro-Hispanic Review, 11*(1/3), 5–10.

Douglas, D. D. (2018a). Black female athletes: The politics of resistance and the struggle to . . . be . . . free . . . *Callaloo, 41*(3), 18–36.

Douglas, D. D. (2018b). Some of us are still brave: Sport and the social production of Black femaleness. In L. Mansfield, J. Caudwell, B. Wheaton, & B. Watson (Eds.),

The Palgrave Handbook of Feminism and Sport, Leisure and Physical Education (pp. 571–587). London: Palgrave Macmillan.

Du Bois, W.E.B. (1903/2003). *The Souls of Black Folk*. Chicago: A. C. McClurg.

Dunbar-Ortiz, R. (2014). *An Indigenous Peoples' History of the United States* (Vol. 3). Boston: Beacon Press

Early, G. (2008). The New Negro era and the great African American transformation. *American Studies*, 49(1/2), 9–19.

Eaton, K. (2013). The centralism of "Twenty-First-Century Socialism": Recontralising politics in Venezuela, Ecuador, and Bolivia. *Journal of Latin American Studies*, 45(3), 421–450.

Edwards, H. (1969/2017). *The Revolt of the Black Athlete*. 50th Anniversary Edition. Urbana: University of Illinois Press.

Edwards, H. (1973). *Sociology of Sport*. Homewood, IL: Dorsey Press.

Edwards, H. (2016a). *The fourth wave: Black athlete protests in the second decade of the 21st century*. [Keynote address]. The North American Society for the Sociology of Sport (NASSS) Conference, Tampa, FL.

Edwards, H. (2016b). The promise and limits of leveraging Black athlete power potential to compel campus change. *Journal of Higher Education Athletics & Innovation*, 1(1), 4–13.

Edwards, H. (2020). *Dr. Harry Edwards—The Plight of Women and Girls in America: Addressing the Challenges*. Elainesir. Retrieved from https://elainesir.com/dr-harry-edwards

Eitzen, D. S., & Sage, G. H. (2012). *Sociology of North American sport* (9th ed.). London: Oxford University Press.

Erenberg, L. A. (2006). *The Greatest Fight of Our Generation: Louis v. Schmeling*. New York: Oxford University Press.

Esson, J. (2015). Better off at home? Rethinking responses to trafficked West African footballers in Europe. *Journal of Ethnic and Migration Studies*, 41(3), 512–530.

Faist, T. (2000). Transnationalization in international migration: Implications for the study of citizenship and culture. *Ethnic and Racial Studies*, 23(2), 189–222.

Faist, T. (2010). Diaspora and transnationalism: What kind of dance partners? In R. Bauböck & T. Faist (Eds.), *Diaspora and Transnationalism: Concepts, theories, and methods* (pp. 9–34). Amsterdam: Amsterdam University Press.

Fanon, F. (1952/2008). *Black Skin, White Masks*. New York: Grove Press.

Fanon, F. (1961/2004). *The Wretched of the Earth*. New York: Grove Press.

Farred, G. (1995). What's my name? Muhammad Ali, postcolonial pugilist. *Dispositio*, 20(47), 37–58.

Farred, G. (2022). *Only a Black Athlete Can Save Us Now*. Minneapolis: University of Minnesota Press.

Fazal, S., & Tsagarousianou, R. (2002). Diasporic communication: Transnational cultural practices and communicative spaces. *Javnost-The Public*, 9(1), 5–18.

Featherstone, D. (2013). Black internationalism, anti-fascism and the makings of solidarity. *Soundings*, 55, 95–108.

FEI (2022). *All-Africa Games*. Fédération Équestre Internationale. Retrieved from https://inside.fei.org/fei/games/cont-regional/all-africa

Fischels, J. (2021, June 28). *Gwen Berry changed Olympic trials protest rules last year and is still protesting*. NPR. Retrieved from https://www.npr.org/2021/06/28/1010995193/gwen-berry-changed-olympic-trials-protest-rules-last-year-and-is-still-protestin

Ford, E. (2020). *Rodeo as Refuge as Rebellion: Gender, Race, and Identity in the American Rodeo.* Lawrence: University Press of Kansas.

Foster, K. (2003). Dreaming of Pelé: Football and society in England and Brazil in the 1950s and 1960s. *Football Studies, 6*(1), 70–86.

Fosty, G., & Fosty, D. (2008). *Black Ice: The Lost History of the Colored Hockey League of the Maritimes, 1895–1925.* Halifax, Nova Scotia: Nimbus Publishing.

Franklin, J. H. (1947/1974). *From Slavery to Freedom: A History of Negro Americans* (4th ed.). New York: Alfred A. Knopf.

Ganguly, D., & Thomas, M. (2004). Cultural politics and iconography: An introduction. *Humanities Research, XI*(1), 1–7.

Gardner H. (1983). *Frames of mind: The theory of multiple intelligences.* New York: Basic Books.

George, N. (1992). *Elevating the game: Black men and basketball.* New York: HarperCollins.

Gilroy, P. (1993). *The Black Atlantic: Modernity and Double Consciousness.* Cambridge, MA: Harvard University Press.

Glick Schiller, N., L. Basch, & C. Szanton-Blanc. (1995). From immigrant to transmigrant: Theorizing transnational migration. *Anthropological Quarterly, 68*(1), 48–63.

Gordon, L. (1996). *Existence in Black: An Anthology of Black Existential Philosophy.* New York: Routledge.

Gorsevski, E. W., & Butterworth, M. L. (2011). Muhammad Ali's fighting words: The paradox of violence in nonviolent rhetoric. *Quarterly Journal of Speech, 97*(1), 50–73.

Graham, M. (2022, December 19). *Kingsley Coman among France players subjected to racist abuse after World Cup final defeat.* MSN. Retrieved from https://www.msn.com/en-us/sports/soccer/kingsley-coman-among-france-players-subjected-to-racist-abuse-after-world-cup-final-defeat/ar-AA15sfoS

Gramsci A. (1971). *Selections from the prison notebooks.* (Q. Hoare & G. N. Smith, Eds. and trans.). New York: International Publishers Co.

Gready, P. (2010). *The Era of Transitional Justice: The Aftermath of the Truth and Reconciliation Commission in South Africa and Beyond.* New York: Routledge.

Green, J. E. (1982). Towards a Political Economy of Negritude. In C. Moore, T. R. Sanders, & S. Moore (Eds.), *African Presence in the Americas* (pp. 55–72). Trenton, NJ: Africa World Press.

Grewal, Z. (2007). Lights, camera, suspension: Freezing the frame on the Mahmoud Abdul-Rauf-anthem controversy. *Souls: A Critical Journal of Black Politics, Culture, and Society, 9*(2), 109–122.

Guridy, F. (2013). Making New Negroes in Cuba: Garveyism as a Transcultural Movement. In D. L. Baldwin and M. Makalani (Eds.), *Escape from New York: The New Negro Renaissance Beyond Harlem* (pp. 183–203). Minneapolis: University of Minnesota Press.

Haislop, T. (2020, September 13). *Colin Kaepernick kneeling timeline: How protests during the national anthem started a movement in the NFL.* Sporting News. Retrieved from https://www.sportingnews.com/us/nfl/news/colin-kaepernick-kneeling-protest-timeline/xktu6ka4diva1s5jxaylrcsse

Hall, S. (2003). Cultural identity and diaspora. In J. E. Braziel and A. Mannur (Eds.), *Theorizing Diaspora* (pp. 233–246). Oxford: Blackwell.

Hamilton, R. S. (1995). Conceptualizing the African diaspora. In C. Moore (Ed.), *African Presence in the Americas.* Trenton, NJ: African World Press.

Haour, A. (2013). *Outsiders and Strangers: An Archaeology of liminality in West Africa*. Oxford: Oxford University Press.

Harris, G. (1994). *Organization of African Unity* (Vol. 7). Oxford: CLIO Press.

Harris, R. (2016, September 25). *Mission accomplished? FIFA disbands racism task force*. The Associated Press. Retrieved from https://www.cbc.ca/sports/soccer/fifa-disbands-racism-taskforce-1.3778251

Hartman, S. (1997). *Scenes of Subjection: Terror, Slavery, and Self-making in Nineteenth-Century America*. New York: Oxford University Press.

Hartmann, D. (1996) *Race, Culture, and the Revolt of the Black Athlete: The 1968 Olympic Protests and their Aftermath*. Chicago: The University of Chicago Press.

Hatcher, A. K. (2021). *Performative symbolic resistance: Examining symbolic resistance efforts of Black professional athletes through a new methodological analytical framework*. [Doctoral dissertation, East Carolina University]. The Scholarship. https://thescholarship.ecu.edu/bitstream/handle/10342/9365/HATCHER-DOCTORALDISSERTATION-2021.pdf

Hawkins, B. (1998). The White supremacy continuum of images for Black men. *Journal of African American Studies, 3*(3), 7–18.

Hawkins, B. (2010). *The New Plantation: Black Athletes, College Sports, and Predominantly White Institutions*. New York: Palgrave-MacMillan.

Henderson, E. B. (1939). *The Negro in Sports*. Washington, D.C.: Associated Publishers.

Heywood, L., & Dworkin, S. L. (2003). *Built to Win: The Female Athlete as Cultural Icon*. Minneapolis: University of Minnesota Press.

Hilliard, A., III. (1998). *SBA: The Reawakening of the African Mind*. Gainesville, FL: Makare Publishing.

Hine, D. C., Hine, W. C., & Harrold, S. (2006). *The African-American Odyssey: Since 1965* (3rd ed., Vol. 2). Upper Saddle River, NJ: Pearson Prentice Hall.

Hodges, C. (2017). *Long Shot: The Triumphs and Struggles of an NBA Freedom Fighter*. Chicago: Haymarket Books.

Holway, J. B. (1988). *Blackball Stars: Negro League Pioneers*. New York: Carroll and Graff.

Holway, J. B. (1989). *Black Diamonds: Life in the Negro Leagues from the Men Who Lived It*. Westport, CT: Meckler.

Horne, G. (1985). *Black and Red: W.E.B. Du Bois and the Afro-American Response to the Cold War, 1944–1963*. New York: SUNY Press.

Horne, G. (1994/2020). *Black Liberation/Red Scare: Ben Davis and the Communist Party*. New York: International Publishers.

Horne, G. (1997). *Fire This Time: The Watts Uprisings and the 1960s*. Los Angeles: Da Capo Press.

Horne, G. (2004). *Race War: White Supremacy and the Japanese Attack on the British Empire*. New York: NYU Press.

Horne, G. (2005). *Black and Brown: African Americans and the Mexican Revolution, 1910–1920*. New York: New York University Press.

Horne, G. (2007). *The White Pacific: U.S. Imperialism and Black Slavery in the South Seas after the Civil War*. Honolulu: University of Hawai'i Press.

Horne, G. (2013a). *Black Revolutionary: William Patterson & the Globalization of the African American Freedom Struggle*. Champaign: University of Illinois Press.

Horne, G. (2013b). *Negro Comrades of the Crown: African Americans and the British Empire Fight the US Before Emancipation*. New York: NYU Press.

Horne, G. (2014a). *The Counter-Revolution of 1776: Slave Resistance and the Origins of the United States of America*. New York: New York University Press.
Horne, G. (2014b). *Race to Revolution: The U.S. and Cuba during Slavery and Jim Crow*. New York: Monthly Review Press.
Horne, G. (2015). *Confronting Black Jacobins: The U.S., the Haitian Revolution, and the Origins of the Dominican Republic*. New York: Monthly Review Press.
Horne, G. (2016). *Paul Robeson: The Artist as Revolutionary*. London: Pluto Press.
Horne, G. (2018a). *The Apocalypse of Settler Colonialism: The Roots of Slavery, White Supremacy, and Capitalism in Seventeenth-Century North America and the Caribbean*. New York: Monthly Review Press.
Horne, G. (2018b). *Facing the Rising Sun: African Americans, Japan, and the Rise of Afro-Asian Solidarity*. New York: New York University Press.
Horne, G. (2019). *White Supremacy Confronted: U.S. Imperialism and Anti-Communism vs. the Liberation of Southern Africa from Rhodes to Mandela*. New York: International Publishers.
Horne, G. (2020a). *The Bittersweet Science: Racism, Racketeering, and the Political Economy of Boxing*. New York: International Publishers.
Horne, G. (2020b). *The Dawning of the Apocalypse: The Roots of Slavery, White Supremacy, Settler Colonialism, and Capitalism in the Long Sixteenth Century*. New York: Monthly Review Press.
Horne, G. (2022). *The Counter-Revolution of 1836: Texas Slavery & Jim Crow and the Roots of U.S. Fascism*. New York: International Publishers.
HuffPost Video (2023). *Gwen Berry: Activist athlete*. HuffPost. Retrieved from https://www.huffpost.com/entry/gwen-berry-activist-athlete_n_60f9525ce4b00fea7fcb27f9
Hylton, K. (2008). *"Race" and Sport: Critical Race Theory*. New York: Routledge.
Hylton, K. (2020). Black Lives Matter in Sport . . . ? *Equality, Diversity and Inclusion: An International Journal, 40*(10), 41–48. https://doi.org/10.1108/EDI-07-2020-0185
IOC. (2021, December 8). *Olympic Games Tokyo 2020 watched by more than 3 billion people*. Retrieved from https://olympics.com/ioc/news/olympic-games-tokyo-2020-watched-by-more-than-3-billion-people
James, C.L.R. (1936). *Minty Alley*. London: Secker & Warburg.
James, C.L.R. (1937). *Cricket and I*. London: Philip Allan.
James, C.L.R. (1963). *Beyond a Boundary*. Durham, NC: Duke University Press.
James, C.L.R. (1963/1989). *The Black Jacobins: Toussaint L'Ouverture and The San Domingo Revolution* (2nd ed.). New York: Vintage Books.
James, C.L.R. (1984). *Party Politics in the West Indies*. Trinidad, WI: Inprint Caribbean.
James, C.L.R. (2012). *A History of Pan-African Revolt*. Oakland, CA: PM Press.
James, C.L.R. (2013). *Modern Politics*. Oakland, CA: PM Press.
James, C.L.R. (2014). *The Life of Captain Cipriani: An Account of British Government in the West Indies*. Durham, NC: Duke University Press.
James, C.L.R. (2022). *Nkrumah and the Ghana Revolution*. Durham, NC: Duke University Press.
James, Lebron [@KingJames]. (2012, March 23). #WeAreTrayvonMartin #Hoodies #Stereotyped #WeWantJustice http://campl.us/il4E [Post]. X (Twitter). https://twitter.com/KingJames/status/183243305428058112?ref_src=twsrc%5Etfw%7Ctwcamp%5Etweetembed%7Ctwterm%5E183243305428058112%7Ctwgr%5Eoocbf0f5

703b96e37717454e5727abodbefb8c57%7Ctwcon%5Es1_&ref_url=https%3A%2F%2Fwww.huffpost.com%2Fentry%2Flebron-heat-trayvon-tweet_n_1375831

Joe Louis knocks out Max Schmeling. (1938, Dec. 31). *The Chicago Defender*. Retrieved from https://www.proquest.com/historical-newspapers/joe-louis-knocks-out-max-schmeling/docview/492610613/se-2

Johnson, J. (1927). *My Life and Battles*. Westport, CT: Praeger.

Joseph, J. (2008). "Going to Brazil": Transnational and corporeal movements of a Canadian-Brazilian martial arts community. *Global Networks*, 8(2), 194–213.

Joseph, J. (2011). A diaspora approach to sport tourism. *Journal of Sport and Social Issues*, 35(2), 146–167.

Joseph, J. (2012a). Around the boundary: Alcohol and older Caribbean-Canadian men. *Leisure Studies*, 31(2), 147–163.

Joseph, J. (2012b). The practice of capoeira: Diasporic black culture in Canada. *Ethnic Studies*, 35(6), 1078–1095.

Joseph, J. (2014). Culture, community, consciousness: The Caribbean sporting diaspora. *International Review for the Sociology of Sport*, 49(4), 669–687.

Joseph, J. (2017). *Sport in the Black Atlantic: Cricket, Canada, and the Caribbean Diaspora*. Manchester, UK: Manchester University Press.

Joseph, P. E. (2006). *The Black Power Movement: Rethinking the Civil Rights-Black Power Era*. New York: Routledge.

Joseph, P. E. (2007). *Waiting 'til the Midnight Hour: A Narrative History of Black Power in America*. New York: Henry Holt and Co.

Kassimeris, C. (2007). *European Football in Black and White: Tackling Racism in Football*. Lanham, MD: Lexington Books.

Katwala, A. (2021, January 4). Lewis Hamilton opens up about activism and life beyond F1. *Wired*. Retrieved from https://www.wired.co.uk/article/lewis-hamilton

Katz, W. L. (2005). *The Black West: A Documentary and Pictorial History of the African American Role in the Westward Expansion of the United States*. New York: Harlem Moon.

Kelley, R.D.G. (2002). *Freedom Dreams: The Black Radical Imagination*. Boston: Beacon Press.

Koshiro, Y. (2003). Beyond an alliance of color: The African American impact on modern Japan. *Duke University Press*, 11(1), 183–215.

Lal, P. (2015). *African socialism in postcolonial Tanzania*. Cambridge: Cambridge University Press.

Lanctot, N. (1994). *Fair Dealing and Clean Playing: The Hilldale Club and the Development of Black Professional Baseball, 1910–1932*. Jefferson, NC: McFarland.

Lanctot, N. (2004). *Negro League baseball: The Rise and Ruin of a Black Institution*. Philadelphia: University of Pennsylvania Press.

Laureus (2000). *Laureus World Sports Awards 2000: Winners & Nominees*. Retrieved from https://www.laureus.com/world-sports-awards/2000

Lawson, W. (1972). *History of the Townships of Dartmouth, Preston, and Lawrencetown, Halifax County, Nova Scotia*. Belleville, ON: Mika Studio.

Leonard, D. J., & King, C. R. (2012). *Commodified and Criminalized: New Racism and African Americans in Contemporary Sports*. Lanham, MD: Rowman & Littlefield.

Levine, L. (1993). *The Unpredictable Past*. New York: Oxford University Press.

Lindsay, V. C. (2019). *Capoeira, Black Males, and Social Justice: A Gym Class Transformed*. New York: Peter Lang.

Lipiäinen, T. (2015). Cultural creolisation and playfulness: An example of capoeira Angola in Russia. *Journal of Intercultural Studies, 36*(6), 676–692.
Litchfield, C., Osborne, J., & Gale, T. (2022). Australian cricket, race, and First Nations Australians: The past and present. *Sport in History, 42*(3), 384–404.
Lomax, M. E. (2003). *Black Baseball Entrepreneurs, 1860–1901: Operating by Any Means Necessary*. Syracuse, NY: Syracuse University Press.
Lomax, M. E. (2014). *Black Baseball Entrepreneurs, 1902–1931: The Negro National and Eastern Colored Leagues*. Syracuse, NY: Syracuse University Press.
Louis, J., Rust, E., & Rust, A., Jr. (1978). *Joe Louis: My Life*. New York: Harcourt Brace Jovanovich.
MacEwan, G. (1960). *John Ware's Cow Country*. Edmonton, AB: Institute of Applied Art.
Magee, J., & Sugden, J. (2002). "The world at their feet": Professional football and international labor migration. *Journal of Sport and Social Issues, 26*(4), 421–437.
Magrath, R. (2022). *Athlete Activism: Contemporary Perspectives*. New York: Routledge.
Maguire, J. (1999). *Global Sport: Identities. Societies. Civilizations*. Cambridge, UK: Polity Press.
Marqusee, M. (1994/2016). *Anyone But England: Cricket, Race and Class*. New York: Bloomsbury.
Marqusee, M. (1995). Sport and stereotype: From role model to Muhammad Ali. *Race & Class, 36*(4), 1–29.
Marqusee, M. (2017). *Redemption Song: Muhammad Ali and the Spirit of the Sixties*. New York: Verso.
Martin, T. (1986). *Race First: The Ideological and Organizational Struggles of Marcus Garvey and the Universal Negro Improvement Association* (No. 8). Dover, MA: The Majority Press.
Marx, K. (1867/1887). *Capital: Volume 1*. Moscow: Progress Publishers.
Mask, M. (2023). *Black Rodeo: A History of the African American Western*. Urbana: University of Illinois Press.
Maynard, J. (2005). "In the interests of our people": The influence of Garveyism on the rise of Australian Aboriginal political activism. *Aboriginal History, 29*, 1–22.
Messner, M. A. (2010). *Out of Play: Critical Essays on Gender and Sport*. New York: SUNY Press.
Moonda, F. (2020a, July 6). *Ngidi says South Africa must take BLM stand like the rest of the world*. ESPN Cricinfo. Retrieved from https://www.espncricinfo.com/story/ngidi-says-south-africa-must-take-blm-stand-like-the-rest-of-the-world-1226283
Moonda, F. (2020b, July 14). *Makhaya Ntini, Vernon Philander, JP Duminy, Herschelle Gibbs sign a letter backing Lungi Ngidi's #BLM stance*. ESPN Cricinfo. Retrieved from https://www.espncricinfo.com/story/ntini-philander-duminy-gibbs-sign-letter-backing-ngidi-s-blm-stance-1226753
Moore, C., Sanders, T. R., & Moore, S. (Eds.). (1982). *African Presence in the Americas*. Trenton, NJ: Africa World Press.
Moore, L. (2017). *We Will Win the Day: The Civil Rights Movement, the Black athlete, and the Quest for Equality*. Santa Barbara, CA: Praeger.
Morse, B. (2021, August 3). *Raven Saunders' X podium protest: What it means and why the IOC is investigating*. CNN. Retrieved from https://www.cnn.com/2021/08/02/sport/raven-saunders-podium-protest-olympics-spt-intl/index.html
Munro, J. (2008). Ethiopia stretches forth across the Atlantic: African American anticolonialism during the interwar period. *Left History: An Interdisciplinary Journal of Historical Inquiry and Debate, 13*(2), 37–63.

Murray, C. (2007, February 6). Black hockey league thrived. *Philadelphia Tribune*, 1C, 2C.

Mwaniki, M. F. (2017). *The Black Migrant Athlete: Media, Race, and the Diaspora in Sports*. Lincoln: University of Nebraska Press.

Nagle, D. (2021, August 29). *Osaka, Medvedev headline opening night at US Open*. ESPN Press Room. Retrieved from https://espnpressroom.com/us/press-releases/2021/08/osaka-medvedev-headline-opening-night-at-us-open/

NBHF. (2022). *José Méndez*. National Baseball Hall of Fame. Retrieved from https://baseballhall.org/hall-of-famers/mendez-jose

Nelson, A. (2011). *Body and Soul: The Black Panther Party and the Fight Against Medical Discrimination*. Minneapolis: University of Minnesota Press.

Newton, H. P. (1973). *Revolutionary Suicide*. New York: Random House Press.

Nichols, E. (1974/1987/2004). *The Philosophical Aspects of Cultural Differences*. Washington, D.C.: Nichols and Associates.

Nkrumah, K. (1970). *Consciencism*. New York: NYU Press.

Nkrumah, K. (1973). *Revolutionary Path*. New York: International Publishers.

Obayiuwana, O. (2017, October 2). *FIFA anti-racism task force: Mission unaccomplished*. Play the Game. Retrieved from https://www.playthegame.org/news/fifa-anti-racism-task-force-mission-unaccomplished

Ogbar, J.O.G. (2004). *Black Power: Radical Politics and African American Identity*. Baltimore: Johns Hopkins University Press.

Ogbar, J.O.G. (2020). Black nationalism. In R. Rabaka (Ed.), *Routledge Handbook of Pan-Africanism* (pp. 89–100). New York: Routledge.

Osmond, G. & Klugman, M. (2022) Through a long lens: Racism, protest, memory and sovereignty in Australian sport. *Sport in History, 42*(3), 366–383.

Patterson, T. R., & Kelley, R. D. (2000). Unfinished migrations: Reflections on the African diaspora and the making of the modern world. *African Studies Review, 43*(1), 11–45.

Pearson, D. W. (2004). Shadow Riders of the Subterranean Circuit: A descriptive account of Black Rodeo in the Texas Gulf Coast region. *The Journal of American Culture, 27*(2), 190–198.

Pearson, D. W. (2021). *Black Rodeo in the Texas Gulf Coast Region: Charcoal in the Ashes*. Lanham, MD: Rowman & Littlefield.

Peck, R. (Director). (2021). *Exterminate All the Brutes* [Documentary film]. HBO Documentary Films. Velvet Film.

Peterson, R. (1970). *Only the Ball Was White*. Englewood Cliffs, NJ: Prentice-Hall.

Prashad, V. (2000). Afro-Dalits of the earth, unite! *African Studies Review, 43*(1), 189–201.

Quan, H.L.T. (2019). *Cedric J. Robinson: On Racial Capitalism, Black Internationalism, and Cultures of Resistance*. London: Pluto Press.

Rabaka, R. (2020). *Routledge Handbook of Pan-Africanism*. New York: Routledge.

Rajshekar, V. T. 1995. *Dalit. The Black Untouchables of India*. Atlanta, Ottawa: Clarity Press.

Ransby, B. (2022). *Eslanda: The Large and Unconventional Life of Mrs. Paul Robeson*. Chicago: Haymarket Books.

Rayl, S. J. (1996). *The New York Renaissance Professional Black Basketball Team, 1923–1950* (Publication No. 9702370) [Doctoral dissertation, The Pennsylvania State University]. Proquest Dissertations Publishing.

Rayl, S. J. (2017). Robert L. "Bob" Douglas: "Aristocracy on the Court, an Architect of Men." In G. R. Gems (Ed.), *Before Jackie Robinson: The Transcendent Role of Black Sporting Pioneers* (pp. 155–178). Omaha: University of Nebraska Press.

Razack, S., & Joseph, J. (2021). Misogynoir in women's sport media: Race, nation, and diaspora in the representation of Naomi Osaka. *Media, Culture & Society, 43*(2), 291–308.

Reuters (2020, June 29). Cricket: West Indies to wear "BLM" logo during England series. *Sport News*. Retrieved from https://www.reuters.com/article/cricket-test-eng-win-gesture-idINKBN2400R0

Rhoden, W. C. (2004, July 21). Sports of the times; Delgado makes a stand by taking a seat. *The New York Times*. Retrieved from https://www.nytimes.com/2004/07/21/sports/sports-of-the-times-delgado-makes-a-stand-by-taking-a-seat.html

Rhoden, W. C. (2006). *40 Million Dollar Slaves: The Rise, Fall, and Redemption of the Black Athlete*. New York: Crown Publishing Group.

Riley, S. (Director). (2011). *Fire in Babylon*. [Documentary film]. Cowboy Films; E & G Productions; ECN Motion Pictures.

Robeson, P. (1958/1998). *Here I Stand*. Boston: Beacon Press.

Robinson, C. J. (1983/2000). *Black Marxism: The Making of the Black Radical Tradition*. Chapel Hill: University of North Carolina Press.

Rodney, W. (1972). *How Europe Underdeveloped Africa*. Baltimore: Black Classic Press.

Rogosin, D. (1985). *Invisible Men: Life in baseball's Negro Leagues*. New York: Atheneum.

Saeed, A. (2002) What's in a Name? Muhammad Ali and the Politics of Cultural Identity. *Sport in Society, 5*(3), 52–72.

Safran, W. (1991). Diasporas in Modern Societies: Myths of Homeland and Return. *Diasporas: A Journal of Transnational Studies, 1*(1), 83–99.

Sage, G. H. (1998). *Power and Ideology in American Sport*. Champaign: Human Kinetics.

Sailes, G. (2010). The African American athlete: Social myths and stereotypes. In G. Sailes (Ed.), *Modern Sport and The African American Athlete Experience* (pp. 55–68). San Diego: Cognella.

Sherwood, M. (2012). Pan-African Conferences, 1900–1953: What Did "Pan-Africanism" Mean? *The Journal of Pan African Studies, 4*(10), 106–126.

Sidanius, J., & Pratto, F. (2001). *Social Dominance Theory: An Intergroup Theory of Social Hierarchy and Oppression*. Cambridge: Cambridge University Press.

Singh, S. (2004). Resistance, essentialism, and empowerment in Black Nationalist discourse in the African diaspora: A comparison of the Back to Africa, Black Power, and Rastafari movements. *Journal of African American Studies, 8*(3), 18–36.

Slate, N. (2012). *Black Power beyond Borders: The Global Dimensions of the Black Power Movement*. New York: Palgrave Macmillan.

Smith, E. (2009). *Race, Sport and the American Dream* (2nd ed.). Durham, NC: Carolina Academic Press.

Stanley, E. (2001). Evaluating the truth and reconciliation commission. *The Journal of Modern African Studies, 39*(3), 525–546.

Stein, D. J., Seedat, S., Kaminer, D., Moomal, H., Herman, A., Sonnega, J., & Williams, D. R. (2008). The impact of the Truth and Reconciliation Commission on psychological distress and forgiveness in South Africa. *Social Psychiatry and Psychiatric Epidemiology, 43*(6), 462–468.

Swan, Q. (2009). *Black Power in Bermuda: The Struggle for Decolonization.* New York: Palgrave Macmillan.

Swan, Q. (2020). *Pauulu's Diaspora: Black Internationalism and Environmental Justice.* Gainesville: University Press of Florida.

Swan, Q. (2022). *Pasifika Black: Oceania, Anti-Colonialism, and the African World.* New York: New York University Press.

Swart, K., & Maralack, D. (2021). Black Lives Matter: Perspectives from South African cricket. *Sport in Society, 24*(5), 715–730.

Talmon-Chvaicer, M. (2008). *The Hidden History of Capoeira: A Collision of Cultures in the Brazilian Battle Dance.* Austin: University of Texas Press.

Taylor, G. (2007). *Capoeira: The Jogo de Angola from Luanda to Cyberspace* (Vol. 2). Berkeley, CA: Blue Snake Books.

Thomas, D. C. (2013). Cedric J. Robinson and racial capitalism: Africana liberation resistance structures and black internationalism in the twenty-first century. *African Identities, 11*(2), 133–147.

Thomas, D. L. (2012). *Globetrotting: African American Athletes and Cold War Politics.* Urbana: University of Illinois Press.

Tolbert, E. (1975). Outpost Garveyism and the UNIA rank and file. *Journal of Black Studies, 5*(3), 233–253.

Tse-tung, M. (1965/1967/2016). *On Contradiction.* New York: Red Star Publishers.

Tshwaku, K. (2020, July 21). SA Rugby takes a strong stand on Black Lives Matter. Business Day. Retrieved from https://www.businesslive.co.za/bd/sport/rugby/2020-07-21-sa-rugby-takes-strong-stand-on-black-lives-matter/

Verdoolaege, A. (2005). Media representations of the South African Truth and Reconciliation Commission and their commitment to reconciliation. *Journal of African Cultural Studies, 17*(2), 181–199.

Vertovec, S. (1999). "Conceiving and researching transnationalism." *Ethnic and Racial Studies, 22*(2), 447–462.

Wallace, B. (2022, November 12). Agents of Change: Sport and Grassroots Political Education for Black Youth. [Conference presentation]. North American Society for the Sociology of Sport Conference, Las Vegas, NV.

Wallerstein, I. (1961/1967/2005). *Africa: The Politics of Independence and Unity.* New York: Bison Books Edition.

Wallerstein, I. (1974). *The Modern World System: Vol. 1. Capitalist Agriculture and the Origins of the European World-Economy in the Sixteenth Century.* New York: Academic Press.

WBUR. (2020, June 22). Mapping Black Lives Matter protests around the world. WBUR. Retrieved from https://www.wbur.org/hereandnow/2020/06/22/mapping-black-lives-matter-protests

White, S. (1995). *History of Colored Baseball.* Lincoln: University of Nebraska Press.

Whitfield, M. (1964). "Let's boycott the Olympics": Olympic champ asks Negro athletes to act. *Ebony Magazine.* Retrieved from https://books.google.co.jp/books?id=RAVl_KwcBuAC&pg=PA95&lpg=PA95&dq=mal+whitfield+boycott&source=bl&ots=Qu6OyS18Bm&sig=bpkFpG3D84VqCM2uCjtidiPmUSg&hl=en&sa=X&ved=0CBoQ6AEwAGoVChMIi8mklOudyQIVQiGmCh2r6g7a#v=onepage&q=mal%20whitfield%20boycott&f=false

Wiggins, D. K. (2018). *More than a Game: The History of the African American Experience in Sport.* Lanham, MD: Rowman & Littlefield.

Wiggins, D. K., & Miller, P. (2003). *The Unlevel Playing Field: A Documentary History of the African-American Experience in Sport*. Urbana: University of Illinois Press.

Wilde, S. (1994). *Letting Rip: The Fast Bowling Threat from Lillee to Waqar*. London: H. F. & G. Witherby.

Wilkins, F. C. (2007). The making of black internationalists: SNCC and Africa before the launching of Black Power, 1960–1965. *The Journal of African American History*, *92*(4), 467–490.

Williams, C. (1974/1987). *The Destruction of Black Civilization: Great Issues of a Race from 4500 B.C. to 2000 A.D*. Chicago: Third World Press.

Williams, E. H., & Bunkley-Williams, L. (2021). What and where is the Caribbean? A modern definition. *The Florida Geographer*, *52*(1), 3–28.

Williams, R. F. (2013). *Negroes with Guns*. Eastford, CT: Martino Fine Books.

Williams, Y. (2012). "They've lynched our savior, Lumumba in the old fashion Southern style": The conscious internationalism of American Black Nationalism. In N. Slate (Ed.), *Black Power beyond Borders: The Global Dimensions of the Black Power Movement* (pp. 147–167). New York: Palgrave Macmillan.

Wilson, P. J. (1973). *Crab Antics: The Social Anthropology of English-Speaking Negro Societies in the Caribbean*. New Haven, CT: Yale University Press.

Woodson, C. G. (1933/2010). *The Mis-education of the Negro*. New York: SoHoBooks.

Yehudah, M. Z. (2020). Refusing to play their games! A Fanonian analysis and Robesonian proposition on sports, race and divestment. In D. Brown (Ed.), *Sports in African American Life: Essays on History and Culture* (pp. 116–137). Jefferson, NC: McFarland.

Yosso, T. J. (2005). Whose culture has capital? A critical race theory discussion of community cultural wealth. *Race, Ethnicity and Education*, *8*(1), 69–91.

Zirin, D. (2008). *People's History of Sports in the United States: 250 Years of Politics, Protest, People, and Play*. New York: The New Press.

Zirin, D. (2021). *The Kaepernick Effect: Taking a Knee, Changing the World*. New York: The New Press.

Index

Abdul-Rauf, Mahmoud, 146
advocacy, 5, 7, 24–25, 38–39, 60, 99, 117, 121, 137, 139, 149, 153, 191n36, 195n32, 197n45
African (Black) Diaspora sporting resistance, 15, 22, 27–31, 44
African Union, 27, 168
agency (agentic resistance), 5, 7, 24, 38, 53, 65, 91, 93, 116, 121, 136, 139, 153, 161, 189n7, 190n26
agentic participatory sporting resistance, 24, 48, 74, 79, 84–85, 93, 107–108, 123, 136, 140
agentic refraining sporting resistance, 93, 123, 140
Ali, Muhammad, vii, 24, 29, 33, 39, 43, 54–61, 128, 143–146
allyship, 73, 108, 123, 149, 152–153, 156, 191n31
anti-apartheid, 2, 11, 22, 25, 37, 85, 129, 150, 158, 164, 167–168, 173, 188n37, 193n6, 194n18, 196n39
Ashe, Arthur, 22, 39, 128–129, 132, 136–138, 158, 167, 195nn26–26
Australian Aboriginal Progressive Association (AAPA), 24, 49, 60, 156, 161

Berry, Gwen, 26, 150–152, 159, 167, 196n36
Black Atlantic, 8–9, 14, 19, 27, 29–30, 43, 57, 73, 89, 91, 120, 153–154, 183n10
Black internationalism sporting resistance, 8, 19, 21–23, 26, 33–37, 43, 125, 167–174

Black Liberation Struggle, 2, 6–12, 19, 30, 50–51, 53, 64, 83, 106, 145, 161, 170
Black Lives Matter (BLM) movement, 22, 26, 37, 119, 141, 147, 167–168, 196n33, 196n36, 196n37
Black Nationalism, 10–12, 14–16, 18–19, 50, 54, 60, 83, 92, 98, 101, 106, 135–136, 163, 166–167, 184n1, 186n15, 195n30
Black Power movement, 12, 18, 55–56, 127, 131, 146
Black Radicalism, 10, 12, 18, 19, 83, 92, 98, 125, 134, 169, 182n30
Black radical tradition, 4, 6, 16, 33, 40, 46, 76, 83, 87, 91, 97, 101, 105, 109, 112, 133, 136, 189n4, 197n1
Black sporting resistance framework, 20–43
Black transnationalism sporting resistance, 22, 31–33, 75–124, 167
Brasilidade fútbol, 63–64, 163

capoeira Angola, 69–74, 164, 169, 188nn40–41, 188nn43–44
capoeira contemporânea, 72–73
capoeira regional, 72–73
Carlos, John, 6, 126, 150, 167, 184n19, 197n46
Carrancistas, 24, 49, 60, 161
collective cultural resistance, 24, 70, 72–74, 87, 89–91, 93, 109, 112, 119–120, 164–165, 167
Colored Hockey League of the Maritimes, 22, 25, 78, 104–110, 112, 123–124, 166

215

Delgado, Carlos, 146–147, 195n32
Douglas, Robert "Bob" L., 110–115, 124, 166

economic activism, 25, 41–42, 91, 93, 96–97, 99, 102, 107, 110–111, 121, 133, 137, 139, 141, 164–167, 191n36, 192n48
Edwards, Harry, 4, 97, 99, 119, 131–136, 148, 167, 169
Ethiopia, 17–18, 28–29, 36–38, 50–51, 68, 139, 185n1, 193n1, 194n15

Freeman, Cathy, 157, 171, 197nn45–46

grassroots activism, 24–25, 41, 74, 88–89, 91, 93, 99, 109, 111, 121, 191n36

Hamilton, Lewis, 26, 152–154, 159, 167, 196n38
Harlem Rens (Renaissance; also referred to as the Black Fives or Rens), 22, 25, 78, 110–115, 124, 166, 191n36, 192n38, 192n42
Hodges, Craig, 146
Holder, Jason, 154
hybrid resistance, 5, 7, 17, 22, 38–40, 56–57, 73–74, 90, 93, 96, 101, 104, 109, 112–113, 115, 119, 121–122, 124, 133, 137–138, 142, 152, 154, 156, 164, 166, 187n34, 190n26, 191n36, 192n48

infrahuman, 46, 80, 183n4, 185n3
inter-diasporic alliances, 49, 53, 56–61, 73–74, 104, 115, 120, 134, 152, 161–162, 167, 170–171

Johnson, Jack, 47–50, 53–55

legal activism, 25, 42, 55, 114, 127–128, 139, 156, 192n39
Louis, Joe, 50–55

mass mobilization activism, 25, 41, 59–60, 68, 91, 93, 95, 99, 111, 119, 121, 133, 137, 139, 151–152, 155, 164–165, 191n36
media activism, 25, 42, 88, 91–93, 99, 130, 133, 137, 139–140, 144, 146, 147–150, 152, 154–155, 165, 196n40
Morales, Amado, 146
music and art activism, 7, 17, 26, 40, 42

native homeland sporting resistance, 67–68, 74, 163
Ngidi, Lungi, 26, 154–155, 159, 167

Obayiuwana, Osasu, 149–150, 159, 167, 196n35
Olympic Committee on Human Rights (OCHR)/Olympic Project for Human Rights (OPHR), 131–136, 158, 168, 193nn7–8, 194n13, 194n16, 194n19
Osaka, Naomi, 26, 152, 159, 167

Pan-Africanism, 10–12, 16–18, 19, 35–36, 44, 50, 54, 58, 60, 64, 68–69, 83, 92, 98, 106, 129, 131, 134, 136, 138, 161, 167–168, 173, 184n1, 186n15, 195n30, 197n1
participatory agentic sporting resistance, 24, 48, 74, 79, 84–85, 93, 107–108, 123, 136, 140
Pelé (Edson Arantes do Nascimento), 62–65
Pickett, Bill, 116–117, 119, 167
pioneering, 5, 7, 24–25, 30, 38–39, 48, 63, 65, 80–81, 93, 99–100, 107–108, 112–114, 117, 119, 121, 123, 136, 152–153, 163–169, 179n12, 190n26, 191n36, 192n48
political activism, 26, 57, 65, 121, 127–128, 133, 137–141, 145, 148, 150–153, 167, 185n10, 193n5, 195n26, 196n36
Polynice, Olden, 147
Pompez, Alex, 99–103

radical imagination of Black sporting resistance, 87, 123, 133, 141, 160–161, 163, 165, 167–174, 197n1
religious activism, 7, 41–42, 59, 109
revolutions/social transformations, 5, 13, 33, 40, 47, 49, 78–79, 92, 96, 125, 143, 150, 168, 173–174, 182, 197n47 (chap. 4), 197n1 (chap. 5)
Richards, Sir Isaac Vivian, 25, 81, 86, 138, 158, 171, 197n46
Robeson, Paul, 26, 33, 42, 53, 103, 126–128, 135, 142–143, 170–171, 184n19, 189n1, 189n13, 194n20, 195n29
Robinson, Eroseanna "Rose," 25, 140–142, 158, 171

Robinson, Jackie, vii, 130, 132, 140, 142, 144, 195n29
Russell, Bill, 139–140, 144

Saunders, Raven, 26, 151–152, 159, 167
scholarly activism, 7, 40–41, 60, 73–74, 91–92, 108, 117, 122–123, 138, 150, 165, 172, 191n31, 196n38
Shadow Riders of the Subterranean Circuit, 22, 25, 78, 115–123, 170, 192n51
Smith, Tommie, 126, 150, 167, 184n19, 193n9, 197n46
sport activism typology, 7, 23, 40–43, 170, 173, 179n16
sporting resistance typology, 7, 23, 37–40, 170, 172
stealth migrant sporting resistance, 24, 67, 74, 81, 83–84, 88, 123, 163
stealth racial empowerment (stealth diasporic sporting resistance), 24, 26, 54–55, 60, 64–65, 74, 161–162, 187n34
sustained cultural empowerment, 5, 7, 24, 38, 40, 83–84, 150, 161, 164, 171, 173–174, 195n30

symbolic activism, 24, 41, 57, 74, 84–85, 93, 133, 137, 141, 146–147, 151–153, 156–157

transnational circuits, 94, 121, 123, 165
transnational communities, 32–33, 78–93, 123
transnational formations, 77–78, 87–90, 103, 110, 113, 121, 123–124, 164
transnationalization, 32, 90–91, 115, 117, 120, 124, 165, 167
transnational kinship groups (networks), 24, 29, 31–32, 76, 89, 94, 104, 113, 123, 166

Universal Negro Improvement Association (UNIA), 16–17, 35, 49, 51–53, 100–101, 156, 161, 168

West Indies cricket, 22, 78, 93, 154
Whitfield, Mal, 139–140, 144
Williams, Henry Sylvester, 17, 106, 166, 170, 191n29
Winmar, Nicky, 6, 26, 156–159, 167, 171, 179n13, 197n44, 197n46

About the Author

JOSEPH N. COOPER is the inaugural Dr. J. Keith Motley Endowed Chair of Sport Leadership and Administration at the University of Massachusetts Boston. His research agenda focuses on the intersection between sport, race, gender, education, and culture with an emphasis on sport involvement as a catalyst for holistic development and positive social change. He is the author of *From Exploitation Back to Empowerment: Black Male Holistic (Under)Development through Sport and (Mis)Education* and *A Legacy of African American Resistance and Activism through Sport*. He is the editor of *Anti-Racism in Sport Organizations*.

Available titles in the Critical Issues in Sport and Society series:

Rachel Allison, *Kicking Center: Gender and the Selling of Women's Professional Soccer*

Jules Boykoff, *Activism and the Olympics: Dissent at the Games in Vancouver and London*

Diana Tracy Cohen, *Iron Dads: Managing Family, Work, and Endurance Sport Identities*

Cheryl Cooky and Michael A. Messner, *No Slam Dunk: Gender, Sport, and the Unevenness of Social Change*

Joseph N. Cooper, *Black Sporting Resistance: Diaspora, Transnationalism, and Internationalism*

Andrew M. Guest, *Soccer in Mind: A Thinking Fan's Guide to the Global Game*

Jennifer Guiliano, *Indian Spectacle: College Mascots and the Anxiety of Modern America*

Kathryn E. Henne, *Testing for Athlete Citizenship: Regulating Doping and Sex in Sport*

Jeffrey L. Kidder, *Parkour and the City: Risk, Masculinity, and Meaning in a Postmodern Sport*

Alan Klein, *Lakota Hoops: Life and Basketball on Pine Ridge Indian Reservation*

Michael A. Messner and Michela Musto, eds., *Child's Play: Sport in Kids' Worlds*

Jeffrey Montez de Oca, *Discipline and Indulgence: College Football, Media, and the American Way of Life during the Cold War*

Joshua I. Newman, Holly Thorpe, and David L. Andrews, eds., *Sport, Physical Culture, and the Moving Body: Materialisms, Technologies, Ecologies*

Stephen C. Poulson, *Why Would Anyone Do That? Lifestyle Sport in the Twenty-First Century*

Aarti Ratna, *A Nation of Family and Friends? Sport and the Leisure Cultures of British Asian Girls and Women*

Courtney Szto, *Changing on the Fly: Hockey through the Voices of South Asian Canadians*

Nicole Willms, *When Women Rule the Court: Gender, Race, and Japanese American Basketball*